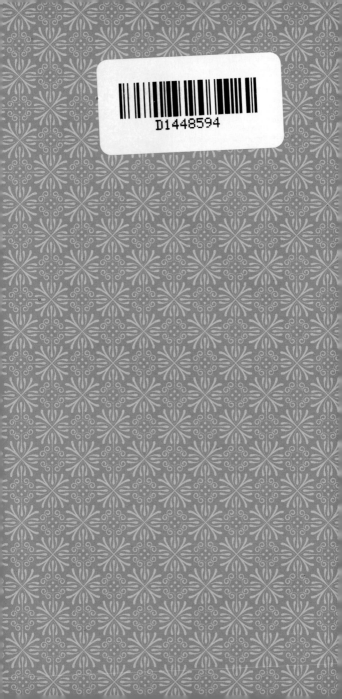

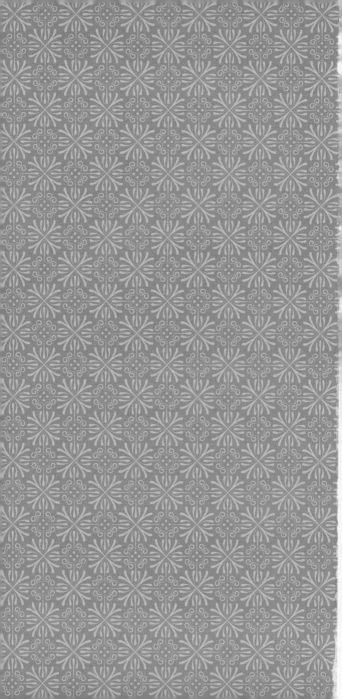

James Sherwood's

DISCRIMINATING
GUIDE TO
LONDON

An unabashed companion to the very finest experiences in the world's most cosmopolitan city

Sir John Soane's Museum

James Sherwood's

DISCRIMINATING
GUIDE TO
LONDON

*An unabashed companion to the very
finest experiences in the world's
most cosmopolitan city*

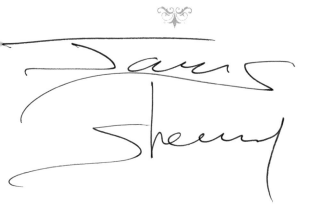

Thames & Hudson

To Gloria and Roger Sherwood

First published in the United Kingdom in 2015
by Thames & Hudson Ltd, 181A High Holborn,
London WC1V 7QX

*James Sherwood's Discriminating Guide
to London* © 2015 James Sherwood
Foreword © 2015 James B. Sherwood

Illustrated by Claire Rollet
Designed by Kate Slotover
Edited by Rosanna Lewis

British Library Cataloguing-in-Publication Data
A catalogue record for this book is available from
the British Library

ISBN 978-0-500-51828-1

Printed and bound in China by Everbest Printing Co. Ltd

To find out about all our publications, please visit
www.thamesandhudson.com. There you can subscribe
to our e-newsletter, browse or download our current
catalogue, and buy any titles that are in print.

Contents

III. Drinks Cabinet

iv. Shops

Furniture & Interiors

Books

Foreword

What a coincidence that the new *James Sherwood's Discriminating Guide to London* should be written by a James Sherwood who is not me!

I am an American who came to Europe in the 1960s and established a shipping company called Sea Containers. I was based in Paris initially, and as a stranger there I relied on the excellent Gault-Millau guide to the city. When I shifted my office to London in the 1970s I found there was no truly discriminating guide comparable to Gault-Millau.

I met a talented journalist, Susan Blackburn, a fellow American. We commiserated with each other on the lack of such a guide, so I decided to commission her to write one. Susan had many friends among important journalists of the day, so she assigned them restaurants to review, their only payment being the cost of the meal. When it came to ranking the establishments by stars, both she and I sampled them. I said I got tired walking the long corridors of huge museums and wanted a shortlist of 'must-see' things on display. When it came to shops, Susan asked her socialite lady friends to recommend the best ones.

I then approached William Heinemann, the British publishers, to publish the book, and they agreed to print 5,000 provided I bought 20 per cent. I did so and sent copies to my customers, friends and associates around the world. That was in 1975. Much to my surprise, Heinemann said the books had sold out, and asked me to produce a new edition, which both Heinemann and Grosset & Dunlap in New York published in 1977. This time 50,000 copies were printed, and they sold out as well. I had visions of Susan continuing to produce the guide, updating it every two years, but she tragically died and with her my guide – until now.

In 2014 I received two handsome books published by Thames & Hudson, which seemed to be dedicated to me on the dust jackets. But a few days later my namesake James Sherwood contacted me and identified himself as the author of the books. He said that Thames & Hudson wanted to take up the reins of my original guide, with him as the author. I readily endorsed the project.

In 1976 I had bought the Hotel Cipriani in Venice, which later became the flagship of a company I founded called Orient-Express Hotels (now called Belmond). Partly because of the success of my *Discriminating Guide* I decided to create a group of hotels and travel experiences that would appeal to discriminating travellers. I brought back into operation the famed Orient-Express train in 1982. Eventually, the company owned fifty properties in twenty-five countries, and it continues to prosper under the name Belmond. We own the Manoir aux Quat' Saisons in Oxfordshire, and that would have been included in James's restaurant list had it been in London.

Producing the new *James Sherwood's Discriminating Guide to London* must have been an enormous task for James. I recall all the galleys that had to be proofed in Susan's day, and the debates about which places were to be included or excluded. Of the twenty-five starred restaurants in the edition of 1977 only eight remain, thanks to the Roux brothers and their sons (Le Gavroche), Richard Caring (Scott's) and a few hotel owners (Connaught). Le Gavroche charged £28 for dinner for two in 1977, plus wine, while Scott's was £22 plus wine. Today, the appetizer alone costs more than that.

In the years since 1977 some restaurants have drifted away from French towards Italian and from Chinese to Japanese, although there are still excellent examples of the former. Brasseries have become increasingly popular. 'Show-biz' cuisine has emerged, with unusually shaped plates, bizarre food combinations, frothy emanations, *amuse-bouches*, pre-desserts, cloches (silver domes) on plates and often so much noise that it is impossible to hold a conversation. I predict that much of this will pass, and the survivors will be those establishments with consistent track records of preparing delicious cuisine and serving it unostentatiously in a pleasing environment. James's recommendations meet these criteria.

Whether it be for food, museums or shopping, I think you will find the new *James Sherwood's Discriminating Guide* of great assistance, whether you are a visitor or a Londoner. I will certainly be using it myself.

James B. Sherwood
Founder and Chairman Emeritus of Belmond Ltd
(formerly Orient-Express Hotels Ltd)

Preface

London is a city of echoes: one that does not repeat itself, but often rhymes. When my writing career in London was in its infancy, a dinner-party guest arrived at a kitchen supper in Clapham with a curious book, published in 1977 and entitled *James Sherwood's Discriminating Guide to London: Fine Dining and Shopping, with a Special Section on Museums and Art Galleries*. I was familiar with my coincidental namesake, the man who single-handedly saved the Orient Express, chaired the charity Venice in Peril and owned the historic Orient-Express Hotels portfolio, including the Cipriani in Venice, the Hôtel du Palais in Biarritz and the Copacabana Palace in Rio. I was not aware, however, that Mr Sherwood's discriminating guide was the 1970s jet-set bible for dining, drinking and dancing in London.

When Louis Vuitton first asked me to contribute to the company's City Guides in 2004, I began following in Mr Sherwood's footsteps around London. At the time of writing I still am, as we begin work on the Louis Vuitton Guide to London 2016. Occasionally, when lost for words, I turn to Mr Sherwood's book for amusement and inspiration. I now know that the authoritative, witty and occasionally caustic tone of *James Sherwood's Discriminating Guide to London* was largely thanks to the late editor Susan Blackburn, who could, like the Dowager Countess of Grantham, produce a withering quip with admirable brevity and accuracy.

It is nearly forty years since the last edition of *James Sherwood's Discriminating Guide to London* was published in the UK and the USA. I wrote to Mr Sherwood, enclosing my previous Thames & Hudson books, in early 2014. We met and he kindly allowed me to use the title and shamelessly copy the compact hardback format that fits into a deep pocket, attaché case or handbag. He also agreed to write a foreword to the edition of 2015. Although all the text is new, we have kept Mr Sherwood's amusing etymology of London restaurants, such as 'Where to eat when you've come into an inheritance', 'Where to eat with your lover' and 'Where to eat in the company of beautiful people'. When Mr Sherwood wrote the original guide, the few smart addresses that allowed such informal attire as blue jeans merited their own special section. Today restaurants in which blue jeans are not acceptable are sadly few, so we have instead included a section entitled 'Where to eat in evening dress'.

Susan Blackburn's note to the *Discriminating Guide* of 1977 begins 'Critics rarely agree,' and, in the spirit of full disclosure, explains that Mr Sherwood and his spies visited well over 300 London restaurants, adding the caveat that 'they don't go in fur coats.' Only half passed the *Discriminating Guide* test. Rather than ignore the also-rans, the *Discriminating Guide* holds the disappointing doors to account in a section titled 'Not for us'. I have retained this section in a reduced format for the new edition, with the proviso 'But should be'. I share Mr Sherwood's particular prejudices on London's culinary landscape – cheek-by-jowl table placement, excessively loud music and oleaginous or arrogant service – and feel it my duty to warn of such hazards, which can imperil a perfectly decent lunch or dinner.

The new edition of *James Sherwood's Discriminating Guide to London* is entirely subjective and entirely written by me. As the original Mr Sherwood cautioned, reviewing a hundred restaurants in a relatively short time would be time-consuming, ruinously expensive and punishing on the waistline, so my equally discriminating friends have reported on the occasional restaurant that I haven't revisited. While we're on the subject of budget, the new edition is not an oligarch's guide to London, although I do, of course, visit some swanky places. Rather, it aspires to be a very particular Londoner's guide to living elegantly without the benefit of a banker's bonus or sovereign wealth fund.

Mr Sherwood's original guide concentrated largely on fine dining, with briefer entries about shopping and a superb guide to museums, including 'Not to be missed' lists collected from the directors of each institution. I have decided to mirror the original format, but have added a new Hotels section and a Drinks Cabinet exploring London's supper clubs, public houses, cocktail bars and cabarets. The original *Discriminating Guide* was a huge success in America, and it is clear that adding hotels is vital if the book is to be as useful to London's guests as to its natives.

Although I endeavour to avoid repetition, there is no disputing that London's social life revolves largely around hotel restaurants, bars, cabarets and ballrooms. So, as well as their listings in the Hotels section, you will find such addresses as Claridge's, the Dorchester and the Savoy in the Drinks Cabinet and Restaurants chapters. I cannot claim to have spent the night in every hotel listed. However, I have visited more London hotel rooms than some ladies and gentlemen for hire, having been invited to attend

fashion and fine jewellery press days or private
views for the Vuitton Guides over the past decade.
I guarantee that I have viewed, if not stayed in, all
the hotels listed.

By its very nature, *James Sherwood's
Discriminating Guide to London* isn't for everyone.
Although there is more than a smattering of addresses
where it is fun to slum it, this book is unashamedly a
celebration of the finest the city has to offer. I have,
however, endeavoured to include delights that do
not require you to pawn the family tiara or sell a
kidney. I hope *James Sherwood's Discriminating Guide
to London* will play a role comparable to that of Her
Majesty The Queen in relation to her numerous prime
ministers: 'to consult, to encourage and to warn'.
I might add 'to amuse' but humour, like criticism,
is also entirely subjective.

I have tried to make this mammoth task more
manageable by choosing addresses that are unique to
and/or characteristic of London. A restaurant, hotel
or shop that also trades in New York or Dubai (the
Ivy, J. Sheekey's) will at the very least have been born
in London. Actually, I'm much keener on restaurants
that fly solo in London and trade abroad than on
those that expand and open doors in every fashionable
neighbourhood of the city.

Finally, a note on those neighbourhoods: you will
notice that the *Discriminating Guide* is extremely fond
of Mayfair, Piccadilly and St James's, postcodes that
constitute the heart of London's West End and tend to
monopolize the attention of natives and visitors alike.
We will, of course, be visiting Knightsbridge, Notting
Hill, Marylebone, Bloomsbury and Clerkenwell; we
might even venture into what's become known as
'fashionable Hoxton, Shoreditch and Spitalfields'

(although we'll make a note to leave our best jewellery in the hotel safe). What I won't do is send you to 'up and coming' neighbourhoods unless they have upped and come. I firmly promise never to take you anywhere that I haven't personally visited, vetted and thoroughly enjoyed.

James Sherwood
www.james-sherwood.com

Note
It is a compliment to the loyalty of London's diners and shoppers, and to the excellence and tenacity of select addresses, that a respectable number of restaurants and shops applauded in this *Discriminating Guide* were trading in 1975, when Mr Sherwood wrote his original edition. Those hardy perennials are annotated &JS.

The Wolseley

I

Restaurants

Where to eat …
to breakfast like a king

CARAVAN £

Exmouth Market is a scene: a pedestrianized Clerkenwell walk where the Margaret Howell- and Grenson brogue-wearing male of the species turns up his jeans to mid-calf, affects tortoiseshell spectacles and cultivates a beard that would make the Amish think twice. Former Market resident Joseph Grimaldi (the clown, not the Monégasque royal) would fit right in. Caravan, a glass-walled corner site with wooden benches spilling out among the food stalls, is where the beards who hot-desk in Clerkenwell's creative agencies come to refuel of a morning. It is thoroughly enjoyable to whip a copy of the *Financial Times* out of your laptop case and watch the puzzled looks on the faces of men who cannot break their fast without the company of an open MacBook Air; it's still more amusing watching trendy dads trying to spoon-feed granola into the mouth of a caterwauling little Mavis or Hector.

Breakfast is not so much served as art-directed to appeal to healthy urban trendies. The 'eggs any style' fry-up is served on a rustic doorstep of sourdough bread with layers of brittle streaky bacon, slow-roasted tomatoes that explode like a love bomb of flavour, and meaty thyme-roasted Portobello mushrooms. Green (read ethically grown, harvested and shipped) coffee is roasted on the premises, earning Caravan 'best in show' for a velvety, rich flat white … no mean feat in a city that has more funky little indie coffee shops per square mile than it has banks. Caravan is a local treasure for serving robust, Dickensian breakfast fare such as baked eggs and smoky black pudding with maple-roast apples. The restaurant seats 48, but I like to perch on a bar stool facing the reclaimed-timber counter – all the better for placing an order with the uniformly fresh-faced and cheerful waiting staff and baristas.

> "*Caravan is a local treasure for serving robust, Dickensian breakfast fare such as baked eggs and smoky black pudding …*"

Healthy breakfasts can be rather joyless, so applause is due to Caravan for serving peanut syrup porridge with cream and orange-scented pancakes with blueberries and vanilla butter: cheerful options all. The weekend brunch menu is slightly more extensive – Welsh rarebit with poached egg and onion jam or ham hock hash with honey-mustard hollandaise – and, weather permitting, a table outside allows you to have a hoot ogling the street theatre. Exmouth Market has a reputation for culinary excellence, and the mighty Moro, Bonnie Gull Seafood Bar and Medcalf are all within spitting distance of Caravan. On a sunny Sunday morning, when they are all packed to the gills, I ponder putting the urban trendies to music. What's that line in Blossom Dearie's 'I'm Hip'? 'Now I'm deep into Zen meditation and macrobiotics. And as soon as I can, I intend to get into narcotics.'

11–13 Exmouth Market EC1
Tel. 020 7833 8115
Tube: Farringdon
http://caravanonexmouth.co.uk

THE RITZ RESTAURANT £££££

It's a rare grand-hotel dining room that resists the siren song of fashion. Asking Philippe Starck to 'freshen up' Le Meurice in Paris was, to me, like letting Val Garland loose on the *Mona Lisa* with her make-up kit. The Ritz Restaurant has not simply resisted change; it would still be recognizable to King Edward VII and his last paramour, Mrs Keppel, who dined there on Escoffier's finest soon after the hotel opened in 1906. The original *Discriminating Guide* declared the Ritz to be 'still London's most beautiful dining room', and forty years later the beauty has not faded: quite the reverse, actually, after its owners, the Barclay brothers, spent ten years restoring the hotel.

The architects Mèwes & Davis understood the psychology of parading wealth when they created the Long Gallery, which runs the length of the Ritz from the concierge to the opulent, enchanting restaurant. The Ritz Restaurant is the finest example of Gilded Age Rococo Revival interiors east of Newport, Rhode Island. The Edwardian interpretation of the style of Louis XVI marries the comforts demanded by a Mrs Astor with the ornate frivolity of Marie Antoinette's Petit Trianon at Versailles: plush Aubusson carpets, gilt festoon chandeliers encircling a celestial *trompe l'œil* oval panel, tasselled silk curtains framing glass

terrace doors and salon chairs as commodious as
thrones. Gilded wall sconces bathe the room in a rosy
gold glow, and the silver, china, glass and linen are all
reminiscent of the richness of the Gilded Age.

There is no better place to breakfast like a
king. The Ritz epitomizes for me how the successful
Londoner begins his or her day: Earl Grey served at
the perfect strength and temperature from a silver
teapot the size of a samovar, luscious eggs Benedict
framed by Royal Doulton china, and, in a silver
rack, toast so uniformly crisp that each piece could
have been spray-tanned. Serving 'the Ritz way' takes
months of training – it is patently obvious that none
of the staff is part-time – and waiters consider it the
Sandhurst of the profession. The breakfast menu lists
sybaritic treats harking back to the Edwardian age,
such as Haddock Monte Carlo (the fish is poached in
champagne), grilled fillet of sole with a lemon and
parsley butter, and even sirloin steak topped with fried
eggs and mushrooms, although the last is not for the
faint-hearted or the hardened of artery.

As you'd imagine, the Ritz Restaurant is
wildly popular for celebratory lunches and dinners
(engagements, anniversaries, divorce settlements and
the like), not least among the Royal Family. Known
as 'the Queen's local', the Ritz hosted Her Majesty's
Golden Jubilee and eightieth birthday dinners in 2002
and 2006 respectively. The 'palace-style cuisine' of the
head chef, John Williams – all reassuringly en croute
and flambé – is of the quality that earned the hotel
Prince Charles's Royal Warrant. The Friday/Saturday
Live at the Ritz dinner dances, when a four-piece band,
crooners and show dancers lead a strictly ballroom
evening, have immense charm for swingers old and
young. It was at the Ritz Restaurant in 1936 that Alice

Keppel voiced her acid drop 'Things were done better in my day' about Mrs Simpson and the Abdication Crisis. The same can never be said of the Ritz.

The Ritz, 150 Piccadilly W1
Tel. 020 7493 8181
Tube: Green Park
www.theritzlondon.com

ST JOHN BREAD & WINE ££

In the nineteenth century Spitalfields was the poorest, most squalid criminal quarter in London, which is why, in 1864, the philanthropist George Peabody chose Commercial Street for his first Peabody Estate social housing. It suits the *pauvre chic* ethos of Fergus Henderson's St John group (honest, under-appreciated British ingredients served in spartan surroundings) to open a restaurant and bakery opposite Spitalfields Market, in the shadow of the spire of Hawksmoor's Christ Church. Like the Smithfield mother ship, St John Bread & Wine is a clean, whitewashed canteen with utilitarian schoolroom desks and chairs and those black flying-saucer ceiling lights that remind one of a Cold War interrogation at Checkpoint Charlie. It's a workman's caff as imagined by the Eameses.

Until St John Bread & Wine opened, in 2003, the East End's most famous breakfast was served at the open-all-hours Brick Lane Beigel Bakery (No. 159, since you ask), where hookers, clubbers, cabbies and major alcoholics still gather for sustenance during the desperate hours. St John Bread & Wine has become famed by the breakfast cognoscenti for serving the definitive bacon sandwich. Here's how it's done: the smoked meat – tender, salty Gloucester Old Spot bacon – is cooked on an open charcoal grill; the bread is a home-baked white sandwich loaf as soft and thick as Joey Essex, cut into doorsteps and lightly toasted on the griddle; and the secret is Henderson's recipe for home-made tomato ketchup.

At £5.90, the SJB&W bacon sandwich is an affordable masterpiece, and – vegans and orthodox Jews excepted – not ordering it for breakfast is tantamount to culinary treason. Nevertheless, the breakfast menu does list all the usual suspects demanded by Millennials, such as granola, yoghurt and honey, porridge and prunes (to keep you regular, as my grandmother would say), poached fruit and pikelets (toasted crumpets) served with jam but infinitely more interesting slathered in full-fat butter and Marmite. Breakfast is served in the narrow window between 9 and 11 am, a fact that should give you a rough idea of the fashionable East End's working hours.

94–96 Commercial Street E1
Tel. 020 7251 0848
Tube: Aldgate East
www.stjohngroup.uk.com/spitalfields

THE WOLSELEY £££

For the benefit of those who have been forcibly or voluntarily absented from London society this past fifteen years, the Wolseley is one of fashionable London's perennial favourites. With the Delaunay, Colbert, Fischer's, the Colony Grill Room and Brasserie Zédel, the Wolseley forms a diamond collet necklace of perfectly faceted West End restaurants. Although it opened relatively recently, in 2003, the dining room feels as urbane as a vintage smoking jacket. Its owners, Chris Corbin and Jeremy King, saw the potential in this Jazz Age car showroom – built for Wolseley Motors next door to the Ritz, to a design by William Curtis – for a grand, glamorous European café in the style of Vienna's Café Sperl or Café Procope in Paris. This they have achieved at the Wolseley, a marbled, mirrored, domed and Doric-columned show-stopper that positively trills with gossip and intrigue from seven in the morning to last orders at midnight. Although Corbin and King restaurants spare us the torture of piped music, one always feels the urge to hum Adele's 'Laughing Song' from *Die Fledermaus* when entering the Wolseley. It's a 'waltz by Strauss' kind of restaurant, you understand.

When I first worked in a newspaper office (the *Sunday Express*, since you ask), breakfast for most fashion folk was a cup of black coffee, a Marlboro Red and a Xanax. How times have changed. Long two-bottle lunches are now considered hopelessly démodé, more's the pity, and important business is conducted over breakfast. The Wolseley waltz begins at 7 am as the *tourier* (pastry chef) delivers the *Viennoiseries* (croissants, pains au chocolat and so on) that are prepared daily on the premises. Within the hour, editors and executives from Hearst and Condé Nast take their seats at the 'inner circle' tables while waiters glide around like dancers in Jonathan Miller's Charleston *Mikado*, delivering silver pots of jasmine tea, tall glasses of hot chocolate, devilled kidneys, caviar omelettes, caramelized halves of pink grapefruit and the old eggs Benedict

> *"It's a 'waltz by Strauss' kind of restaurant, you understand."*

and Bloody Mary one-two for those who might have overindulged at last night's awards ceremony.

Corbin and King staff are choreographed and drilled like Busby Berkeley chorines to move seamlessly and in unison, with never the clatter of cutlery or the shatter of glass. They will not bat an eyelid should you go off-piste for breakfast and ask for the Wolseley's Pimms Royal Ice Cream served with a splash of champagne to go with your Bucks Fizz. I think you can always tell a restaurant by the newspapers you are offered while you wait for an errant guest. Breakfast time at the Wolseley means the *Financial Times* and the *International New York Times*, titles that please the key catchment of early-rising high-achievers such as hedge-fund boys, media moguls, fashion PRs and St James's bachelors. Of course, at breakfast you will be denied a sighting of Katy Perry, the Beckhams, Madonna, Daniel Craig, Miss Moss or Jude Law, all of whom have dined here. Depending on your appetite for famous faces in public places, that could be a good thing.

160 Piccadilly W1
Tel. 020 7499 6996
Tube: Green Park
www.thewolseley.com

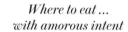

Where to eat ...
with amorous intent

ANDREW EDMUNDS £££

One always warms to a new acquaintance who suggests lunch at Andrew Edmunds. Chances are we will become great friends or end up in bed together. This Hogarthian eighteenth-century town house is shorthand for understated, unpretentious food that plays a supporting role to a superlative wine list priced as if an overindulgent uncle has taken the sting out of the bill. It's like a Masonic handshake for excellent taste. Interior designers are paid ludicrous sums to imitate the stripped-back, sepia-toned old Soho patina of Andrew Edmunds, but such charm cannot be bought or manufactured. Wild flowers spill out of china jugs, tall candles illuminate the bar/dining room at night and menus are brief, simple and handwritten.

The ground-floor and basement dining rooms are reminiscent of a Cruikshank coffee house: a hugger-mugger of booths and back-to-back chairs that encourage you to 'lean in' – hence Andrew Edmunds' reputation as a hunting ground for the second wives' club. The kitchen is an antidote to the pernicious trend for overcomplicated dishes and obnoxious menus that demand twenty questions to decipher. In fact, I'd go so far as to say that Andrew Edmunds was serving a simple, seasonal British menu thirty years before it became a trend. Whereas elsewhere you'll be charged a tenner if a tomato is classified as 'heritage', Andrew Edmunds presents a dressed crab, mouth-watering plate of charcuterie or salt cod, fennel and orange salad entrée at a decent price.

You would insult the wondrous wine list by ordering by the glass. The primary selection is weighted with marvellous bottles under £30, such as a 2010 Marquese Antinori Chianti Classico or a 2011 South African Chenin Blanc, that go down like a Madame Claude girl. Typical of Edmunds, the crown jewels of the cellar are modestly listed as 'Additional Wines'. How can you not love a restaurant that offers a bottle of Pol Roger for £45 and a magnum for £95? The menu is, I think, at its best during the game season, when you can tear into a pheasant leg and punish a full-bodied Pinot Noir on a cold autumn afternoon before progressing to a plate of Neal's Yard cheeses and a half bottle of Muscadet.

Mr Edmunds keeps an antique print shop next door, and a private club upstairs, the Academy, which serves as a den for the literary, artistic and theatrical set, who remember or regret not knowing the Soho of the Colony Room, Piano Bar and Jeffrey Bernard. I once bought a print of Gainsborough's 1871 portrait of Queen Charlotte from Andrew Edmunds. A week later I received a phone call saying he would like me to have King George III as well, because it was a pity to break up the pair. Now that's the mark of an elegant mind.

46 Lexington Street W1
Tel. 020 7437 5708
Tube: Oxford Circus/Piccadilly Circus
www.andrewedmunds.com

BOB BOB RICARD £££

Bob Bob Ricard creates a *Last Days of the Romanovs* aura of the reverent and the risqué that appeals to famous faces in public places. Like a grand duchess in flight, one is briskly handed from doorman to footman to maître to waiter – each murmuring your name with a slight bow – and ushered to a richly upholstered booth hidden from prying eyes by peacock-blue velvet curtains. The light is sinfully low and the room shimmers with the glint of Byzantine mosaics, mirrors, marble and Pullman carriage brass. It's an Orient Express carriage reimagined as a Fabergé egg. Bolshevik restaurant critics sneered at the 'Press for

Champagne' button, but the men my friend Mr Barker calls 'randy dandies' have thawed many a heart thanks to such a simple device. As many a restaurant has learned to its cost, theatre is absurd without stealthy, smooth service. When you press for champagne at Bob Bob, it arrives as if by magic.

Dining at Bob Bob Ricard has all the sense of anticipation of opening night at the Ballets Russes. The Russian-English cuisine reflects the nationalities of the owners, Leonid Shutov and Richard Howarth, and strikes just the right balance of flamboyance and familiarity. You could start by toasting the evening with vodka shots served at -18 degrees and light bites of Petrossian caviar, but I fear one can get carried away ... feet first like Mag Wildwood in *Breakfast at Tiffany's*, as it happens. The twice-baked Stinking Bishop cheese soufflé is darling, as is a salad of goat's cheese and beetroot, sliced so thinly it resembles a stained-glass window on a plate. Although I consider it close to treason to grill or bake an oyster, surprises such as venison steak tartare served with a raw quail's egg and lobster macaroni cheese are to be applauded. A new star dish – poached Loch Duart salmon served with warm cucumber, mustard and dill – has supplanted the chicken Kiev that is still mourned as one might a lost lover.

Bob Bob Ricard's wine list is intentionally concise, and its upper register is modest in its mark-up. It is exceptionally convivial to hunker down for the evening in one's booth, endlessly pressing the buzzer for more bottles of Taittinger Brut Reserve, and you are never asked to relinquish the table at the point of a bayonet, as is common in some of the West End's more avaricious addresses. Here, there is always time for a little more delicious gossip and another spoonful of shared Eton mess *en perle*. The Club Room below Bob Bob Ricard is as sparkling as a Van Cleef *minaudière* and serves the same menu as Bob Bob but later, and at tables surrounding a glamorous backgammon-board dance floor. The club room is like a threesome between *Bullets over Broadway*, *Boardwalk Empire* and *The Cotton Club*.

1 Upper James Street W1
Tel. 020 3145 1000
Tube: Piccadilly Circus
www.bobbobricard.com

GASTRO ££

Drumroll, please, for one of the very few restaurants we consider worth the trek to south London. When I lived in Clapham North, twenty years ago, the High Street was like a depressed Serbian suburb. The only supermarket would routinely run out of potatoes, a scrap-metal merchant still traded, and it was clear from the sweet smell emanating from a dodgy booth called Granny's Pantry under the railway arches that the old girl smoked weed. The consolations of living in Clapham were the elegant Old Town, a super art-house cinema on Venn Street and, opposite, a bistro called Gastro that couldn't have been more Parisian if Édith Piaf had crouched outside warbling 'L'Accordéoniste'.

With its zinc bar, tank of live lobsters, stripped wooden tables and stained-glass windows, Gastro was and is a charming anomaly in Clapham. The kitchen is faultless when it comes to the classics: fish soup (a gift that keeps on giving), dressed crab served with home-made mayonnaise, *coq au vin* and bouillabaisse. The *vin de table* is perfectly respectable, although

I always enjoy a Ricard aperitif, served as it should
be with a jug of water at room temperature. Gastro is
particularly magical by night, and, if there are sweet
nothings to be whispered, I recommend the tables for
two that line a dark corridor adjacent to a generous
communal dining table. The service is gratifyingly
brisk, unless of course you happen to be French, in
which case you'll be greeted like a long-lost brother-
in-arms to la Résistance. The interiors, which are
reminiscent of a Brassaï photograph, lend themselves
to those who want to be alone but not indefinitely.

67 Venn Street SW4
Tel. 020 7627 0222
Tube: Clapham Common

J. SHEEKEY OYSTER BAR £££

Marilyn Monroe, who wasn't dumb and wasn't
blonde, observed astutely that 'glamour cannot be
manufactured.' This applies to restaurants as well as
to the most fabulous 1950s blonde: you either have
it or you've had it. The pretty people who hover like
dragonflies over any new opening in London may give
a frisson of sex appeal, but, as we all know, they're
about as loyal as Guy Burgess. So it is with huge
respect, a standing ovation and a rush of endorphins
that we applaud the perennial glamour puss opened
by Josef Sheekey in 1896, when Queen Victoria was
still on the throne.

J. Sheekey is the pearl in the oyster of West End
theatrical restaurants. Its patina of timeless chic has
been formed by decades of patronage by stars of stage
and screen, whose portraits adorn its walls. In typical
luvvie fashion, Sheekey's loiters like Lili Marlene in a
down-at-heel pedestrianized court that snakes along

the haunch of the Noël Coward Theatre. The mirrored glass façade and top-hatted doorman leave one in no doubt that this is a place of greater safety for famous faces. You might well think the restaurant provides the best seats in the house to see the portraits of Simon Callow, Kenneth Branagh, Stephen Fry and the dames Judi Dench and Maggie Smith come to life, but for us its beating heart is the adjoining Oyster Bar, which opened in 2008.

The Oyster Bar specializes in plump crustaceans, refined small plates and adulterous couples, so the atmosphere fizzes with champagne and seduction. The Hollywood art deco interiors by Martin Brudnizki glitter like the fender of a vintage Rolls-Royce. One feels like making terribly dry quips about the potency of cheap sheet music. Needless to say, seats around the horseshoe counter are at a premium and, once won, rarely relinquished. As a glamorous theatrical agent rightly said of lunch at Sheekey's, 'It's a false economy to order champagne by the glass', knowing full well you'll easily polish off a bottle each and still be here when the pre-theatre crowd arrives. The fabled crustaceans are the centrepiece of the bar and languish on a mountain of dry ice like a Radio City Music Hall *Tribute to Neptune* as designed by Vincente Minnelli.

The stars of the menu are the dozen mixed oysters served with spicy wild boar sausages, a gargantuan whole Devon cock crab, the half lobster mayonnaise and the bravura crab bisque that's always tip-top because the *Tribute to Neptune* is stripped down twice daily. J. Sheekey's famous fish pie is served in the Oyster Bar with a buttered spinach that would make a nun kick a hole through a stained-glass window. But of late, we're rather taken by the Japanese-

Peruvian fusion influence creeping in, resulting in dishes such as bass ceviche and tempura squid. If you serve as much time as we do in Sheekey's, you will inevitably see familiar faces like Jude Law, Benedict Cumberbatch, Sheridan Smith and Daniel Radcliffe darting in and out between shows. But the real stars of the Oyster Bar are the handsome, amusing and efficient staff, who must have seen it all in their time but don't tell tales.

28–35 St Martin's Court WC2
Tel. 020 7240 2565
Tube: Leicester Square
www.jsheekeyoysterbar.co.uk

Where to eat ... when you've
come into an inheritance

HÉLÈNE DARROZE AT THE CONNAUGHT £££££

London's restaurant critics are a contrary, sometimes feral pack of attack dogs that should be approached with extreme caution. When Hélène Darroze opened her restaurant at the prestigious Connaught hotel (see entry) – replacing the critics' favourite, Angela Hartnett – *The Guardian* savaged the menu as 'the stupidest, most overwrought proposition apparently created by the random word generator'. One wonders if a marriage had broken up or root-canal work was completed on review day. Why a newspaper with socialist tendencies should even bother reviewing a hotel restaurant patronized by the very people it would like to string up on the nearest lamp post is a mystery. Fast-forward to 2015, and Hélène Darroze at the Connaught is one of only eight restaurants with two Michelin stars in London, and a much-loved favourite of the moneyed Mayfair establishment.

The pleasing oak-panelled Edwardian dining room shows the light touch of the interior designer India Mahdavi, with contemporary elements such as a surprisingly pretty Damien Hirst canvas and deliciously deep club chairs covered in gaily patterned floral brocade. Being a fourth-generation chef from Landes, with a second Michelin-starred restaurant (in Paris) that bears her name, Darroze is messianic about finding and naming the best producers in Europe. Should they wish, each guest is given a solitaire board filled with white marbles, on which the day's key ingredients are printed. Food intolerance – both real and imagined – is endemic in London, so this game is a rather clever conceit. If you'd rather use the menu (spoilsport), you'll find each dish headlined by the key ingredient, be that foie gras, artichokes, lobster, sweetbreads or wild strawberries.

Darroze is an artist, and the pedestrian prose on the menu doesn't do justice to her exquisite food. 'Lamb, carrot, tandoori, Greek yoghurt & mint' couldn't sound less tempting, but the dish itself is a masterpiece of subtlety and style. It's like describing Klimt's *Lady in Gold* as 'middle-aged woman in yellow'. Inheritance permitting, we would recommend submitting to the nine-course tasting menu (£155) with accompanying wine (£125). For a hotel that is more than 200 years old, the wine list is as weighty as the Gutenberg Bible and longer than the Domesday Book. Conceding choice is a great luxury, and I'm ashamed to say my palate wouldn't appreciate a Louis Roederer Cristal champagne for £1050 any more than my wallet would be prepared to take one for the team.

For most, dinner at Hélène Darroze at the Connaught is for high days and holidays. But should you be invited, cancel elective surgery for the pleasure.

The Connaught, Carlos Place W1
Tel. 020 7107 8880
Tube: Bond Street
www.the-connaught.co.uk/mayfair-restaurants/
helene-darroze

HIBISCUS £££££

Criticizing a meal at Hibiscus is rather like standing in front of a Matisse collage in Tate Modern and debating whether that precise shade of blue could be a tone lighter. The Lyonnais chef Claude Bosi takes a wild, fauvist approach to flavours. His experimental cuisine plays brilliantly with combinations of savoury and sweet flavours that may surprise – raspberry adding character to a pork belly, for example, and lobster ravioli – but always delight. From his parents' restaurant in Lyon, Bosi moved to Paris, and before reaching his thirtieth birthday had trained under Michel Rostang, Alain Passard and Alain Ducasse. He opened the two-Michelin-star Hibiscus in Ludlow in 2000 before bringing the restaurant to Maddox Street, London, in 2007.

Hibiscus has always been a haven of civility and charm, but we found the dining room too beige and too polite; diners whispering as if they're in church and waiters gliding silently as though on casters don't add to the levity of the proceedings. However, a recent return visit with a fashion PR chum was a revelation. The interior designer Alexander Waterworth's peacock-blue banquettes and fine-art photography curated by Maxine Davidson give the room character while not taking anything away from the serenity of the decor.

It's a balancing act to serve haute cuisine in a way that combines knowledge, formality and friendliness. The ladies and gentlemen at Hibiscus are perfection one and all. Of course, you long to spend hours here, but you are treated as though you're the last of the big spenders even when ordering a swift two-course lunch with a glass of wine. Spring onion and lime king prawn consommé was a soup of the gods, and veal cheeks with parsnips and truffles the star of the autumn menu. On being shown blood-peach soufflé with roasted almond sorbet and Neal's Yard cheeses on the pudding menu, we felt that only a blowpipe and poisoned dart would remove us from the premises. For that reason, we're including Hibiscus in our 'Inheritance' section because we long to return and spend the evening with Monsieur Bosi and his tasting menu.

29 Maddox Street W1
Tel. 020 7629 2999
Tube: Oxford Circus
www.hibiscusrestaurant.co.uk

LE GAVROCHE £££££ • &JS

The original *Discriminating Guide* wrote expansively about the original Gavroche on Lower Sloane Street when the father and uncle of the present chef, Michel Roux Jr, ruled the kitchens. In an era when 'the lady's or guest's menu will be *sans* prices', Le Gavroche won the plaudit: 'Few restaurants can match it at its best, and the originality of the chef and the effort of the staff deserve the praise they are becoming used to.' Minor criticism included questioning whether it was 'de rigueur for the waiter to ask clients to decide

how a chef should cook cuts of meat for which he
has invented special sauces', and commenting that
'wine glasses should be more carefully watched in
a restaurant where the wine is not left on the table
(or even within arm's reach).' Mark-ups for the 1964
Château Margaux (£5.50 at auction and £31 on the
list) led to the conclusion that 'probably your best bet
is to follow the French fashion of drinking Champagne
throughout': a Veuve Clicquot 1969 for £11.

Le Gavroche has lived on Upper Brook Street
since 1981 and has thrived under the direction of Roux
Jr since 1991. A new kitchen was installed in 2014,
with the Chef's Library private dining room. The
subterranean dining room is relatively unchanged,
with its collection of Chagall and Picasso prints and
its curious animals sculpted from cutlery as table
centrepieces. The interiors are classic Mayfair old
money (warm, soft and rich), from the 'red room'
bar to the dining room circled by green-velvet
banquettes. Jackets are required, and if you consider
this an affront to self-expression, there are countless
alternatives. As Judy Garland told the CBS executives,
'If you want the girl next door, go next door.'

Le Gavroche still serves the Soufflé Suissesse
about which the original *Discriminating Guide* was
sniffy (ordinary, moist, bland), but this soufflé cooked
on double cream is flavoursome, rich and deliciously
blasphemous in the age of tedious allergies and
dietary requirements. We would say it's best to check
in your diet with your pashmina at Le Gavroche,
but don't underestimate Roux Jr's light touch with
Scheherazadian ingredients. Lobster mousse with
Aquitaine caviar and champagne butter sauce and
the grilled scallops with clam minestrone are pretty,
light entrées that in no way made us regret sharing

the roast suckling pig for two. Nor did the not-so-little piggy deter us in any way from sharing the superb coconut and white-chocolate cream pudding served with a mango and lime salad. It is rather pointless to criticize individual dishes at Le Gavroche, because you aren't going to be served a bad one. Of course, it isn't cheap, but as the original *Guide* succinctly put it, 'one doesn't come to the Gavroche to be thrifty.'

43 Upper Brook Street W1
Tel. 020 7408 0881
Tube: Marble Arch
www.le-gavroche.co.uk

UMU £££££

Off Bond Street and behind the fashion flagships of Bruton Street, Bruton Place is a deceptively humble mews. The Guinea (on the site of a tavern built in 1423) is a de facto beefsteak club for Mayfair's most dashing hedge-fund buccaneers. The old and new establishment meet at Gavin Rankin's Bellamy's, where Her Majesty The Queen has dined, and the tailors Timothy Everest and Thom Sweeney have windows on this relatively closed world. Umu has been hiding for a decade in the corner of Bruton Place behind a dark wood sliding door. Like its neighbours, it doesn't need to show off because it is unique: the only Kyoto-influenced restaurant in the UK, serving the purest Japanese cuisine under the direction of head chef Yoshinori Ishii.

From the moment one is greeted at the gorgeous raw timber desk (of stacked logs cut like a terrine) designed by Jae-Hyo Lee, one is in the hands of angels. We have never encountered a waiter with such a charming, calming manner and superlative knowledge.

As we order sashimi, he explains that Ishii has trained his Cornish fishermen in the Edo dynasty technique of dispatching fish swiftly and without trauma. Rather like a Mafia hit, this involves a stiletto piercing above the neck and at the base of the tail fin. We also learned that Umu's vegetables, herbs and fruit are grown at Nama Yasai in East Sussex, the UK's first organic farm to be run on Japanese principles.

Our waiter encouraged us to allow Ishii to select our sashimi, and we were most taken with the substantial bites of salmon and the fan of wafer-thin Cornish white fish usuzukuri, which quite simply melted when bathed in

"From the moment one is greeted ... one is in the hands of angels."

chirizu and wasabi soy sauce. The beauty of Umu is not necessarily in the specialities. We were served a sea urchin dish that was perhaps a step too far for the palate without the aid of sake. But a smartly dressed Umu salad, a delicate shiromiso (Kyoto-style white miso) and green tea without a trace of bitterness are things of beauty. Although we didn't partake, Umu has one of the longest sake lists in the world that demands a rematch, and flies in ingredients from Tokyo daily, which might explain why it is the preferred restaurant for Japanese expats in London. A word on the competition: we adore the original Nobu in the Park Lane Hilton. But with over twenty-five doors worldwide, Nobu has become the McDonalds of the super-rich, hence our preference for Umu.

14–16 Bruton Place W1
Tel. 020 7499 8881
Tube: Bond Street
www.umurestaurant.com

Where to eat ... in the company of beautiful people

BERNERS TAVERN ££££

Chapeau to Studio 54 legend-turned-hotelier Ian
Schrager for turning faded Victorian dowager the
Berners Hotel into the sexy, super-chic London
Edition. A precedent was set when Philippe Starck's
surreal interiors for the Sanderson hotel (see entry)
wowed London when it opened opposite the Berners
in 2000. At that time Berners Street was considered
to be on the wrong side of Oxford Street, but radical
redevelopment of the Tottenham Court Road district
has significantly smartened up the approach to the
London Edition.

Perhaps the name 'tavern' is ironic, because any
dining room less redolent of a tavern I have yet to see.
The old Berners Hotel restaurant had ceilings high
enough to rival the Savoy ballroom, with impressive
fan and scroll stucco detail as intricate as royal icing.
The designer of Berners Tavern, Yabu Pushelberg (try
saying that after a Martini or two), has amplified the
scale of this monumental dining room by stacking gilt-
framed paintings and photographs to the ceiling, in an
echo of an eighteenth-century *vernissage* at Somerset
House. A towering amber-hued backlit bar hits you
from the hotel lobby, and cries out for the presence of
a film noir villainess in a black lace half-veil with an
enigmatic smile, provocatively sipping a vodka stinger.

There's an Edwardian glitter and grandness
to the room that is reflected in the refinement of
the contemporary British menu, directed by the
Michelin-starred chef Jason Atherton, alumnus of

Pierre Koffmann, Marco Pierre White and Ferran Adrià. My date recommended the egg, ham and pea risotto, and I ordered the dish as a starter-size main course – this being a fashionable feint these days for London lunches. Although exquisitely presented, with a perfectly cooked crispy quail's egg, creamy risotto and juicy lardons, the portion made one want to sink to one's knees and ululate with hunger and the pain of missed opportunity. Paucity aside, lunch was a delight and the service beautifully refined. By night the Berners Tavern is a much sexier proposition, where one can overindulge in Lake District chateaubriand, foie gras and roasted baby artichoke for two, with a rich, soporific bottle of Malbec. The scalloped banquettes that run dead centre down the length of the dining room are for those who aren't troubled by admiring eyes.

The London Edition Hotel, 10 Berners Street W1
Tel. 020 7908 7979
Tube: Tottenham Court Road
www.bernerstavern.com

CECCONI'S ££££

Here, as at Caffè Florian in Venice's Piazza San Marco, if you linger in a window seat long enough the fashionable world will walk by and, more often than not, walk in. Not coincidentally, the eponymous founder, Enzo, was general manager at Venice's Cipriani Hotel before migrating to London to open Cecconi's in 1978. In the past, the corner site between Old Bond Street and Savile Row was shielded from the street by rather bizarre fringe curtaining reminiscent of a strip joint. The fringe was shed in 2004, when Nick 'Soho House' Jones took over, to reveal Ilsa

Crawford's fabulous designs for the dining room:
jazzy humbug-striped marble floors, emerald-green
upholstery and – centre stage, flanked on three sides
by tall bar stools – a bar that has Prosecco on tap.

At Cecconi's you will always see old friends, new
faces and old friends with new faces. The denizens
of Sotheby's, Ralph Lauren, Graff, Vogue House
and the many hedge-fund offices secreted around
Mayfair treat Cecconi's like the local Italian, often
taking morning coffee, a light lunch, an aperitivo and
a nightcap there all on the same day. The restaurant
manager, Giacomo, places regulars like chess pieces,
always finding appropriate tables a discreet distance
from ex-wives and so forth. Cecconi's is a treasure
because you can dash in pre-theatre for a seat near the
cicchetti counter and order a swift plate of meatballs
and tomato sauce with a fresh peach Bellini, or lunch
on superlative beef carpaccio with a tart Venetian
dressing and a glass of Chablis.

I find Cecconi's at its most seductive for a
languorous dinner, however. The low, dramatic
lighting at night is magic: it's as if Clarence Sinclair
Bull, the man who shot Garbo, had art-directed
every angle and conspired to give guests cheekbones
like the reclusive Swede. It would be churlish not
to order a cucumber and mint Martini and a plate
of *zucchini fritti* while the waiters dart like swallows
between the tightly packed tables. The classic pasta
dishes, such as spaghetti lobster, crab ravioli and
pappardelle with beef and chicken-liver ragu, are
specialities of the house, although we'd have preferred
the pappardelle slightly more al dente than it was
served on a recent visit. The veal Milanese has the
requisite crunch of breadcrumbs and tenderness of
meat, and the perfectly pink beef *tagliata* served with

wild mushrooms and sautéed spinach is a triumph of flavours. Cecconi's home-made tiramisu is justifiably famous, although we preferred a plate of burrata to soak up the second bottle of Chianti Classico.

5A Burlington Gardens W1
Tel. 020 7434 1500
Tube: Green Park
www.cecconis.co.uk

SCOTT'S ££££

Scott's is the Koh-i-Noor in the crown of Richard Caring's London restaurants. Mount Street is the smartest, most fashionable street in Mayfair, and Scott's has been a resident since 1968, although the restaurant itself dates back to 1851. It was to Scott's that Laurence Olivier took Marilyn Monroe on her only trip to London in 1956. A facelift by the interior designer Martin Brudnizki in 2006 spared no expense, hence the sparkling floors that look as though they've been looted from the Ravenna mosaics, the magnificent green-marble oyster bar and walls smothered with contemporary Brit artworks by Damien Hirst, Gary Hume, Tracey Emin and Martin Creed. Celebrity is oxygen to Scott's, and such big beasts as Prince Harry, Anna Wintour, Tom Ford and the Beckhams are invariably on display like crustaceans for the delectation of fellow diners.

Scott's is not the restaurant to book if you don't wish to be scrutinized or to dress up. Ladies have been known to pop first into Nicky Clarke on Carlos Place for a blow-dry, just to be on the safe side. That said, it is heaven when the doorman tips the top hat and you are led to a banquette knowing you've scrubbed up well. We prefer the bar at the centre of the room because it gives such a good view of the society waxworks, their skin as stretched and transparent as bass ceviche. Scott's is famed for seafood, so it would be churlish not to order a dozen mixed oysters with wild boar sausages, even though the price would make you think they'd sent Tom Daley to dive for them. The *plateau de fruits de mer* with lobster is decorative and decadent, and the classics – shellfish bisque, sole meunière, lobster thermidor – are served with all the respect that is their due.

The raw dishes and miso-blackened salmon give the nod to Nobu, and the roasted cod with beans, chorizo and Padrón peppers has proved a popular choice with the size zeros, but we cannot dine at Scott's without ordering asparagus drowning in hollandaise, buttered spinach and that wicked bisque served with cream and cognac. We wouldn't expect anything less of Scott's than unimpeachable savouries (herring roe on toast, Welsh rarebit, Vacherin Mont d'Or with endive salad) and crisp Muscadet Sèvre et Maine ordered by the glass (£8.75) and swiftly followed by the bottle (£32). Although the passion-fruit crème brûlée is a dream, we'd rather top and tail our meal with an Aperol spritz. Few reviews of Scott's avoid mentioning the Saatchi-Lawson 'incident', and ours is not one of them. Did Scott's benefit from being the scene of the crime when Charles Saatchi was photographed on the Mount Street terrace with his hands round then-wife Nigella Lawson's throat? Frankly, you can't buy that kind of publicity.

20 Mount Street W1
Tel. 020 7495 7309
Tube: Bond Street
www.scotts-restaurant.com

SPRING ££££

The progress of the chef Skye Gyngell from the
bucolic charms of her Petersham Nurseries restaurant
to the pomp of Somerset House's New Wing – an
eighteenth-century wing on the site of a Stuart royal
palace – raised a few eyebrows. But how could she
resist? This is the first time in 150 years that this part
of Somerset House has been open to the public, and
the suite of rooms occupied by Spring makes one purr
with satisfaction at the sheer scale and serenity of the
architecture. The 'long walk' approach to Spring is
reminiscent of the Royal Opera Arcade in St James's,
with café tables leading to a bar and reception to the
left. Tables are set in an enchanted forest of black
olive trees in the atrium. The main dining room is
lofty, light and symmetrical, with tall arched windows
framing banquette tables and lovely bouquets of
balloon chandeliers hanging the length of the room.
We were seated next to the white marble bar at a
table for two, on pleasing caramel-leather chairs that
immediately won the rosette for most comfortable
place to park one's behind in a London restaurant.

The waiters are cute as a button in Egg
Breton-striped tees, canvas trousers and plimsolls,
perhaps an echo of Somerset House's history as
the Admiralty Office. Waitresses in billowing Egg
smocks flit around as if they're in a production of
A Midsummer Night's Dream. The sommelier was as
startled by our order of Pinot Blanc La Cabane by
the glass as we were by his emerald-green Trager
Delaney trousers. Now, ordinarily we don't like
waiters who look perturbed by our order (two main
courses), but the salad he suggested – organic leaves
with Caesar dressing and candied walnuts – was an
absolute delight.

Service was efficient and friendly without being overfamiliar, and the pace was leisurely and entirely at the tempo we like for a Sunday lunch. The Pinot kept coming (when will we ever learn that ordering by the glass is a false economy?), and the main dishes were substantial but light. The Dorset crab was flaked to perfection and tasted sublime with sourdough slathered in tomato and olive oil. Ravioli of ricotta with sage butter looked dull, but our guest was rapturous and did not deliver on her promise to save a mouthful. Puddings – including an outstanding prune and Armagnac tart – were sweet and simple. A few too many of the main courses were priced over £30, which is less forgivable when a side order is recommended. But Spring at Somerset House is a magnificent dining room, run efficiently by a good-looking group of staff. What's not to like?

Somerset House New Wing, Lancaster Place WC2
Tel. 020 3011 0115
Tube: Temple
www.springrestaurant.co.uk

Where to eat …
with important clients

34 £££££

It is the law of the financial jungle that clients visiting London will be bitterly disappointed if they aren't entertained at the most fashionable restaurant *du jour*, such as the Chiltern Firehouse. We think they'll be bitterly disappointed if they are. There's no margin for error when you're entertaining a 'king of

the monkeys' client, or indeed a queen bee. The last
thing you want is an altercation at the door, a table
in social Siberia or Miss Azerbaijan at the next table
making eyes – or, worse, not making eyes – in your
direction. We were put off the Chiltern Firehouse
when an overenthusiastic critic wrote that 'even God
would have to wait for a table.' Really? Really!

From the day it opened in 2011, Caprice Holdings'
34 has proved a safe pair of hands for the financially
blessed to entertain their peers. Grosvenor Square
is London's Bible Belt for hedge funds, and the rich,
gleaming neo-art deco interiors of 34 are reassuring
for those who don't have to look twice to see that no
expense has been spared. Even the champagne glasses
have a gimmick: they were modelled on Kate Moss's
left breast to celebrate her fortieth birthday. (No
fool, owner Richard Caring: Miss Moss is famously
flat-chested.)

The menu has been designed for every
eventuality, from reverse snobbery (lobster macaroni,
meatballs and spaghetti) to a Belshazzar's feast
of teriyaki Wagyu beef and Alba truffles, loin of
Glencoe venison and a superlative twenty-eight-day-
aged Scottish rib-eye steak on the bone cooked on
the restaurant's Argentinian parrilla grill. The wine
list is an arpeggio that jumps swiftly from a £36
Samaur 'The Caper' 2012 to the Olympian heights of
a Château Lafite Rothschild 1982 Pauillac *premier cru*
for £6,850. Should a deal be sealed, one can always
split a bottle of £400 Krug Rosé or toast it in limited-
edition Glenallachie single malt. The crude nude label
is drawn by 34's house mascot, Tracey Emin, after
whom the upstairs private dining room is named. It
is a compliment to Martin Brudnizki when we say
that the low-lit, sophisticated interiors make it look as

though 34 has been a London institution for as long as the old Savoy Grill.

34 Grosvenor Square W1
Tel. 020 3350 3434
Tube: Bond Street
www.34-restaurant.co.uk

CITY SOCIAL ££££

Since 2011, when the rising star Jason Atherton became a limited company and opened his first London restaurant, Pollen Street Social, his name has appeared above the door at Social Eating House, Little Social, Berners Tavern, Typing Room and now City Social. Tower 42 (formerly the NatWest Tower) is a bête noire of mine: a black, brutal 'school of Mordor' slab of architecture completed in 1980 that still looms over the Square Mile. Opening City Social in such a Castle Dracula, one could think only that Atherton and his partner, Restaurant Associates, were eyeing bankers' bonuses like a vampire watching a haemophiliac shave. The private entrance to City Social from a pedestrianized concourse leads you down diabolically dark corridors as you are handed from checkpoint to a dedicated lift that takes you up to another low-lit, corporate atrium.

But nothing quite prepares you for the drama of City Social. The 24th floor has been opened up since Gary Rhodes's tenure, and now the restaurant, bar and private dining rooms encircle Tower 42 with floor-to-ceiling windows that lay London at one's feet. Interiors designed by Russell Sage echo deco and bathe the restaurant in a rich bronze sheen created by rosewood, brass, reflective ceilings and smoked glass. Generous leather-lined banquettes face windows that frame high-rises such as the Gherkin, the Walkie-Talkie and the Shard. Our corner table for two gave us a ringside seat of crisp summer sun followed by an electric storm that made my guest feel as though she were dining on the flight deck of the Death Star.

Atherton's menu, designed with the City Social's head chef, Paul Walsh, feigns simplicity (uncooked and cooked entrées, pasta and rice, main dishes and grill) but is in fact incredibly sophisticated. A pretty flower-strewn plate of delicate yellow-fin tuna, tart cucumber salad, wafers of radish, dabs of avocado purée and ponzu dressing was outstanding, as was the risotto of ceps with veal sweetbreads and Madeira glaze. There's a nod to St John-style nose-to-tail cuisine with dashes of pig's trotter and black pudding, but the main theme is exceptionally cooked British ingredients: Romney Marsh rack of lamb, Dorset plaice, whole Dover sole or *côte de boeuf* finessed with subtleties such as samphire and citrus sabayon or a citrus butter sauce. For the clients who still quaff claret at lunchtime (God bless you, one and all), there are such suitably robust dishes as whole Scottish lobster served with duck-fat chips, and charcoal-grilled steaks.

Tower 42, 25 Old Broad Street EC2
Tel. 020 7877 7703
Tube: Bank
http://citysociallondon.com

THE GREENHOUSE ££££

When we first discovered the decked garden courtyard leading to the Greenhouse, we naturally thought the menu would be Japanese. It made us think of the secret garden behind Tokyo's Hotel

Okura, transported to the heart of Mayfair. This scores for important clients who might have been expecting anything but calm and bucolic charm. The 'do not disturb' atmosphere extends to the politely decorated dining room with generously spaced tables that preclude eavesdroppers overhearing one's plans for world domination. Chef Arnaud Bignon's award-winning French seasonal menu simply lists ingredients. We approve of this pragmatism, which means one doesn't have to ask the waiter endless questions like a distressed refugee at the Afghan border of the Khyber Pass.

If presenting food were a beauty contest, we would give the Greenhouse the sash and tiara over, say, Alain Ducasse at the Dorchester. We're not fans of towers that need an hour's council of war with your guests to decide on a strategy for breaching the bloody things. Presentation is uncomplicated at the Greenhouse, but the colour palette is quite simply beautiful and reminded us of the cooking of Fernand Léger. Bignon paints with flavour: native lobster, watermelon, lime and peanut was a memorable entrée, and, of the main courses, turbot, carrot, coconut, tamarind and ginger was a joy, as was the Limousin veal romanced by flavours of plum, tarragon and prune. We must pause before the cheese plate to applaud London's set lunches. A two-course set lunch at the Greenhouse is £35 – less than a cab and a cocktail.

"If presenting food were a beauty contest, we would give the Greenhouse the sash and tiara ..."

Now, there are impressive wine lists and there are those that you can mistake for Donald Rumsfeld's bank statement. The wine list at the Greenhouse stretches to over 100 pages, with numerous bottles that cost thousands. Unless you happen to be a Master of Wine or the cellar man at Berry Bros & Rudd, we would recommend you commandeer the services of the sommelier, who will make a wise choice once given a rough sketch of flavour and finances. If – as is mournfully common these days – your guests insist on spring water, we thoroughly recommend the booze-soaked rum baba pudding, if it's on the menu; it's served with strawberries soused in aged balsamic vinegar. When bound for home or office, do point out 21 Hay's Mews. It was home to Ian Fleming, the creator of James Bond, in the late 1940s.

27a Hay's Mews W1
Tel. 020 7499 3331
Tube: Green Park
www.greenhouserestaurant.co.uk

HAWKSMOOR SPITALFIELDS £££

Are we alone in being terribly proprietorial about our favourite restaurants? We can't begrudge childhood chums Will Beckett and Huw Gott their success in finding a smart formula – superlative grass-fed, dry-aged, all-British beef cooked to perfection on a charcoal grill – but we're not sure whether we like Hawksmoor rolling out the Spitalfields original to Seven Dials, Guildhall, Air Street, Knightsbridge and possibly beyond. To be fair, each Hawksmoor has its own personality, but it is our prerogative to like the original Dickensian schoolroom-style interiors in the East End, with blackboards, parquet floors, exposed brick walls and a largely carnivorous menu. It's an environment that comforts public schoolboys, Old Street's bearded techies and financiers relieved to escape their glass towers in the Square Mile.

We always think of Dickens's Mr Bumble and the feast served to the workhouse trustees in *Oliver Twist* when served a 400g rib-eye steak on the bone at Hawksmoor. It is grilled to a crust, which gives way to pink flesh marbled with the fat that gives the native-breed beef such succulent flavour. Odes have been written to Hawksmoor's recipe for anchovy or Stilton hollandaise and triple-cooked chips. Surf and turf has always been an anomaly to us – rather like dungarees and diamonds – but should you wish for a garlic-buttered lobster chaser for your chateaubriand, then fill your boots.

> *"Odes have been written to Hawksmoor's recipe for anchovy or Stilton hollandaise ..."*

Hawksmoor has remained loyal to beasts reared on the Ginger Pig's North Yorkshire farmlands, although the menu does include guest breeds, such as Herefords and Lincolnshire Reds. The list of reds (wines, that is) is as long as a Chinese telephone directory. We polished off a bottle of Ramón Bilbao Black Label Rioja 2012 – decently priced at £35 – with indecent haste. What we like is the slow progression of the prices that eases ever upwards: a Michele Satta Syrah 2009 (£75), Margaux du Château Margaux 2009 (£100), Sine Qua Non Upside Down Grenache 2009 (£300) and Château Lafite Rothschild 1985 Pauillac (£1,700). If you're pushing the boat out among friends, a magnum of Luigi Bosca Malbec (2011) for £100 is a winner with Hawksmoor's Sunday lunch: rare roast beef, duck-fat roast potatoes,

Yorkshire puds, carrots, greens and bone-marrow gravy. The bar next door at 157b is a gleaming coppered, turquoise-tiled cave and a star in its own right.

157a Commercial Street E1
Tel. 020 7426 4850
Tube: Old Street
www.thehawksmoor.com

Where to eat ...
for the ladies who lunch

CAFE MURANO £££

Diffusion-line restaurants such as Café Murano, Angela Hartnett's perkier little sister to her Michelin-starred Queen Street address, Murano, are to be treasured like a loved one's locket. A faster, slightly less formal pace coupled with a star chef is just the thing to blow the cobwebs away in the heart of St James's Street's world of gentlemen's clubs. Reservations are taken at the bar, the nifty waiters wear blue jeans and the room is neat and easy to navigate. For lunch we liked the round six-seater Mafia table in the corner at the back of the restaurant, underneath the conservatory skylight, although the bar stools look fun for cocktails and a post-theatre supper.

An entrée of succulent, firm slivers of peach, crunchy endive, moist little snowballs of gorgonzola and blanched almonds perfectly balanced flavours and textures. Try to resist filching a tentacle from your guest's warm octopus bathed in pesto with firm chickpeas, and do fight protein envy when you see the platter of beef carpaccio as red as a Tudor rose. Being in the kind of company where nobody wanted to show off or spend ludicrous amounts of money, we took the 'third from the top' test with the wine list. It is an old trick to offload overpriced filth, working on the premise that no one likes to appear a cheapskate and order the house. Although, if a sommelier so much as raises an eyebrow when you order from the lower register of the wine list, simply ask why those wines are listed in the first place. Anyway, Café Murano passed the 'third from the top' test, and our trust was rewarded with a light, crisp Pinot (£34) that proved to be a terribly easy drink. The tide didn't go out on a single glass, and yet we weren't hustled into an o'er-hasty new bottle. Needless to say, this being a Friday lunch, we did order another two bottles, and jolly nice they were too.

With fashionable folk round the table, we ordered a couple of dishes each from the *primi* menu. The taglioni saturated with squid ink was judged best in show because chef was so generous with the succulent crabmeat. We can't bear 'breathe and they're gone' side orders, so were most impressed by a huge dish of plump, tender runner beans served with a drizzle of chilli and garlic that turned one of our party into a Gollum protecting 'the Precious'. You have to love a restaurant that proposes a bowl of fresh cherries as a pudding; we ordered them as a chaser to Hartnett's iced slice of chocolate and hazelnut parfait ... and to soak up the last drop of the Pinot. Coco Chanel famously said

> *"You have to love a restaurant that proposes a bowl of fresh cherries as a pudding ..."*

'The best things in life are free. The second-best things are very, very expensive.' Restaurants like this prove her wrong.

33 St James's Street SW1
Tel. 020 3371 5559
Tube: Green Park
www.cafemurano.co.uk

LE CAPRICE ££££

Let's take a minute to consider the acquisition by the billionaire Richard Caring of the Corbin and King crown jewels Le Caprice, the Ivy and J. Sheekey's (also known as Caprice Holdings). Corbin and King made a mint and stole London's heart restoring faded, once-fashionable restaurants. They played *mein Host* so deftly that Hollywood actresses and West End producers would weep with gratitude just to be noticed by them. Caring's refits to these London treasures make us feel a little as though we are seeing a familiar face after an extreme lift. We comfort ourselves that the surgery will relax with time. Le Caprice still has the black-and-white David Bailey portraits acquired by Corbin and King, and the impossibly charming host Jesus Adorno, who has been there since 1981. At the time of writing, an expansion plan has yet to be approved and we can't help but think 'Praise be', because the annex to Sheekey's Oyster Bar has lost the intimacy of that lovely room.

For now it is business as usual at Le Caprice, which lives in a cul-de-sac downstream of the Ritz's Arlington Street entrance. Its proximity to the Ritz and the Wolseley makes Le Caprice prime paparazzi territory, and it is not unusual to spy Joan Collins, Graydon Carter, Victoria Beckham and Naomi

Campbell arriving in a blaze of flashbulbs. As with many perennially fashionable restaurants, Le Caprice isn't particularly fancy. Neither is the menu. One can order a Caprice burger, fish and chips with minted pea purée and a rather amusing tikka masala made with monkfish and prawns. But, as at all Caprice Holdings restaurants, chef Andrew Mclay has added sashimi plates, miso-marinated black cod, and prawns with chilli and yuzu dressing to please the delicate stomachs of the international rich.

Our favourite table in Le Caprice is the banquette at the end of the bar. For once, a bar stool is not recommended; there's a narrow conduit between the bar and the first restaurant tables that on a busy serving makes you feel like a human piñata. The outstanding dish on our last visit to Le Caprice was a salad of crispy duck and pomelo with spicy cashew nuts, and the steak tartare was, as always, satisfying and well-seasoned. Although we don't have a sweet tooth, Le Caprice's plate of iced berries laced with white chocolate sauce could win a contest for most popular pudding in London.

Arlington Street SW1
Tel. 020 7629 2239
Tube: Green Park
www.le-caprice.co.uk

KOFFMANN'S AT THE BERKELEY £££

Should you ever question the importance of flowers in a restaurant, consider Koffmann's at the Berkeley. The McQueen floral displays – naturalistic, French Impressionist vases of sunflowers, irises, peonies and cabbage roses – seem to drift from the light-filled ground floor down to the mezzanine bar and into the subterranean dining room below. You step from the streets of London straight into the rustic southern French countryside, where Pierre Koffmann was born and which inspired his two-Michelin-starred menu. The ladies who lunch here are following in the footsteps of the Duchess of Cornwall, who chose Koffmann's for an intimate lunch with the then Kate Middleton before her wedding to Prince William in 2011.

Koffmann's three-Michelin-starred La Tante Claire was a culinary academy and inspiration for the hellfire club of London chefs Gordon Ramsay, Marcus Wareing, Jason Atherton and Marco Pierre White. He now shares the Berkeley with Wareing's restaurant Marcus. The latter serves some of the most inventive plates of food in London, but the decor doesn't have the charm or lightness of Koffmann's. Ladies who lunch trust Koffmann to serve food that maximizes flavour but doesn't make the gold buttons on one's Chanel bouclé jacket pop. The entrées alone – duck consommé and tortellini, fresh crab salad, avocado and grapefruit, hot foie gras, chicory and Sauternes sauce – would suffice if followed by Koffmann's magnum opus: pig's trotter stuffed with sweetbreads and morels. Even the puddings, which include pistachio soufflé and matching ice cream, won't send one screaming for a spinning class ... whatever that might be.

Our last visit to Koffmann's was for a pre-theatre dinner (three courses for £28), and we could rave about the beef cheek ravioli, stuffed guineafowl and dark chocolate mousse. The subterranean dining room is most satisfying by night, although we do like the tables with views over Wilton Place for lunch. Koffmann's wine list is tailored to cover

any eventuality of a ladies' lunch: a cheeky glass of
Laurent-Perrier (£13) for a delicious gossip, a carafe
of Sancerre (£28) when an affair is ended, and at
least a bottle of Fronton Rosé (£35) if the subject
of the day is a divorce settlement. Lord knows what
the duchesses of Cornwall and Cambridge ordered
for their pre-royal wedding lunch; the ladies and
gentlemen at Koffmann's are far too discreet to say.

The Berkeley, Wilton Place SW1
Tel. 020 7235 1010
Tube: Hyde Park Corner
www.the-berkeley.co.uk/knightsbridge-restaurants/
koffmanns

SOTHEBY'S CAFÉ £££

As small and neat as a prenuptial agreement,
Sotheby's Café, on the ground floor of the Bond
Street auctioneer, is quite simply one of London's
finest restaurants. Most of the tables are secreted
in a discreet alcove lined with vintage Cecil Beaton
portrait prints (Sotheby's owns the archive), but
I always prefer the few tables roped off from the main
reception, in full view of the screens showing the day's
auction as it happens. Because it's Sotheby's, the lobby
is like a safari park where you can observe the world's
wealthy in their natural habitat.

As one would expect from so diminutive a
restaurant, Sotheby's Café is almost always fully
subscribed for breakfast, lunch and afternoon tea, so
booking is advisable. The auction house's proximity
to Vogue House on Hanover Square makes its café
an unofficial canteen for *Vogue*, *Tatler* and *World of
Interiors* editors. Chef Laura Greenfield's menu and
the wine list chosen by Sotheby's wine department

head girl, Serena Sutcliffe, prove that brevity and quality always ace loquacious, overambitious offerings.

Greenfield's menu is seasonal and changes weekly. In fact, her *Sotheby's Café Cookbook* is something of a cult on the Upper East Side of Manhattan, where size-zero light bites are essential for the ladies Tom Wolfe christened 'social X-rays'. The rich tend to be no-nonsense and incredibly economical with their time, so Sotheby's Café has the one-course lunch (chilled pea and mint soup, classic lobster club sandwich or roast corn-fed chicken breast served with mashed potatoes, peas, and lemon and thyme sauce, accompanied by a pretty, perfumed Gavi di Gavi or house champagne) down to a fine art.

Sotheby's, 34–35 New Bond Street W1
Tel. 020 7293 5077
Tube: Oxford Circus
www.sothebys.com

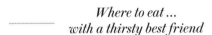

Where to eat ...
with a thirsty best friend

10 CASES ££

In the late seventeenth century, the site that is now 25 Endell Street contained one of London's fashionable bagnios, a medicinal spring bath that became known locally as Queen Anne's Bath. Today, Londoners prefer the medicinal properties of wine to those of spring water, and they queue on Endell Street for the ten tables at 10 Cases: a crisp little wine bar with bentwood chairs, chequerboard floors, blackboard menus and wine lists handwritten on wall-mounted rolls of brown paper. It's a tight fit, with bar stools around the counter, but it comes into its own when the shutters open and café tables spill out on to the pavement.

The owners of 10 Cases, Ian Campbell and Will Palmer, have stuck to their guns in proffering a rolling stock of ten cases of white and ten cases of red (plus fizz and rosé), so the wine list offers something new to try from smaller producers. All are sold by the glass, carafe or bottle, which we consider civilized and sensible. Colleagues do tend to think ill of you if you order a bottle over lunch these days, and it's always depressing to eat good food with a cheerless glass of disappointing house wine. It is one of London's great pleasures to sit at the counter of 10 Cases grazing on plates of charcuterie, duck rillettes, sautéed soft-shell crab (a dream) and salted radishes while sipping a Riesling from the Red Newt Cellars in New York State.

The menu at 10 Cases purports to be minimal – three starters, three main dishes and three puddings – but if ever there were a restaurant that demands sharing plates, this is it. We would suggest asking the knowledgeable waiters and barmen to recommend a red as robust as the grilled *côte de boeuf* for two, or a fizz that finesses a small plate of swordfish carpaccio flavoured with mango and chilli dressing. It's a nice touch that still and sparkling mineral water on tap is gratis, and that one is never, ever hurried. The Cave à Vin next door is a handsome vintner's shop with occasional tables and a private dining room should you wish to imbibe in private. It also has one of those dangerous enomatic wine-tasting machines – basically a jukebox for Cave à Vin's list – that, like the House of the Rising Sun, has been the ruin of many a young man.

16 Endell Street WC2
Tel. 020 7836 6801
Tube: Covent Garden
www.10cases.co.uk

BENTLEY'S OYSTER BAR £££

When the *Gentleman's Magazine* announced Lord George Cavendish's plans to construct the Burlington Arcade in 1817, it noted: 'What first gave birth to the idea was the great annoyance to which the garden of Burlington House is subject from the inhabitants of the neighbouring streets throwing oyster shells over the walls.' It is a sign of the changed times that Lord George's Piccadilly Palace is now the Royal Academy of Arts, and what was considered a humble street food two centuries ago is now a delicacy.

Bentley's opened on Swallow Street, a pedestrianized cut between Piccadilly and Regent Street, in 1916. Osbert Lancaster's illustrated guide *London: Night & Day* (1951) noted its 'emphasis on fish food'. Today Bentley's ground-floor oyster bar is a Folies-Bergère of crustacean delights, and in 2015 it celebrates ten years under the ownership of Richard Corrigan. There's a fine dining room upstairs that you'll glimpse if you powder your nose, but sitting up there isn't half as amusing as taking a seat downstairs at the original marble counter and watching oyster man Filippo Salamone shucking a dozen Lindisfarne lovelies and constructing iced platters of *fruits de mer royale*.

The oyster bar is lively rather than leisurely. You sit cheek-to-cheek at the bar or shoulder-to-shoulder in a tight line of tables while waiters duck and dive straight down the middle. It's not the kind of place to discuss selling the family tiara to Bentley & Skinner or offloading a tiny Titian on to one of the St James's Street dealers. But Bentley's is unbeatable for a gossip, a robust lobster bisque, a fillet of Dover sole with Jersey royals and spinach, and a gargle of Gavi di Gavi. Although I firmly believe that seafood, like watches, benefits from simplicity, Bentley's has tipped its hat to the sushi/ceviche trend with delicate plates of scallops, chilli and lime, tuna, soy and mirin and salmon, oyster and wasabi. The outdoor enclosure on Swallow Street is lovely for a three-hour lunch if you're at leisure on a sunny afternoon, although it is rather dwarfed by the flash Gaucho Argentinian restaurant terrace next door.

11–15 Swallow Street W1
Tel. 020 7734 4756
Tube: Piccadilly Circus
www.bentleys.org

CIAO BELLA £

Every Londoner should have a go-to local restaurant where everyone knows your name, your order and your poison. For us it is the Bloomsbury Italian Ciao Bella, which opened in 1983 and has been owned by host Felice Pollano since 1999. It's hard to know how to describe Ciao. Day and night it is as giddy and raucous as a Mafia wedding in Calabria. The al fresco tables are fought over by flash local rogues, fey Bloomsbury setters, flush foreign students and smart Fitzrovians. Inside, both upstairs and down, there's a celebratory atmosphere that is permissible in London only when the bill per head is unlikely to top £50.

You'd think a restaurant with so many covers and a menu that goes way beyond the usual pizza, pasta and risottos would be average at best. Locanda Locatelli it ain't, but you could walk the Tuscan hills barefoot for weeks and not find *minestrone della nonna*, Italian-style carbonara and rare grilled lamb chops served with al dente broccoli as consistently delicious. I'd go so far as to say the further you stray from the Pizza Express dishes the better you'll fare, but I wouldn't wish you to miss out on the house calzone, as taut and airy as a barrage balloon.

From about 7 pm the queues begin to form outside Ciao Bella, and the passing show becomes street theatre for the outside tables. If you dislike engaging with fellow diners and prefer to eat in monastic silence, Ciao is not for you. The acoustics in the dining room play merry Hamlet with your hearing, particularly if you're seated at the communal table that runs the length of the room or close to the piano that is punished nightly with renditions of 'That's Amore' and 'Happy Birthday'. The mood outside is a little more sedate, unless you happen to dine on an evening when our nearest and dearest take our monthly table for eight and hammer the house Chianti. You know you're family when you've graduated to linen napkins and a bottle of the good grappa is left on the table after dinner.

> *"... I wouldn't wish you to miss out on the house calzone, as taut and airy as a barrage balloon."*

86–90 Lamb's Conduit Street WC1
Tel. 020 7242 4119
Tube: Holborn
www.ciaobellarestaurant.co.uk

BARRAFINA £££

We have never quite grasped the mentality of people who queue outside restaurants that won't take bookings. Neither do we much like restaurants that won't take bookings, for that matter. It's all very well for Soho hipsters to press their noses against Barrafina's window like the Bisto Kid as they pose in the queue on Frith Street. But many of us have quite enough uncertainties to deal with day to day, and prefer restaurants that don't add to our distress and frustration. When Barrafina Soho first opened, in 2007, we recall feeling rather sorry for the tapas bar that was basically an empty marble counter wrapped around an open kitchen. Talk about naïve! Within half an hour, the twenty-six stools were taken, queues were forming and we were hoovering up small plates that were a tarantella of sharp, intense flavours with lashings of Manzanilla. Barrafina was awarded its first Michelin star in 2014.

Its owners, Sam and Eddie Hart (proprietors of Fino and Quo Vadis), modelled the menu at Barrafina on their favourite restaurant, Cal Pep in Barcelona. Now usually we take a dim view of turning a jewel into a chain, and always believe the original site holds the soul of the restaurateur (rather like one of Lord Voldemort's Horcruxes). In Barrafina's case, the second dining room on Adelaide Street (more Charing Cross than Covent Garden) is a winner. For starters, the corner site is much larger than that of the original, and the marble counter more generous and even curvaceous in part. The menu has also been reconsidered by the head chef, Nieves Barragán Mohacho. We fell in love with *croquetas* stuffed with crab and béchamel sauce, *chipirones*, courgette flowers stuffed with Catalan cheese, and the simplicity of a plate of salted tomatoes with a drizzle of olive oil. The red shrimp (*carabineros*) made us want to applaud.

Barrafina Adelaide Street has specialities that are too strong for our palate: fried sea anemone marinated in vinegar, milk-fed lamb's kidneys or brains and suckling pig's ears. But one need not engage with nose-to-tail dining, and there is always the specials board, which changes twice daily and will reward you with Barrafina classics such as a salad of mackerel and beetroot or a middle white pork cutlet with Jerusalem artichokes. The beauty of a no-bookings policy is, of course, that you can't be moved on like an unwelcome encampment of travellers in Surrey. So, should you wish to write off the afternoon, order another bottle of rosé and keep grazing until a week on Tuesday, you're welcome to do so. Adelaide Street is pedestrianized and rather down-at-heel, so we'd really rather not queue, particularly not after dark. Avoiding the 1 pm and 8 pm rush hours is therefore advisable. If you're at leisure, Barrafina would be a winner for a late lunch after a day at the National or National Portrait galleries.

"... should you wish to write off the afternoon, order another bottle of rosé and keep grazing until a week on Tuesday, you're welcome to do so."

10 Adelaide Street WC2
Tel. 020 7440 1456
Tube: Charing Cross
www.barrafina.co.uk

Where to eat …
when you want to be alone

DUCK & WAFFLE ££

Marina van Goor's Eenmaal was opened in 2015:
a restaurant concept imported to London from
Amsterdam and New York, that offers only tables
for one. The idea is presumably a cool room full of
creative types in black polo necks and 'statement'
spectacles individually designing apps, writing
screenplays or composing sonatas, rather than
embittered singletons in the Slough of Despond
weeping into their sauerkraut. Either way, it's all
too contrived for us, and no less gimmicky than the
ludicrous Clerkenwell spot Dans le Noir? where you
dine in the pitch black served by blind waiters. We kid
you not: google it.

   We wouldn't dream of being so presumptuous
as to ask why you'd like to be alone, but it usually
involves getting away from a place or a person. In the
absence of being at liberty to get on a boat, plane or
train, there's nothing quite so satisfying as taking the
glass lift on the exterior of the City's Heron Tower to
Duck & Waffle on the 40th floor. This is a very useful
friend in London because it is open twenty-four hours
and its views over London by night or day make you
feel that you've risen above it all. We love being alone
up there humming Cole Porter's 'Down in the Depths'
as we order – depending on the hour – a Bloody Mary
or an English breakfast tea so strong you could trot a
mouse over it.

   London is not a twenty-four-hour city in the style
of New York or Tokyo, so addresses such as Duck &

Waffle that deliver on their open-all-hours promise are extremely unusual. We remember very well joining the meatpackers at Smithfield Market for a 6.30 am hair of the dog in the Cock Tavern when the licensing laws were still tight. But that's another story. This being the City, Duck & Waffle is not full of louche lushes or saucer-eyed clubbers in the desperate hours between midnight and 6 am, when breakfast is served. If you happen to be there in the small hours, you're much more likely to find smart financiers taking a break from an all-nighter for a sustaining duck-egg cocotte, half-dozen rock oysters, legendary ox-cheek doughnut or eponymous crispy confit of duck leg, toasted waffle, fried duck egg and mustard maple syrup.

We don't wish to stereotype Duck & Waffle as some sort of *Lost in Translation* twilight zone, however. The full English breakfast served in the restaurant on top of the world will keep you energized like the Duracell Bunny, and the all-day menu does offer dishes with neither ducks nor waffles: 500g Longhorn rib-eye steaks, whole roasted Shropshire chicken and sea bass. Whatever time of day one chooses to visit Duck & Waffle, one is rewarded by the view of London beneath, with people scurrying round the City like ants. Seen from that perspective, they really don't seem to matter at all.

Heron Tower, 110 Bishopsgate EC2
Tel. 020 3640 7310
Tube: Liverpool Street
www.duckandwaffle.com

GREEN'S £££

Green's opened in St James's only in 1982, but it is spoken of in the same breath as gentlemen's clubs

White's, Boodle's and Brooks's. Its founder, Simon Parker Bowles (a former brother-in-law of the Duchess of Cornwall), and investors, the lords Daresbury and Vestey, know how to please the clubbable gentlemen. Political grandees and Palace officials gather in the booths at Green's to dine on lobster thermidor, haunch of venison and the house speciality, Smoked Haddock Parker Bowles: a piece of poached fish shouldering a mountain of herby mashed potato and served with a poached egg.

Green's is not quite nursery fodder, but it couldn't be more British if it waved the flag of St George and sang 'Rule Britannia' at the Last Night of the Proms. The beer-battered fish and chips with minted mushy peas and the bangers and mash wouldn't look out of place on a pub menu, but they do come as something of a relief if you've had one too many tasting menus in the West End involving such eccentricities as carrot meringue or raspberry ravioli. Service is as smooth as the castors on a carving trolley, and presentation is first-class.

Although we do enjoy dining at Green's in company, the seats at the bar are entirely appropriate for a brief lunch alone, whether it be half a dozen quail's eggs, a large plate of smoked salmon and scrambled eggs, half a dozen Loch Ryan oysters, or scallops and black pudding. This being a family restaurant in all but name (most of the diners probably went to school or Sandhurst together), the wine list doesn't presume that anyone has anything to prove. There's very little over £50 on the list of reds and whites, and of the 'Fine Wines' listed – only half a dozen – none insults the intelligence or goes beyond £100 anyway. Should you have the time, indulge in a glass of port and a plate of Paxton & Whitfield cheeses. Established in 1797, when George III was still on the throne, Paxton's has been at 93 Jermyn Street since 1896, and supplies all the St James's clubs and restaurants worth their salt.

36 Duke Street St James's SW1
Tel. 020 7930 4566
Tube: Green Park
www.greens.org.uk

HONEST BURGERS £

Whenever we have felt an Edward Hopper *Nighthawks* moment coming on in the last twenty years, we have always headed for a corner stool at Ed's Easy Diner on Old Compton Street for a classic burger with griddled onions and crunchy, fat fries. So the boom in what has, rather distastefully, become known as 'dirty food' passed us by. The Young raved about Five Guys, Shake Shack, Burger & Lobster, Honest Burger and Flesh & Buns, but we couldn't see the point of eating American diner food in anything other than a pastiche American diner complete with jukeboxes, bubblegum machines and posters of James Dean. We always dismiss posh burger joints as we do designer jeans: they don't improve on the raw ingredients but they add a zero to the price.

However, happening to be in Notting Hill, we chanced upon Honest Burgers on the Portobello Road. Not wishing to sit in the window, we dived downstairs and rather liked the timber-clad basement with its brightly lit bar and stripped-back 'I'm finishing my screenplay' tables that one person can colonize with a ruled pad or an iPad. Much as Ed's Easy is a joy, its burgers don't compare to Honest Burgers': a patty made from succulent Ginger Pig-farmed beef served pink in a tower of smoked bacon, mature cheddar, pickled cucumber, lettuce and red-onion relish. Honest Burgers' triple-fried rosemary-salted fries are worth the taxi fare alone when dipped in home-made bacon ketchup. It's terribly Notting Hill to ask for a gluten-free bun and replace chips with a side of cabbage, carrot and kohlrabi coleslaw. But does anybody interesting have a gluten intolerance?

Honest Burgers is the brainchild of youngish pups Tom Barton and Philip Eeles, who met at the University of Brighton, sold premium burgers at music festivals from a tent and opened their first restaurant in Brixton. They now have eight Honest Burgers restaurants in London, but – to their credit – have not changed the formula one iota to play to various postcodes. The secret of their success is that each restaurant does what it says above the door without fuss but with great skill and sincerity. We've visited Honest Burgers in Soho and King's Cross, but prefer the larger Portobello dining room downstairs. Apparently Richard 'Four Weddings and a Funeral' Curtis, the comedian David Walliams and various members of the Freud family are fans. But with a bit of luck you won't bump into them.

189 Portobello Road W11
Tel. 020 7229 4978
Tube: Ladbroke Grove
www.honestburgers.co.uk

YAUATCHA £££

Alan Yau's zhoosh Chinese dim sum tea house Yauatcha pleases on many levels. It hovers like an alien spaceship, emanating a blue glow from blank windows, on the corner of Berwick Street Market in

Soho, one of the last outdoor fruit, veg, flowers and narcotics vendors in the West End, where Virginia Woolf used to go for 'slightly flawed' silk stockings sold on a barrow. The ground floor of Yauatcha is a rather dainty, light-filled tearoom where the boys and girls from the Hearst offices down Broadwick Street sip holistic white tea from painted Chinese porcelain teacups and nibble pretty multicoloured macaroons prepared by the pastry chef, Graham Hornigold.

We prefer to dive downstairs to the dim sum restaurant in the basement, which looks like a glam nightclub on the Shanghai Bund. An electric-blue tank filled with exotic fish runs the length of the bar, low black tables are starkly (and sensitively!) spotlit, and the waiters are on the right side of nonchalant, although you wonder why they have to bother with bar work between Dior shows. Soho is one of those places in London where dining alone makes you a figure of fascination ... especially when you keep your dark glasses on in a basement. Yauatcha is famed for its dim sum – it earned a Michelin star in 2004 and still has it – so we'd be inclined to order favourites such as steamed king crab dumplings, pork and prawn Shu Mai, pan-fried chicken and shiitake mushroom dumplings. Venison puffs are popular, but we've never been fond of anything en croute, whether Chinese or British, so usually pass.

Chinatown is still stuffed with harshly lit restaurants with basic service and bog-standard food. Do you ever wonder whether the crispy ducks rotating on spits in the windows on and around Gerrard Street are actually varnished plastic? We bring this dearth of good Chinese restaurants up because Yauatcha's menu goes much further than dim sum and oolong.

We like to visit and play the takeaway game: ordering chicken and sweetcorn soup, sesame prawn on toast, half a crispy aromatic duck and a main dish, such as jasmine tea-smoked ribs with egg-white fried rice (cooked with dried scallop and asparagus). Yauatcha is the best Chinese restaurant in London, and we guarantee that you'll never order a takeaway again once you've tasted the classics cooked properly and served in such a chic dining room. A second Yauatcha opened in Broadgate in 2015.

15–17 Broadwick Street W1
Tel. 020 7494 8888
Tube: Tottenham Court Road
www.yauatcha.com/soho

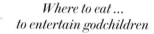

Where to eat ...
to entertain godchildren

BOCCA DI LUPO £££

Don't know about the howl of the wolf, but we laughed like hyenas reading that Bocca di Lupo considers itself 'a small and humble trattoria at heart'. From the day Jacob Kenedy and Victor Hugo opened it in 2008, this Archer Street dining room has been mobbed by foodies and families with weekend homes in Chiantishire. This is regional Italian food and wine at its best, served with no fuss or pretention. Bocca di Lupo is a jolly good place to take a godchild for the theatre when seated at the kitchen counter, and to challenge an appetite that may have been warped by parents with fantasy food intolerances.

We tend to order everything as a small plate to broaden the culinary horizons, not to mention to leave less for us to consume should our guest not take to the lamb sweetbreads with artichokes and sage, or the veal saltimbocca. The menu at Bocca di Lupo changes daily, but favourites such as sage leaves with anchovy, pappardelle with duck ragu, tagliatelli with porcini mushrooms, and roast pork and foie gras sausage seem to be hardy perennials. The prices aren't small or humble. When we ordered four grilled wild tiger prawns, we resorted to an old *Round the Horne* gag: 'Are those prawns wild?' 'No, outrageous!' However, we'd be content with a sharing plate of tagliata and enchanting, simple side dishes such as borlotti beans with tomato and basil, and spinach with pine nuts and raisins.

Bocca di Lupo's wine list is long and exclusively Italian. For fish, a bottle of Trebbiano Le Coste 2013 (£21.50) is perfectly decent, and the Montepulciano Samael 2013 (£25.50) is more than a match for the tagliata. Sadly, unlike Italy, London frowns on anyone who serves a child a thimble-full of wine, but do not despair: you can always promise underage godchildren a lemon sorbet beaten with vodka and Prosecco. Bocca di Lupo is also a winner for godchildren because, should they grow restless, you can always send them across the road to Gelupo for home-made ice cream in a cup or cone that they can bring back to the restaurant while you polish off a *bomba calda* (apricot jam doughnut) and an Aperol spritz.

12 Archer Street W1
Tel. 020 7734 2223
Tube: Piccadilly Circus
www.boccadilupo.com

CHINA TANG ££££

Most of us would find a coach party from Belgrade
a more welcome sight outside a favourite restaurant
than the paparazzi. But for godchildren, knowing a
joint is a favourite of Kate Moss, Stella McCartney and
Naomi Campbell is like catnip. We'd go so far as to
say that China Tang may be top of the list of London
addresses that Miss Moss has been papped leaving,
looking over-refreshed. Well, *Honi soit qui mal y pense*,
as they say. The glamorous interior of China Tang is
reminiscent of the Shanghai's Paramount Ballroom
in its 1930s prime, or the 'Anything Goes' opening
number of *Indiana Jones and the Temple of Doom*. Of
course, you're spoilt for choice in the Dorchester, with
Alain Ducasse and the new Bruno Moinard-designed
Dorchester Grill, but for the young, China Tang has
that scent of decadence that always excites.

What Sir David Tang has bankrolled is essentially
a terribly posh Chinese that serves much the same
food as the joints on Gerrard Street but cooked
to Dorchester standards and served in billionaire
art-collector surroundings. To avoid squabbling and
wasting time trying to please everyone, we would
encourage you to order one of the banquet menus
(from £75 per person) that has China Tang favourite
Peking duck as its centrepiece, plus favourites spring
rolls, chicken satay, scallop dumplings, hot-and-sour
soup and stir-fried beef in black pepper. If you're
dining with godchild in the singular, we recommend
the lobster lettuce wrap, the soft-shell crab fried with
egg yolk, the salt-and-pepper squid and the steamed
fish with ginger and spring onions.

Some restaurants suit the late shift, and we find
that China Tang is one of them. It's great fun after the
theatre or cinema, and, quite frankly, if your guest

wants to see stars then s/he will have a much better chance the closer the clock gets to midnight. The bar at China Tang is always entertaining, particularly on a Tuesday evening when Kitty LaRoar and Nick of Time (the Monroe and Sinatra *de nos jours*) perform. A word of warning: if you look at China Tang's website, please don't think ill of the 'secret guests' pages of famous faces looking less than their best in the company of Sir David. They make the bar and restaurant look hideously lit, and the reverse is the case. Perhaps it was Richard Young's night off when those pictures were taken.

The Dorchester, 53 Park Lane W1
Tel. 020 7629 9988
Tube: Hyde Park Corner
www.chinatanglondon.co.uk

DINNER ££££££

Treating godchildren to ludicrously expensive restaurants, such as London's only three-Michelin-star doors (Alain Ducasse at the Dorch and Gordon Ramsay), is rather over the top and sets the bar too high for any future treats. Besides, fine dining can be a humourless affair, and the last place the Young want to be is an environment in which they feel they ought to be sitting on their hands with a copy of Debrett on their heads. Dinner, Heston Blumenthal's two-Michelin-star restaurant in the Mandarin Oriental Hotel, is London's culinary equivalent of Willy Wonka's Chocolate Factory. The Mandarin Oriental looks grand and austere: as *The Telegraph*'s critic Ben McCormack put it, 'the foyer is as marbled as a Medici tomb.' The surprise at Dinner is a glass wall exposing a Heath Robinson kitchen with mechanized spits roasting capons and pineapples.

The gimmick at Dinner is a history of food told by dated dishes such as Rice & Flesh (1390), Chicken cooked with Lettuces (1670), Earl Grey Tea-cured Salmon (1730) and Brown Bread Ice Cream (1830). Our godchildren took great delight in pointing out that the chocolate-bar pudding (allegedly 1700) pre-dated such a thing by 150 years, and that Twinings didn't formulate Earl Grey tea much before 1831. But that's the beauty of Dinner. It makes you think and challenge Mr Blumenthal ... or, should we say, the head chef, Ashley Palmer-Watts, who is the heart and soul of the Knightsbridge restaurant. Despite his fame Blumenthal is a risk, so the Mandarin Oriental is to be applauded for not playing it safe.

One can't lunch or dine at Dinner without ordering Meat Fruit, a *trompe l'œil* mandarin orange with dimpled skin and stalk that is in fact a creamy chicken-liver and foie-gras parfait encased in mandarin-flavoured jelly and served with rustic grilled bread. Whether such a thing was served in 1500 we do not know, but 'subtleties' (*trompe l'œil* dishes) were popular at the early Tudor court. The onion, apple, mead and mustard flavours surrounding the roast Iberico pork chop (1820, since you ask) give the lie to the perception of Blumenthal's food as overcomplicated science project. His Tipsy Cake soused in Sauternes, brandy and vanilla cream, served with roasted pineapple, makes one want to dance a minuet, as they did when it was first eaten in 1810 at the Prince Regent's parties.

Mandarin Oriental Hotel, 66 Knightsbridge SW1
Tel. 020 7201 3833
Tube: Knightsbridge
www.dinnerbyheston.com

LA BODEGA NEGRA ££

Not to be confused with the pleasant Mexican café
round the corner on Moor Street, the La Bodega
Negra supper club we recommend (same owner,
different vibe) is disguised as a neon-lit sex shop
with signs reading 'Peep Show' and 'Adult Video'.
To denizens of Soho, the naughty neon is a giveaway,
because the Internet has pretty much seen off the
porn and peep that gave Soho its deliciously seedy
character. Anyway, 9 Old Compton Street is your
doorway downstairs to the tequila and mezcal chapter
of the La Bodega Negra story. Since opening in 2012,
the basement has sung its siren song to London
nighthawks such as Lily Allen, Prince Harry, Paloma
Faith, Harry Styles, Keira Knightley and (cue the
department of no surprises) Kate Moss and her
husband, Jamie Hince.

Now, one might rather paint one's bottom blue
and dance down Mount Street whistling the theme
tune to *Braveheart* than languish in a Soho basement
where a bottle of tequila costs anything from £80 to
£500. But imagine the kudos you're earning by taking
your godchildren to such a godforsaken, noisy place.
Remind yourself that not so long ago everyone – you
included – smoked in Soho basements like this. So
at least you'll emerge without lungs like a pit pony,
even if your wallet is a few monkeys lighter depending
on the stamina of your party. Should you be foolish
enough to invite more than ten to cram into one of the
coal-hole booths, you'll get the dedicated services of a
taco-and-tequila hound of a hot waiter.

Although ordinarily when it is tequila o'clock
food becomes about as appealing as a quiet night
in with a crossword puzzle, we do urge you to eat at
La Bodega. Solids are allegedly good for us, and the

menu is really rather fine. A selection of tacos is sensible – soft-shell crab, lamb with drunken salsa, beef with *salsa fresca* – and the ceviche is surprisingly good with the lethal liquid stuff. Tequila isn't compulsory, and as the responsible adult it might be wise for you to keep to three or four frozen margaritas, in which case a half roast chicken or an octopus-and-chorizo skewer might be politic. But far be it from us to lecture. Eat, drink and be merry; everyone else at La Bodega Negra will be doing exactly the same and they certainly won't think you should be old enough to know better.

9 Old Compton Street W1
Tel. 020 7758 4100
Tube: Leicester Square
www.labodeganegra.com

Where to eat ... when entertaining a dowager

BELVEDERE £££

One would no sooner visit Belvedere in Holland Park without the benefit of sunshine than one would the nude bathing ponds on Hampstead Heath. The summer ballroom of Holland House, a grand Jacobean mansion that was largely destroyed in the Blitz, is one of the most romantic places in London for a *fête champêtre*. The two-tier ballroom (originally the seventeenth-century stable block) is set in 54 acres of formal grounds landscaped with elaborate parterres, a rose walk and a Japanese garden framing an artificial lake. In high summer, when tables are set on the terrace, Belvedere is as picturesque and carefree as a Fragonard painting.

Belvedere's parquet ballroom floor is framed by soaring arches, mullioned windows and celestial silk curtains and surrounded by galleries. There is acres of space between the round tables, and a rather nice curtained alcove lined with banquette seating that is most appropriate if you are entertaining a dowager. The upper balconies, where the orchestra once played, feel as distant from the ballroom floor as the gallery in the Royal Albert Hall. Overall, the mood set by the late interior designer David Collins is a gavotte between the formal and the frivolous, although we fail to see the point of a Warhol Marilyn or Damien Hirst's butterflies in an otherwise pretty, nostalgic and classically well-proportioned room.

As you might think, Belvedere is popular for wedding receptions, and this is reflected in the sometimes o'er-fussy main dishes, which taste a little perfunctory and reminded me of many a mass-catered awards dinner at the Natural History Museum. If, like us, you visit Belvedere only on a summer's day, the choices are simple and satisfying: a robust gazpacho flavoured with orange and coriander; Parma ham and roasted figs; cold poached salmon with a well-seasoned green salad; and a bottle or two of Château de Pampelonne Rosé.

Holland Park, Abbotsbury Road W8
Tel. 020 7602 1238
Tube: Holland Park
www.belvedererestaurant.co.uk

BELLAMY'S £££

The name of handsome, rakish Mark Birley still hangs like a bat in the minds of dowagers who remember the glory days of his Berkeley Square

nightclub Annabel's (opened in 1963) and his private
dining rooms Harry's Bar, annexed by Richard
Caring in 2007. Birley inspired devotion in almost
all his employees, and established at his nightclubs,
restaurants and members' bars a culture of
understated excellence that is inherited in the
manner of blue blood or porphyria. Bellamy's is
directed by a triumvirate of Annabel's men: former
managing director Gavin Rankin, chef Stéphane
Pacoud and barman Luigi Burgio. Opened in 2004,
it was named after the club in Evelyn Waugh's *Sword
of Honour* trilogy, an establishment that was in
turn a thinly disguised caricature of White's on
St James's Street.

Rankin describes Bellamy's as 'a club without
a sub', and that rather neatly sums up the feeling of
six degrees of separation when sitting down to lunch:
Sally over there is the godmother of Harry, who went
to school with Tom and Jerry, who both slept with
Lucy, and so forth ... The dining room is bright and
polite, a Mayfair interpretation of a Franco-Belgian
brasserie with jazzy posters and formally laid tables
with gleaming silver, crystal and linen pressed to a
sheen. The menu proves that everything old is new
again. It's very refreshing to be served a prawn and
avocado cocktail and roast pheasant with Brussels
sprouts when every chef east of Soho hasn't realized
that we're all bored of 'heritage' tomatoes and
belly pork.

The menu at Bellamy's is simple in construction
and sophisticated in cooking: smoked eel mousse,
rillettes of duck and a salad of artichoke heart and
haricots verts are all classic entrées, and Dover sole,
entrecôte of beef, jugged hare and roast partridge
are typical main dishes. The Table D'Hôte menu

(under £25 for three courses) is miraculous, as is
the exclusively French wine list. We have known
dowagers to drink – we think of Waugh's description
of Sebastian Flyte 'sip sip sipping like a dowager' in
Brideshead Revisited – but we heartily approve of a
restaurant that will serve a 2009 Châteauneuf-du-
Pape by the glass (£12). Bellamy's Bar is much loved,
not least at lunchtime, when the blue-suited boys in
Cleverley shoes set aside global finance for half an
hour and order a toasted open sandwich of potted
shrimp or Black Forest ham and olive oil.

18/18a Bruton Place W1
Tel. 020 7491 2727
Tube: Bond Street
www.bellamysrestaurant.co.uk

THE GORING DINING ROOM £££££

An acquaintance of ours who recently lunched at
the Goring exclaimed: 'I looked at my watch and
it was 1932!' The dining room at the Goring does
indeed feel like the sort of place to which a chap
could return after decades in Kenya and the waiter
would remember that he preferred mint jelly to sauce.
Traditionalists absolutely adore the Goring, hence
the proliferation of High Anglican priests in full rig,
courtiers from nearby Buckingham Palace and ladies
(with or without the capital L) who can spot natural
pearls from 10 miles off. The late Queen Elizabeth
The Queen Mother dined at the Goring at least once
a year, and her favourite dish, Eggs Drumkilbo (a
symphony of lobster, eggs, mayonnaise and sherry),
is on the menu in her honour.

The dining room at the Goring is reassuringly
pale and interesting – designed by the Queen's

nephew David Linley – although a dowager would probably prefer Edwardian lead-crystal chandeliers to the rather strange fairy lights hanging from the ceiling. But the room has a sense of occasion, and you are entertained royally by the fascinating cast. The lunch menu is a joy because the daily special never fails to please: it might be perfectly prepared fish pie, leg of lamb, steak-and-kidney pudding or beef with Yorkshire pudding. The Goring's glazed lobster omelette is heroic, but we feel it belongs to another artery-hardening century, much like the Savoy's Omelette Arnold Bennett.

Although we heartily approve of seeing Oscietra and Beluga caviar on a dinner menu, we do wonder if anyone but an early twentieth-century Russian grand duchess would consider a £600 serving of caviar an amusing prelude, rather than a mere rip-off. We are never endeared to restaurants that insist on adding supplementary charges to dishes with 'premium' ingredients, so our lorgnettes positively steam up when we see potted shrimps or a leg of lamb marked up. As for side orders of greens being proffered for a fiver and a £1 donation to the Prince of Wales's Countryside Fund, we think cheaper prices for English-grown veg would do much more for farmers than hijacking London diners in the manner of Dick Turpin. But the Goring is nothing if not polite, pretty and blessed with impeccable manners. We'd rather be in this dining room than anywhere else when entertaining a dowager.

The Goring, Beeston Place SW1
Tel. 020 7396 9000
Tube: Victoria
www.thegoring.com

WILTONS ££££ • &JS

Our hearts lift when we are greeted with the warm
'Welcome home sir, madam' at Wiltons. We have
made a covenant that only guests for whom we have
the greatest fondness are to be invited to lunch or
dinner at Wiltons, because it is – all bias intended
– the restaurant we hold dearest above all others in
London. As reassuringly traditional as Elgar's *Pomp
and Circumstance*, Wiltons' menu and service echo
a smarter, gentler and more patrician age. It is a
pleasure to take a glass of
special cuveé with oysterman
of thirty years, Sammy, at
the bar and listen to Michael
the house manager read the
catechism of 'my lord', 'your
Grace', 'Your Highness' and
occasionally 'Your Majesty' as

> *"As reassuringly traditional as Elgar's* Pomp and Circumstance *..."*

he greets Wiltons' guests. You do, of course, pay for
the privilege of staff as practised as the cast of *The
Mousetrap* and food that Escoffier couldn't fault.

Should hanging ever become legal again in
England, and in the case that a last meal was required,
we would request half a dozen Jersey rock oysters
shucked by Sammy, honey-glazed gammon (served
from the carving trolley every Thursday lunchtime)
and lashings of special cuveé. It is terrific fun to
lunch in the Oyster Bar, which was sensitively and
successfully redecorated by Philip Hooper in 2014,
but for special occasions we all like to dine
in Barbara's section, ideally in one of the high-backed,
velvet-upholstered booths set with glass etched for the
restaurant's Edwardian premises in Bury Street.

Service is as smooth as the State Opening of
Parliament, but there is nothing fussy or pretentious

about head chef Daniel Kent's presentation of great British food: a peerless lobster bisque, roast sirloin of Mey selection beef served with buttered spinach, sole meunière off the bone, a light caviar omelette or a robust roast leg of Romney Marsh lamb. The Jimmy Marks Room, named after the restaurant manager from 1942 until 1976, is a private dining room that is booked annually by all the editors of Condé Nast UK and the Newhouse family. Wiltons has been owned by the Hambro family since 1942, when Olaf Hambro was lunching there and a German bomb scored a direct hit on nearby St James's Church. The owner, Bessie Leal, despaired of the future, so Mr Hambro instructed that she add the price of Wiltons to his bill.

You will not find a finer historic London restaurant for oysters, fish and game, and I include Scott's, Rules and Sweetings. Nor will you find as discreet and convivial a gathering of influential ladies and gentlemen from the royal household, the Palace of Westminster and the many hedge funds now located in St James's. When George William Wilton established his oyster, shrimp and cockle stall in the Haymarket in 1742, George II was king. By 1884 Wiltons had been awarded its first Royal Warrant as Purveyor of Oysters to Queen Victoria, and today it is one of the very few London restaurants where the Queen and the Duke of Edinburgh have dined privately. Wiltons is quite simply a pedigree chum for those who value discretion, charm and terribly good manners.

55 Jermyn Street, SW1
Tel. 020 7629 9955
Tube: Piccadilly Circus
www.wiltons.co.uk

Where to eat ... outdoors

AMPHITHEATRE RESTAURANT AND TERRACE ££

Those of us in the know about the Royal Opera
House restaurant's terrace tables betray the secret only
under extreme duress: Chinese burns, thumbscrews
or sustained exposure to Lesley Garrett CDs.
But seeing as it's you: people presume that the
Amphitheatre restaurant on top of the Royal Opera
House is open only to those attending a performance.
This is correct in the evening, but from May to
September it can be booked for lunch by members
of the public, whether it's a matinée day or not. When
the weather is kind, the glass doors are opened and
tables are set for lunch on the terrace overlooking
Covent Garden Piazza.

Finding the terrace, however, involves trials
as taxing as those faced by Tamino and Pamina in
Mozart's *The Magic Flute*. One has to negotiate security
next to the box office, climb the stairs into the Paul
Hamlyn Hall (a spectacular glass conservatory as tall
as a cathedral) then take an escalator reminiscent of
the Grandstand at Royal Ascot to the top floor, where
the Amphitheatre is discovered behind a glass wall.
The terrace is a fascinating place to sit because you're
parallel to the wing where the Royal Ballet School
rehearses and where armies of tailors, milliners,
jewellers and wig-makers create costumes for new
productions. A tier above the Amphitheatre is the
artistes' terrace, where you can see the ballet boys and
girls furiously smoking cigarettes.

The terrace menu is seasonal and echoes the
operas and ballets that are being performed that

season. Thankfully, the head chef doesn't take the brief too literally, so you're not going to be presented with an empanada just because Christine Rice is giving her *Carmen* in the auditorium. Theming only goes so far as a cream-filled choux-pastry cygnet for *Swan Lake*, or Eton Mess served in a china teacup for *Alice's Adventures in Wonderland*. The modern European menu is prima-ballerina light: a smooth gazpacho drizzled with basil oil, roasted cod served with herb lentils and chive crème fraiche, and a smoked chicken Waldorf salad. The tempo is sharp as a pin because the kitchen is drilled to serve bang on the *entr'acte* for tables attending a performance.

Royal Opera House, Bow Street WC2
Tel. 020 7212 9254
Tube: Covent Garden
www.roh.org.uk

BOULESTIN £££ · &JS

Named after 'culinary ambassador to the English' Marcel Boulestin, who dazzled 1920s London with his cookbook *Simple French Cooking for English Homes* and his eponymous restaurant (opened in 1923), Boulestin offers with its menu an homage to nostalgic French cuisine. The esteemed original in Covent Garden – a favourite of Serge Diaghilev, Ivor Novello, Lady Diana Cooper and the future King Edward VIII – closed its doors in 1994, fifty years after Boulestin's death. Mr Sherwood Sr's review ended: 'Unless emergency measures are taken, Boulestin will disappear with Covent Garden Market.' Of course, the market was saved with no little thanks to Robert Carr MP, and Boulestin staggered on for another twenty years before becoming extinct.

How smart of its owner, Joel Kissin, to resurrect Boulestin in gentlemen's clubland St James's, currently undergoing a multimillion-pound redevelopment by the Crown Estates and so much smarter than Covent Garden. Boulestin is in the shadow of the Tudor clock tower of St James's Palace, and next door to Berry Bros & Rudd, wine merchant by Royal Appointment (founded in 1698). Boulestin and Berry's share a gaslit courtyard, Pickering Place – once famous for gambling dens and duelling – where al fresco tables are laid under vast umbrellas of cream calico.

Rather than reviving Boulestin's lost splendour (the hammer horror idol Vincent Price called it 'one of the grandest restaurants in London'), the St James's Street dining room is classically understated: a chessboard floor and skylight lead the eye from the tables of Café Marcel at the front of house, past the bar and into the lean main dining room, which is well-hung with mirrors so one can see who's who, who's with who and (if you can lip-read) what's what. It being a summer day, we ate in the courtyard, and very lovely it is too if you don't mind being a little close to other tables for comfort. Fusion food is becoming a game of Russian roulette in London's restaurants, so it was a joy and a pleasure to peruse exclusively classic French dishes prepared by the head chef, Andrew Woodford, more than half of them taken from Monsieur Boulestin's cookbooks.

We would walk the length of the rue de Rivoli to find a fish soup as magnificent as Boulestin's. It was served with do-it-yourself garlic-and-saffron-buttered croutons and Gruyère that melted beautifully into the bisque. That alone, with a half-bottle of 2012 Domaine Thomas Sancerre, would suffice for a swift lunch, but we ploughed on, sharing a pleasantly tart sweet-cured herring with potato and dill and the poached egg in aspic before tackling a rich, robust *daube de boeuf*. The chocolate and salted-caramel mousse was indecently good. It was very pleasant to be served the flavours one expects without any guerrilla tactics from a kitchen trying to improve on trusted and true food. Boulestin St James's is a triumph.

5 St James's Street SW1
Tel. 020 7930 2030
Tube: Green Park
www.boulestin.com

HAM YARD BAR & RESTAURANT £££

We have noted Tim and Kit Kemp's genius in finding lost corners of central London for their portfolio of hotels. Ham Yard, the last slice of Soho left undeveloped after the Blitz and a stone's throw from Piccadilly Circus, is the location of Firmdale's £100 million new-build. The Kemps have created an urban village with independent shops (florists, jewellers, nail bars) surrounding a central courtyard and a hotel with residential apartments, a private cinema, a bowling alley and a roof garden. When we first visited Ham Yard we thought the exterior a tad grim and municipal, but the interiors popped with Kit Kemp's signature mash-up of jazzy mismatched furniture, contemporary art and bold, busy wallpaper.

It is a pleasure to lunch in the Ham Yard restaurant, not least because it scores for providing miles of banquette seating and plush felted dining chairs in orange and grey, meaning none of your guests has to make the numb bum sacrifice. Many Londoners take the 'two starters' option these days, and Ham Yard produces exquisitely presented and substantial small plates, such as shaved asparagus and truffle salad with fennel and radish, and a delicate confection of seared scallops, tempura courgette flower, crushed peas, chilli and rocket. Champagne cocktails served in Madame de Pompadour coupes hit the spot – as bittersweet as a Cole Porter lyric – but took forever to arrive. That said, Ham Yard had only been open a week, so it would be churlish to criticize. Besides, the waitresses were utterly endearing in a 'first day at school' fashion.

Returning to Ham Yard, we found the courtyard transformed with al fresco lunch tables elegantly set with crisp white linen, sparkling glass and glittering silver. The waiters practically danced from kitchen to courtyard, and a bottle of sparkling Shiraz was at our table before we'd even had time to settle our feathers. Sitting in the sun dissecting sea trout served with puy lentils, salsa verde, fennel and watercress with a side dish of buttered Jersey Royals and knocking back the Shiraz made for a memorable, pleasurable late summer lunch. And any restaurant that puts Arctic Roll on the puds menu has our vote.

Ham Yard Hotel, 1 Ham Yard W1
Tel. 020 3642 2000
Tube: Piccadilly Circus
www.firmdalehotels.com

THE RIVER CAFÉ ££££

For at least a generation of Londoners with an SW postcode, Ruth Rogers and Rose Gray's *River Café Cookbook* (1996) with its graphic blue-and-white cover was as essential in the kitchen as shop-bought aioli and a Filipino maid called Consuela. Opened in

1987 in a rather inaccessible Thames-side industrial block where Rogers's husband, Sir Richard, runs his architectural practice, the River Café was one of the first restaurants in London to place an open kitchen counter and a wood-burning stove centre stage. It is right to say without hubris that the River Café's *cucina rusticana* dishes gathered from all regions of Italy revolutionized the way we ate in London. Perhaps it signalled the death of haute cuisine and a growing appreciation of cooking the best organic ingredients simply and serving them like a kitchen supper.

Of course, the River Café had its detractors, who objected to being charged £20 for a bowl of risotto and disapproved of the left-leaning media and politico class annexing an expensive restaurant that was masquerading as a rustic kitchen. The BBC did seem to have a block booking for most of the 1990s, and you couldn't move for Yentobs, Braggs, Frostrups and Lawsons. It was hardly surprising that the television chefs Jamie Oliver, Hugh Fearnley-Whittingstall and Tobie Puttock (no, me neither) were discovered at the River Café, since you couldn't swing a Fendi Baguette without hitting a commissioning editor in the kisser. You might still see the odd famous face at the River Café, but those heady days have gone, along with the BBC's White City studios.

Rogers now flies the River Café solo after the sad death of Ruth Gray in 2010. We've never been much enamoured of the dining room or of sitting next to the wood-burning stove, which looks like the apparatus in a Tuareg crematorium. But on a bright spring or summer's day, there isn't a prettier table to be had in London than one of those placed among the raised beds of herbs and flowers in the River Café courtyard, overlooking the Thames. Put a blood orange, Campari and Prosecco aperitivo in our hands and the anxieties of London life melt away. You're not going to be served a bum dish at the River Café, but our favourite four courses comprise prosciutto with Chanterais melon, handmade pasta stuffed with buffalo ricotta, courgette, courgette flowers and parmesan, a succulent wood-roasted Anjou pigeon and a slice of indecently rich Chocolate Nemesis.

Thames Wharf, Rainville Road W6
Tel. 020 7386 4200
Tube: Hammersmith
www.rivercafe.co.uk

Where to eat …
for a light lunch

DAPHNE'S £££

There has been a Daphne's on Draycott Avenue since 1963, when the theatrical agent Daphne Rye turned her hand to the restaurant game and packed the joint post-theatre with friends such as David Niven, Laurence Olivier and Alec Guinness. In her time working for Binkie Beaumont's company H. M. Tennent, Rye discovered Richard Burton, who briefly became her lodger. When she eloped to Mallorca, leaving Tennent, the wag Richard Clowes quipped: 'It's the only known case of the sinking ship leaving the rats.' Perhaps the interior designer Martin Brudnizki was inspired by Rye when he redecorated in 2014 after a fire. There's definitely a touch of the camp theatricals about the 1950s Murano glass chandeliers and the pink marble bar.

We love Daphne's: always have. It is minutes from 'Chelsea Beach' (the Fulham Road), the conservatory roof retracts in the summer and it has the loyalty of It girls past, present and future. The lightest lunch we've ever had at Daphne's since the refurb is a couple of stiff Truffled cocktails, damnable concoctions of gin, honey, lavender, lemon and 'the witch' (Strega). But the Italian menu is rather too good to have an *Absolutely Fabulous* liquid lunch. The ladies (and gentlemen) of South Ken and Chelsea do like their raw food, and Daphne's does a terrific tuna tartare with avocado and wild fennel, black figs, gorgonzola and hazelnuts; you can also request the yellow fin tuna in the nude (the fish, that is) rather than grilled. We thoroughly endorse Daphne's duck tortellini, but would be equally satisfied with two side dishes of fried courgette and broccoli served with garlic, chilli and toasted almonds.

> *"... it has the loyalty of It girls past, present and future."*

It is nice to see that Daphne's still has the wit for which its founder was famous. The cocktail menu is punctuated by neat little aphorisms from the twentieth century's most lovable soaks. From Sinatra, 'Alcohol may be man's worst enemy but the Bible says to love your enemy.' From Dino, 'If you drink don't drive. Don't even putt.' But we digress. For a light bite with an old friend who doesn't have a kind word for anyone or the self-awareness to say 'when', Daphne's your gal.

112 Draycott Avenue SW3
Tel. 020 7589 4257
Tube: South Kensington
www.daphnes-restaurant.co.uk

LIMA FLORAL £££

Most of us would struggle to name Peru's most famous export after Mario Testino and Paddington Bear, but in recent years we all seem to have been dancing a marinera to the doors of London's many Peruvian restaurants, Coya, Lima, Ceviche and Emanuel to name just a few. It begs the question of who sets the fashion for food in London. It's not the public, because we didn't all wake up one morning and conclude that we were famished for anticuchos, quinoa and purple potatoes. It's not the critics, who are largely reactive and leap on a 'two's a trend' story. Novelty will always attract the smart set, but they dash like stage-door Johnnies from one restaurant opening to another, caring only about the drama and little for the food.

The answer, as with most things in life, is investors, such as the Venezuelan Gabriel Gonzalez, who worshipped Virgilio Martínez Véliz's cooking at Centra in Peru and resolved to bring his menu to the West End of London. Lima London opened in Fitzrovia in 2012 and was the first Peruvian restaurant in Europe to earn a Michelin star. A second, Lima Floral, opened in 2014 on a corner site that has been a Jonah for previous restaurants but not, we suspect, this one. The ground-floor dining room is fresh as paint; to be precise, petrol-blue paint brightening up industrial pillars and whitewash on the brick walls. A Kandinsky-esque mural in an alcove is a well-judged splash of colour in an otherwise minimalist interior.

We fully expected to loathe Lima Floral. A sweet but dizzy girl on the desk couldn't work the computer system, and we lent her our pen to write down the reservation and mobile number. On arrival she suggested we go downstairs for a pisco, and I'm afraid the smutty schoolboys in our party found this hilarious. None of us could understand the short lunch menu, and the dishes we could decipher – dry potato stew, goat's cheese, onion ashes and red shiso – sounded like a ghastly food trial on *I'm a Celebrity ... Get Me Out of Here*. We were seated in the aforementioned alcove, which echoed like the Whispering Gallery in St Paul's Cathedral, so we had to move.

And yet, when the food arrived it was a revelation: sea bream ceviche with tiger's milk, avocado, crispy onion and cancha corn was a triumph, as was the main course of chicken chalaca, decorated (and I use the word advisedly) with raw asparagus. If you like the big flavours of Peruvian yellow chilli pepper, purple potato and Amazonian tomato, the head chef, Robert Ortiz, delivers a masterclass. A couple of joyless eco handwringers have commented that bringing Peru to London is irresponsible, but, as Gonzalez says, of 245 products on the menu, only 18 are imported from Peru. The mantra is 'authenticity, seasonality and freshness', and Lima Floral keeps all three promises.

14 Garrick Street WC2
Tel. 020 7240 5778
Tube: Leicester Square
www.limafloral.com

THE MODERN PANTRY ££

The loft-living, Scandi noir-watching, Rapha-cycling natives of Clerkenwell are spoilt for choice when it comes to cool restaurants. Hix, Polpo, St John and Smiths of Smithfield are all thriving, and we are huge fans of Bill Granger's newbie, Granger & Co., with its raised dining room like the prow of a ship overlooking Clerkenwell Green. We've also had many an amusing weekend brunch at Bistrot Bruno Loubet on St John's

Square. But we are consistently impressed by
Anna Hansen's Modern Pantry, which opened in
2008. Canada-born and New Zealand-bred Hansen
trained under Fergus 'St John' Henderson and co-
founded Marylebone's the Providores. Housed in
a handsome Georgian town house stripped back
and decorated with minimalist, industrial furniture,
the Modern Pantry is tailor-made for affluent
urban trendies.

On the ground floor is a café space with neat rows
of white tables and window seats. It's all too close for
comfort should you wish for a private conversation,
but there is a more grown-up arrangement in the
first-floor dining room. This being Clerkenwell, there's
rather a lot of tofu and kale on the menu. I'm afraid
our heart sinks like a leaper from Westminster Bridge
when we see tofu on a menu, but we do heartily
approve of the love Hansen gives to vegetables. We
ordered marinated venison haunch and took as much
pleasure from the smoked carrot purée and braised
leeks as we did from the game. We particularly
liked the wine recommendations on the menu to
match particular dishes. Charred sweetcorn, smoked
ricotta and tarragon fritters complemented the 2013
Sauvignon Blanc perfectly. We also liked the codes
on the wine list, which pointed us towards particular
flavours, such as rich and powerful reds and zesty and
refreshing whites.

The Modern Pantry is a totally rounded
operation. Hansen's *Modern Pantry Cookbook* is to
Clerkenwell in the twenty-first century what *The River
Café Cookbook* was to Fulham in the twentieth. Behind
the café is a delightful little *traiteur* space where one
can buy hampers, deli dishes, artisan sandwiches
and gorgeous bottles and jars of home-made chutney,

jam and preserves. We haven't taken the private dining room on the second floor, but are reliably informed that fashion locals such as Hussein Chalayan and Sarah Burton (creative director of Alexander McQueen) are huge fans.

47–48 St John's Square EC1
Tel. 020 7553 9210
Tube: Farringdon
www.themodernpantry.co.uk

ROKA ££££

There's an old superstition in New Orleans that the coffin is tossed into the air several times as a funeral procession passes a place where the deceased was happiest. Roka on Charlotte Street is definitely on our shortlist. Summer Sunday lunches there, when the floor-to-ceiling windows are flung open and unlimited Moutard NV is served for a supplement of £25, are magic – not that one needs the incentive of champagne on tap to dine on world-class Japanese robatayaki cuisine in such a chic, amusing dining room.

It's folly not to book at Roka, because we don't think it's had a tumbleweed moment since it was opened by the chef Rainer Becker and investor Arjun Waney in 2004. A ringside, rather low seat at the polished, sinuous hardwood bar surrounding the robata grill is rather fun, and you do feel like cheering your man as he gives a rack of asparagus spears a good basting with sweet soy sauce and sesame. We're not great fans of devouring salty dishes of edamame beans like a demented chipmunk, and prefer instead to order Roka's superlative white miso with slivers of scallop and spring onion immediately, and the 'bring me the

head of Carmen Miranda' sashimi platter on a pillow
of crushed ice with spectacular fronds of foliage.
Dishes come as they are cooked, so it is smart to
order such palate-cleansers as a tower of spinach
leaves with delicate sesame drizzle or crispy prawn
and avocado dipped in sweet soy to balance the big
flavour of the specialities, which include lamb cutlets
grilled in Korean spices
and a juicy, plump piece
of blackened cod.

*"... we don't think
it's had a tumbleweed
moment since it was
opened ..."*

Although the full Roka
menu is served in the Shochu
Lounge bar below, to eat
there is rather like booking
tickets for the must-see
play in the West End and spending the first act in
the theatre bar. You want to eyeball the drama of the
robata grill and not be deprived of the pleasure of
critiquing dishes as they sail past, though we must say
there aren't many 'don't fancy yours much' moments.
When it isn't Champagne Sunday at Roka, do take
advantage of the sake menu. Don't ask us why, but
we always fool ourselves that when served warm, sake
is non-alcoholic. What the hell! Warm sake is the
alcoholic equivalent of slipping into a floor-length
mink coat. Roka has opened doors in Canary Wharf,
Mayfair and Aldwych, not to mention Hong Kong; we
flatly refuse to visit any of these, and still pretend that
it has not spawned a chain.

37 Charlotte Street W1
Tel. 020 7580 6464
Tube: Goodge Street
www.rokarestaurants.com

Where to eat ... with dedicated followers of fashion

THE CLOVE CLUB £££

Facebook and Twitter have a lot to answer for. Pity the poor chefs who don't prepare plates of food ready for their close-up, à la Norma Desmond. We long for the day when a restaurant imposes a zero-tolerance policy on cameras, as the West End theatres do. There's nothing more off-putting than sitting next to a couple thrusting their iPhones into your tortellini, having already shot their plates from every angle. We don't approve of the food paparazzi even if, as at Clove Club, plates are pretty as a picture (albeit one painted by David Hockney).

We were familiar with the chef Isaac McHale and his front of house partners-in-crime Daniel Willis and Johnny Smith from their pop-up, which became permanent, above the 10 Bells (see **Drinks Cabinet**). We also remember Shoreditch Town Hall (built in 1865, the year Mrs Beeton died) as a near-derelict husk before it was brought back to life. The viaduct end of Old Street is still grim and dreary, making the cerulean-blue Town Hall door leading into the Clove Club a welcome sight.

The Clove Club, which opened in 2013, has had its detractors, who believe a set menu is pretentious and an emphasis on overlooked British ingredients a pose. We would ordinarily agree that there's a good reason chefs overlook ingredients, and fight like Boadicea to order what we – rather than the chef – want to be served. We weren't particularly enchanted by the austere dining room, where all the attention was directed towards the blue-tiled open kitchen. But then we remembered that we're in the East End; the Clove Club isn't Wiltons, nor would it wish to be. McHale's food is audacious – buttermilk fried chicken served on a bristling nest of pine twigs being a new classic of taste and presentation – and made with an awful lot of love for seasonal ingredients, such as wood pigeon (which are made into sausages), Cornish skate and pheasant (baked in hay). It is the fashion to pepper a menu with obtuse references. We thought red orache was something naughty sailors picked up on the docks, until we were told it was spinach. We'd be much more impressed if chefs used the RHS language and called it *Atriplex hortensis*. Nevertheless, the Clove Club produces exceptional food.

Shoreditch Town Hall, 380 Old Street EC1
Tel. 020 7729 6496
Tube: Old Street
www.thecloveclub.com

DABBOUS ££££

In the 2000s we used to joke about the oddball club kids who lived in Old Street, wore Jeremy Scott and had Japanese friends. These days East End boys can kiss goodbye to fashion unless they have a ginger beard, a gym-toned physique, turn-ups and brogues. When Ollie Dabbous opened his first eponymous restaurant in Fitzrovia in 2012, we wondered why the critics were falling over themselves to praise the talented unknown. Then we saw the first of many newspaper and magazine profiles and understood. Bingo: ginger beard and moustache, gym-toned physique, turned-up jeans and white 'Brando in *The Wild One*' T-shirt. Ha! Here, we thought, is a classic case of looking the part: cometh the hour, cometh the man, and all that. Would the critics Messrs Gill, Coren, Rayner and Parker Bowles, and old mother Maschler from the *Evening Standard*, have made such a fuss if Ollie didn't look the part?

Wrapping this cynicism around us like a Blackglama mink stole, we ventured to Whitfield Street – a drear boulevard adjacent to Tottenham Court Road – and thought 'department of no surprises' when we arrived in the bare industrial dining room with exposed metal vents on the ceiling and concrete on the floor. We stepped gingerly downstairs to Oskar's Bar, which looks like the cellar in Ekaterinburg where the Russian tsar and his family were shot, and rolled our eyes theatrically at the cocktail list: Rye Rye Rye Delilah? Beer Grylls? Rum Direction? Rice Rice Baby? The ambassador from planet fashion in our party ordered a sloe gin punch and the negativity dissolved like the Wicked Witch of the West when introduced to liquid. Home-made sloe gin, lemon and pink grapefruit teased with a top-up of ginger ale and topped with mint and cucumber: bravo Oskar!

Having tottered gently back upstairs to the dining room, our party was entirely seduced by Dabbous. We didn't even rise to the bait of our bêtes noires – 'heritage' tomatoes and 'hen's' eggs – on the menu. (As *The Guardian*'s Jay Rayner wrote, 'the cock's not going to b***** lay the thing, is it?') It may sound fatuous to say the ingredients lead Dabbous's menu – Jersey Royals, globe artichoke, asparagus, turnip tops – but the flavours he achieves are anything but naïve. Asparagus served with a dipping 'egg yolk' of rapeseed-oil mayonnaise and toasted hazelnuts was brilliant, as was a signature coddled egg, mushroom and smoked butter served in the eggshell. Valentines have surely been written to the barbecued Iberico pork served with a savoury acorn praline, but we saved our love for British cheeses served with a honey-glazed baked apple and toasted sourdough bread. It is the kind of flavour combination that makes you think a chef is really thinking of giving pleasure, not of showing off or teaching lessons. In short, if Ollie Dabbous gets his beard clipped and his suit cleaned, it could be a match.

39 Whitfield Street W1
Tel. 020 7323 1544
Tube: Goodge Street
www.dabbous.co.uk

GYMKHANA ££££

The Edwardian India of the Raj, when British king-emperors ruled and the maharajas retained their palaces, is an intoxicating tot of colonial history to sip in twenty-first-century Mayfair. Gymkhana's owner, Karam Sethi, has judged the interior perfectly. The ceiling fans, cut-glass wall lamps and hunting trophies from the cabinet of a long-forgotten maharaja of Jodhpur suggest the gentlemen's clubs of the princely Indian states without descending into parody. London is no stranger to gourmet Indian food. Veeraswamy, London's first Indian restaurant, was opened in 1926, and in recent years Benares and Tamarind have held their Michelin stars, not to mention Sethi's Marylebone restaurant, Trishna.

So why has London gone absolutely wild for Gymkhana? We are of course familiar – even overfamiliar – with Anglo-Indian food, even if only of the Brick Lane indeterminate-meat-in-molten-lava variety. What we perhaps don't expect is interesting fish and game cooked in the tandoori oven and on the sigri charcoal grill that is at once intriguing and vaguely familiar. The taste of our duck dosa was tender and strong when scooped on to a buttery flatbread and smothered in cooling coconut chutney. Wild tiger prawn and red pepper chutney was a thrill, as were fried south Indian chicken wings.

Having been armed with one Quinine Sour (Gymkhana's take on the G&T using tonic syrup, curry leaf and egg white), physical force had to be used to persuade us to move on to wine rather than order another for each hand. The waiters were outstandingly well-briefed to lead us through the many menus, and to deter us rather than encouraging us to order too much food. Pig-cheek vindaloo in red chilli and garlic masala sounds more threatening than it actually was, and we adored a dish that apparently involved quail. On the strength of a baby aubergine side order, we'd like to try the vegetarian dishes next time we visit Gymkhana. A quick peek downstairs at the bar confirmed that another date with a Quinine Sour was imminent, and we adored the private dining rooms – coal holes stretching out under Albemarle Street – furnished with what Sethi calls 'inky blue leather love booths'.

42 Albemarle Street W1
Tel. 020 3011 5900
Tube: Green Park
www.gymkhanalondon.com

HOI POLLOI ££

East End foodies send up flares every month to announce the arrival of a new hipster dining room,

and, like bright young things on a treasure hunt in
the 1920s, those of us who don't call Bethnal Green
home leap into cabs or on to buses to keep *dans le
vent*. The Clove Club (see entry), Typing Room (see
Hotels) and Hoi Polloi at the Ace Hotel have all been
designated the must-eat destination in the East End.
2014's candidate for Miss Shoreditch High Street was
Hoi Polloi, the brainchild of Pablo Flack and David
Waddington, the lovely chaps behind Bistrotheque and
various pop-ups that had popped off before we caught
on. They were chosen to 'curate' the first Ace Hotel
restaurant outside the US. Ace has been much derided
for its pretensions – offering complimentary DJ decks
in every room, alongside other such essentials as
soap and towels – but Hoi Polloi deserves nothing
but respect.

Once your olfactory sense has been seduced
walking through Hattie Fox's That Flower Shop to Hoi
Polloi, you are greeted by pleasing design. Interiors by
Edward Barber and Jay Osgerby's Universal Design
Studio are surprisingly warm, tactile and welcoming.
The main dining area is enclosed with fluted timber
wall panels, and Philippe Malouin's brass pendant
lights cast a warm glow over tabletops lined with
flecked linoleum. Banquette seating invites one to
linger and contradicts the London lore that all seating
in East End restaurants must be Bauhaus severe and
schoolroom hard. *Round the Horne* characters Julian
and Sandy appear to have written a beyond camp
cocktail menu, listing the Dilly Boy, Wet Luppers and
Lily Law, but fortunately we speak fluent Polari, so
we asked the serving homi to nish the naff trade and
bring us a bona Fantabulosa.

The menu at Hoi Polloi is served from 7 am to
1 am. We'd rather drink bleach than watch the hipsters

breakfasting on lemongrass smoothies, organic yoghurt and granola, but Hoi Polloi is a fine place to meet for a boozy lunch or dinner. There's nothing fancy on the menu. You want crab salad, radish and toast? That's what you get. Chicken broth, dumpling, cabbage and roast corn is honest and easy. We adore the poached lobster salad served with brioche and lobster mayo, and have no scruples about ordering dripping chips to go with it. When the cocktail glass has been forcibly removed from our hand we can weave around the nursery slopes of Hoi Polloi's wine list and know we're not going to be disappointed. And whereas dedicated followers of fashion very rarely demonstrate a sense of humour – or even a pulse – we have noticed that the boys and girls at Hoi Polloi do seem to be letting their topknots down.

Ace Hotel, 100 Shoreditch High Street E1
Tel. 020 8880 6100
Tube: Old Street
www.hoi-polloi.co.uk

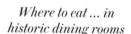

Where to eat ... in historic dining rooms

QUALITY CHOP HOUSE £££

In 1869, when the Quality Chop House first opened its doors, Clerkenwell was a rough working-men's quarter of London, and the solid-wood booth seating (still in situ) was designed to make sure the men ate quickly. The food was good, cheap and honest. Well, two out of three certainly ain't bad since Will Lander and Josie Stead took over this much-loved Grade II-listed dining room, which suffered the indignity of briefly being rebranded as a meatball restaurant. We have always loved the main Chop House, with its linoleum floor, bum-numbing benches and multiple mirrors, but we love it much more now the tables are decorated with meadow flowers in milk bottles and the booths have been upholstered. The café room next door is equally charming, and the juxtaposition of blackboards, mismatched antique china, Sheffield plate cutlery and occasional café tables is just right.

What we like about the Quality Chop House is its diminutive size. It reassures us that the menus are indeed devised each morning according to what produce has been delivered, and keeps the chefs on their toes when specials prove popular or ingredients run out. That said, the magnificent Q butcher's shop on the premises makes running out of chops unlikely, and also bodes well for the quality of the meat served as well as that sold. Call it autosuggestion, but we find it terribly hard to resist always ordering a chop as thick as a telephone directory, new potatoes and a mountain of kale and washing it down with a bottle of 2008 Caiarossa Pergolaia Toscana. But even if we're committed to the set dinner, we know we are in good hands.

We've shared cassoulet at the Quality Chop House that deserved a *Légion d'Honneur*, and would fight for the venison mince served on dripping toast. Highland beef and ale stew or Somerset kid served with purple sprouting broccoli and swede fondant are also favourites from the set dinner menu. But, to be honest, quality and simplicity are aces that are repeatedly played at the Chop House. Side orders are the bridesmaid in many establishments, yet we found ourselves falling in love with a plate of watercress, chicory and pickled walnuts. You have to tip the top hat to Lander and Stead for taking on this historic dining room. Although the Chop House is round the corner from Exmouth Market's culinary string of pearls (Moro, Medcalf, Bonnie Gull, et al.), the restaurant and Q shop aren't on a street that will give it much love or passing trade now *The Guardian*'s offices are gone. But still, you'll struggle to book a table.

88–94 Farringdon Road EC1
Tel. 020 7278 1452
Tube: Farringdon
www.thequalitychophouse.com

QUO VADIS £££

Like many a woozy roué, Soho is as sentimental as it is debauched. H. V. Morton hits the nail on the head when he writes 'Soho is largely decayed Georgian ... [with] men and women working there dreaming of somewhere else.' We adore Soho's transience but also its survivors, such as Kettner's (1867), Bar Italia (1949) and L'Escargot (1927). We also ask a minute's silence to mark the closure of the legendary drag cabaret Madame Jojo's (1962), spuriously shut down at the end of 2014. Reinventing a Soho institution is risky. There's been a restaurant on the site of Quo Vadis since 1926, when its founder, Pepino Leoni, arrived in London. The oldest of the houses annexed by Quo Vadis pre-dates Queen Anne. An impoverished Karl Marx lived in No. 28 – what he described as 'an old hovel' – between 1851 and 1856, and there he wrote *Das Kapital* and buried three children. Quo Vadis survived a putsch in 1996, when Marco Pierre White and Damien Hirst smothered it in BritArt and nouvelle

cuisine. White and Hirst fell out spectacularly, and
Marco replaced Damien's artworks on the walls of Quo
Vadis with his own, which was probably preferable to
Hirst replacing White in the kitchen.

Today Quo Vadis is in the capable hands of Eddie
and Sam Hart, the darlings who brought us tapas-
inspired Soho and Covent Garden hotties Barrafina
and Fino in Fitzrovia. We all breathed a sigh of relief
at the opening in 2008, but it wasn't until 2012, when
the chef Jeremy Lee took the helm at Quo Vadis, that
the menu got into a mood more suited to Soho. As
befits a district long famed for its ladies of the night,
Soho is all fur coat and no knickers. It has a penchant
for eating comfort food in grand surroundings. The
QV dining room has a placid grandeur, with light
spilling through the stained-glass windows, but age
and character make it much more welcoming than
those beige panic rooms in Mayfair that keep out all
but the disgustingly rich.

Lee's menu is succinctly put and artfully
presented, with amusing sketches by John Broadley
that make the cards collector's items. It is a British
version of the grand European café menu revived by
Corbin and King: a smoked-eel sandwich, a seasonal
chopped salad, dressed crab and mayonnaise or a
shoulder of mutton with chickpeas and spinach.
There are ludicrously reasonable specials, such as
the £20 three-course theatre menu – chicken-liver
paté, grilled bream and potato salad, and Campari
and pomegranate sorbet – and staples of English
cuisine, such as salt cod, leeks, salsify and almonds,
that wouldn't be out of place on an eighteenth-
century dining table. Quo Vadis introduces itself as
'a charming dining room where we offer our menu
amended merrily and daily', adding: 'We also boast

two handsome private dining rooms both beautifully appointed and very well attended to.' Quo Vadis tells no lies. It is a Soho sensation.

26–29 Dean Street W1
Tel. 020 7437 9585
Tube: Tottenham Court Road
www.quovadissoho.co.uk

RULES ££££

It is terribly trite to trot out the bare facts about London's oldest restaurant, Rules – purveyor of 'porter, pies and oysters', established by Thomas Rule in 1798 – whose history spans nine monarchs from George III to our present Queen. The grand old man of Maiden Lane was a literary favourite (Dickens, Thackeray, Waugh, Greene, Betjeman) and a theatrical haunt (Irving, Olivier, Chaplin, Barrymore, Gable). Rules might easily have become a time capsule, labouring its past and resting on its laurels, but the menu still has star quality and the dining room a charm that defies imitation. Who else would even try to get away with displays of dried flowers that look like first-night bouquets thrown when Henry Irving and Ellen Terry took their bows at the Theatre Royal Drury Lane?

The decor at Rules is not dissimilar to a plush Victorian bordello, with scarlet velvet banquettes, *Vanity Fair* 'Spy' cartoons, alabaster busts, hunting trophies and hothouse plants all artfully bathed in nostalgic gold light beneath a stained-glass dome. Service is terribly old-fashioned and formal – hurrah! – with 90 staff serving 90 guests seated in the main dining room. Rules is famed for its game and for its Belted Galloway beef reared on owner John Mayhew's

Perthshire estate. One doesn't so much dine as feast on twenty-eight-day-aged rib of beef with creamy dauphinois potatoes and crisp Yorkshire pudding (an embarrassment of riches if ever we saw one), wild boar and mushroom pie, wild rabbit hotpot and whole roast crown of pheasant served with sausages, bacon and braised carrots.

History buffs are usually disappointed when they try to capture the essence of another age in an interior with great provenance. At Rules one can easily imagine Evelyn Waugh's Agatha Runcible and Miles Malpractice surreptitiously snorting 'naughty salt' under the next table, or P. G. Wodehouse's Bertie Wooster, Gussie Fink-Nottle and other chaps of the Drones Club daring one another to down tankards of champagne and scorching plates of pheasant curry as a rag. Out of the corner of your eye you might even see a handsome couple surreptitiously disappear upstairs as the Prince of Wales (later Edward VII) and Lillie Langtry did in the late 1870s. As you'd expect from such a character, Rules has a rich and deep wine list that specializes in wines from the Rhône valley and tops out at £180 for a magnum of Châteauneuf-du-Pape 2005. The house Côtes du Rhône 'Est-Ouest' Domaine André Brunel 2010 is a steal (£25), and the Rules cocktail (Dubonnet and Tanqueray No. 10 gin with brown sugar, Angostura bitters and champagne) is addictive. Private dining rooms are named after regulars Graham Greene and John Betjeman, the

> *"At Rules one can easily imagine Evelyn Waugh's Agatha Runcible and Miles Malpractice surreptitiously snorting 'naughty salt' under the next table ..."*

latter of whose campaigning in the 1960s helped
to save Covent Garden Market and Rules from the
wrecking ball.

35 Maiden Lane WC2
Tel. 020 7836 5314
Tube: Covent Garden
www.rules.co.uk

SWEETINGS ££

There's an old saying that in the event of nuclear
war Christie's and Sotheby's would still be open for
business and ready to auction off the debris. We might
add that Sweetings would still be on the corner of
Queen Victoria Street, where it has traded since 1889,
serving whitebait and skate wings in black butter to
the survivors. Of all the facts about Sweetings' history,
we love the thought of Henri de Toulouse-Lautrec
and Francis Bacon – subversive artists separated by
almost a century – walking its marble mosaic floors to
find a corner where they could devour smoked eel and
tankards of white wine.

This being the City, Sweetings has a dictatorial,
no-nonsense approach that appeals to public
schoolboys. Lunch is served between 11.30 am and
3 pm Monday to Friday. There are no reservations,
you sit where you're put and coffee is discouraged.
Sweetings has had five owners in its long life, the latest
being Mr Barfoot, who was a Billingsgate fishmonger
by trade before assuming guardianship of the curved
corner site in 2000. The menu simply does not change,
and is almost exclusively fish and shellfish: lobster
bisque, home-made gravadlax, scallops and bacon
and potted shrimp to start, followed by comforting
fish pie, cod steaks in parsley sauce, Dover sole and

wild turbot with mustard sauce. The quality is not up to Wiltons or Bellamy's but, frankly, who cares when you're walking in the footsteps of, ahem, such giants as Toulouse-Lautrec?

Puds like jam roll, spotted dick and syrup pudding appeal to boys who still like their bottoms smacked (albeit by stern ladies in Shepherd Market rather than nannies), and there are of course the savouries for which Sweetings is famed: buck rarebit, roes on toast and an English cheese plate. The wine list is brisk, and favours white wines. We enjoyed a nice Vouvray from the Loire (£36; also served by the glass), and we would be lying if we said we didn't punish the ports – house and vintage – that aren't listed on the menu. As traditional as a Poole's chalk-stripe three-piece and orderly as a furled umbrella, Sweetings is an echo of an older world of certainty, in which everyone knew their place.

39 Queen Victoria Street EC4
Tel. 020 7248 3062
Tube: Mansion House
www.sweetingsrestaurant.com

Where to eat ...
Sunday lunch

CORRIGAN'S MAYFAIR ££££

We were the first to applaud when a new crop of 'all brick and floorboards' independent wine shops, tapas bars and organic delicatessens such as Polpo, Vinoteca, Ottolenghi and Fernandez & Wells appeared in central London in the Noughties. What's not to like about laid-back, low-key dining rooms that serve good, unpretentious modern European food and wines from small, family-owned vineyards? But, like all hipster singletons, they matured and expanded into chains, albeit in key areas like Marylebone, Clerkenwell, Soho and Notting Hill. So, much as we love them, we won't include these Sunday lunch staples in the *Discriminating Guide.*

Corrigan's Mayfair couldn't be less low-key if it tried. Neither does it reflect the apparently sunny soul of Irish charmer Richard Corrigan. Upper Grosvenor Street is paved with diplomatic passports and dollar bills, and Corrigan's Mayfair gives local residents the grand entrance to which they are accustomed. Martin Brudnizki has made a super job of the interior, in which practically every available surface is upholstered in Smythson blue leather. The lighting is elective surgery-friendly, and the coy references to the fish and game at which this restaurant excels don't detract from the statuesque elegance of the room. We recommend Corrigan's Mayfair for a lavish family lunch, preferably when a prodigal son is being welcomed back or a dowager is poised to reveal the contents of her will. Facetiousness aside, it is a comfortable if rather swish dining room for all generations.

"Upper Grosvenor Street is paved with diplomatic passports and dollar bills ..."

The Sunday lunch menu is served between noon and 4 pm. It is a ridiculously cheap £29 for three courses, and Mr Corrigan doesn't skimp on the number of dishes to choose from or the quality of the ingredients. That said, we're hardly likely to visit a Corrigan restaurant and not order at least half a dozen oysters to keep our Singapore Sling company. The herb-crusted lamb served with gem lettuce (codenamed Cara Delevingne because it is this year's model ingredient) is satisfying, but we couldn't resist breaking our own rules and paying the £10 supplement for Corrigan's rib of beef. Although it opened in 2008, Corrigan's Mayfair has the gravitas to be thought a similar vintage to Le Gavroche.

28 Upper Grosvenor Street W1
Tel. 020 7499 9943
Tube: Marble Arch
www.corrigansmayfair.co.uk

HIX OYSTER & CHOP HOUSE ££££

As chef director of Caprice Holdings, Mark Hix filled the nosebags of London tastemakers at Scott's, the Ivy and the Rivington Bar & Grill. In the short time since he opened Hix Oyster & Chop House in Smithfield, in 2008, he has conquered London with his restaurants in Brown's Hotel, Selfridges, Soho, infinity and beyond. When we're in the mood we like Hix's chicken and steak concept, Tramshed, in the East End, and the bar below Hix Soho (see **Drinks Cabinet**) is sinfully handsome. But on Sundays W1 belongs to shoppers rather than leisurely lunching parties, so we lean towards a table at Hix's former sausage factory/fish restaurant behind Smithfield Market in Clerkenwell.

Some restaurants immediately make you reach for the calculator to work out how much has been blown on interior decoration to make a so-so room spectacular. Hix Oyster & Chop just works. There's a marble bar/counter where it ought to be, occasional tables standing on wooden floorboards and further seating on raised platforms giving a relatively small room lots of character, privacy and interest. Hix offers a £27.95 three-course Sunday lunch surrounding star turns Glenarm 'mighty marbled sirloin' with Yorkshire pudding or chicken with sage-and-onion stuffing. We consider it close to treason to visit Hix without ordering half a dozen mixed oysters with spicy boar sausages and flying the flag with a glass or bottle of British Nyetimber Classic Cuvée 2008. However mighty and marbled the sirloin, it doesn't hold a candle to a sharing plate of Glenarm Estate porterhouse steak with home-made horseradish, spring greens, roasties and cauliflower cheese. Another Hix speciality are set feast menus for parties of eight, built around a whole roasted chicken with skin as crisp as Donatella Versace, a roast suckling pig or oysters and steaks.

> *"We consider it treason to visit Hix without ordering half a dozen mixed oysters with spicy boar sausages ..."*

Hix is not cheap, but we fully expect to pay top dollar for such fine-quality beef cooked to perfection on the site of the world's oldest surviving meat market. The fact that our ancestors also burned martyrs here at the command of Henry VIII and his children adds another layer of history to this blood-soaked sacred ground. But we digress. As we said, Hix is not cheap, so we weren't very impressed when the 'Mark Suggests' wines on the list were £75 and £93 respectively. To quote Mandy Rice-Davies, 'He would say that, wouldn't he?' We were also nonplussed by the wines boxed and listed under 'Big Guns', which hit a high-water mark of £503 a bottle. It would have been much chicer had Hix recommended a perfectly decent red, such as the £22 Montepulciano d'Abruzzo 2011, as well as his bottles for big spenders.

36–37 Greenhill Rents, Cowcross Street EC1
Tel. 020 7017 1930
Tube: Farringdon
www.hixoysterandchophouse.co.uk

SIMPSON'S-IN-THE-STRAND ££££

The original coffee house and cigar lounge was opened in 1828 by Samuel Reiss and reached a peak of excellence and fame in the second half of the nineteenth century, when John Simpson extended the restaurant and christened it Simpson's Grand Divan and Tavern. It was he who made Simpson's London's home of chess, where the 'Immortal Game' (Anderssen versus Kieseritzky) was played in 1851. The booths replicated in Simpson's today were designed for the playing and observing of chess games, and the silver domed carving trolley on casters was invented at 100 Strand so as not to disturb play. In 1904 Simpson's was redecorated completely by Rupert D'Oyly Carte, whose father, Richard, had opened the Savoy hotel next door in 1889. Art deco touches were added in the 1930s, when the Savoy was jazzed up, including Knight's Bar on the first floor: a woefully forgotten little gem of a cocktail bar that is almost always deserted.

> *"The booths replicated in Simpson's today were designed for the playing and observing of chess games …"*

The original *Discriminating Guide* considered Simpson's-in-the-Strand 'Not for Us', explaining that 'the general air of decay has not lifted since our last edition [and] the beautiful rooms are still carpeted in stains and served by often un-shaven waiters in dirty white jackets.' Our reply would be 'better mild decay than utter destruction.' The fact that Simpson's was always the poor relation to the Savoy meant that its interiors are relatively untouched. The Savoy's latest guardian, Fairmont, has given Simpson's a little love, resulting in the absence of decay, stained carpets and unshaven waiters in dirty jackets. The odour of boiled cabbage has gone, leaving the atmosphere clear for the ghosts of E. M. Forster, P. G. Wodehouse and Arthur Conan Doyle, all of them Simpson's men.

Simpson's is unashamedly Edwardian in pace and personality. The ground-floor dining room, which admitted ladies only from 1984, is charming, even though you will be sharing it with far more tourists than locals. Fashion has caught up with the 'Best of British' philosophy upheld by master chef Thomas Davey, who renamed the menu a 'Bill of Fare', a tradition upheld to this day. The formality and ritual of the silver carving trolley (do remember to tip the carver £5) would certainly reassure eminent Victorian guests Dickens, Disraeli and the Count d'Orsay. We do agree with Mr Sherwood Sr that 'any cooking that's not on the trolley is institutional', but we don't think it any the worse for that. You will not find a finer Sunday lunch in London than Simpson's twenty-eight-day-aged roast rib of Scottish beef served with

> *"The formality and ritual of the silver carving trolley (do remember to tip the carver £5) would certainly reassure eminent Victorian guests …"*

Yorkshire pudding and side orders of Savoy cabbage and roast potatoes in miniature copper pots. Do visit Wodehouse's 'restful temple of food'. Even the most sinister hangover can be cast down with Simpson's Ten Deadly Sins fried breakfast washed down with a glass of champagne or a Bloody Mary.

100 Strand WC2
Tel. 020 7836 9112
Tube: Charing Cross
www.simpsonsinthestrand.co.uk

ST JOHN £££

The smug marrieds and consciously coupled in Clerkenwell would have one's balls for sweetbreads if one dared to classify St John's 'nose-to-tail' menu, loaded with dishes involving offal, too visceral for all but the alpha male. There is nothing sybaritic about the spartan dining room with whitewashed walls, school pegs for coats and refectory furniture in the former packing room of this Georgian town house, which had been a smokehouse for ham and bacon, a squat and a venue for illegal raves before the founder of St John, Fergus Henderson, took it on in 1994. Henderson is one of the few game-changing London chefs; he was on to locally sourced, sustainable, ascetic food when Ollie Dabbous was still in a papoose, and he wrote the Ten Commandments of cooking with tongue, cheeks, tail, trotters, chitterling, tummies and hearts.

St John is a bison's stride away from Smithfield meat market (where else?), and its upper floors housed *Marxism Today* in the late 1960s and East End fashionistas Katy Grand (editor of *Love* magazine) and Luella Bartley in the 1990s, so it goes without saying that it would be folly to whip out a copy of the *Daily Telegraph* when waiting for your guest in the bar and bakery. Flippancy aside, St John is one of London's outstanding kitchens: it balances clean, complementary flavours such as crispy pig's skin, chicory and sorrel, lamb tongues with green beans and anchovy, ox liver, chard and mustard or lamb sweetbreads with turnips and bacon. If, like me, you don't have a sweet tooth, St John is one of the few restaurants where puddings – such as Eccles cake and Lancashire cheese or brown-bread ice cream – appeal.

> "... the St John bakery makes the best bread north of Paris ..."

The brisk service and plain English food appeal to tastemakers such as Jay Jopling, Janet Street-Porter, Kate Moss, Zaha Hadid and Jude Law as an antidote to the pomp of the West End. Chapeau to St John for its pragmatic, predominantly French wine list, with at least twelve bottles of either colour under £40. St John doesn't tend to have quiet nights, but I've had as much fun in the rough-and-tumble of the bar ordering Welsh rarebit on doorsteps of home-baked white bread and drizzled with Lea & Perrins as I have joining the grown-ups in the dining room. If you're local, the St John bakery makes the best bread north of Paris, and no Clerkenwell kitchen supper would be complete without St John's Bag-in-a-Cardboard-Box, containing four bottles of the house Saint-Loup Rouge 2012.

26 St John Street EC1
Tel. 020 7251 0848
Tube: Farringdon
www.stjohngroup.uk.com/smithfield

Where to eat ...
pre- and post-theatre

BRASSERIE ZEDEL ££

Before the Second World War, London was a city of ballrooms. The belle époque splendour of Piccadilly's former Regent Palace Hotel has been all but erased, but the basement ballroom remains intact. In the 1990s it was the *mise-en-scène* for Oliver Peyton's hot box the Atlantic Bar & Grill, one of the most decadent nightspots of its era and something of a blur for those of us who were over the age of consent at the time. Fashion moved on or the cops moved in, I don't recall, but the ballroom went to sleep until Chris Corbin and Jeremy King, the reigning monarchs of London's fashionable restaurant scene, brought it back to life as Brasserie Zedel.

There aren't many staircases in this town that make one curse leaving your fox fur, cigarette holder and brace of salukis in diamond collars at home, but Zedel certainly has one of them. Turn a corner and you're at eye level with a crystal chandelier as you descend to the circular reception area, which had a cigarette kiosk before PC became your GP. Past the red-velvet-curtained art deco Crazy Coq's cabaret and the Bar Americain, you make a very grand entrance to the gilded ballroom, reminiscent of a Vanderbilt mansion in Newport, Rhode Island. Rent *Hello Dolly* and skip to the Delmonico's scene and you've got the gist. Waiters in white aprons dance around the parquet floor, and every seat gives a terrific view of fellow diners ... a plus or a minus, depending on the company you keep.

If, like us, you dress for the theatre, Brasserie Zedel is one of those interiors that reward your efforts. The more one puts on the ritz, the more one's face fits in to this divine throwback to the age of tortoiseshell compacts and diamond-encrusted opera glasses. However, unlike Corbin and King's Wolseley and Delaunay, Brasserie Zedel undercuts the loco London prices that drive away the pretty but penniless people who always decorate a room. The *prix fixe* menu is an almost impossible £11.95 for three courses of such brasserie classics as endive salad with Roquefort, onion soup, steak tartare, snails and puds such as *crêpes à l'orange* and *bombe glaceé*. The price, the location and the late hours Zedel keeps make it the perfect place for a pre- or post-theatre supper. The pink-tinged lighting is too bright for us at lunchtime, but is more forgiving at night. The ground-floor café isn't particularly our cup of tea and doesn't quite prepare dinner guests for the sumptuous spectacle below, but perhaps it gives the element of surprise for which the showmen owners are noted.

20 Sherwood Street W1
Tel. 020 7734 4888
Tube: Piccadilly Circus
www.brasseriezedel.com

GREAT QUEEN STREET £££

Opened in 2007 by the chef Tom Norrington-Davies – an alumnus of the original gastropub, Clerkenwell's Eagle – Great Queen Street brought a robust, no-nonsense home-cooked approach to chichi theatreland. The long, low-lit dining room, with walls painted brick red, scuffed floorboards and Victorian workhouse tables and chairs interspersed with the odd church pew, doesn't give an inch to comfort, let alone luxury. and yet there's barely a table free by the time the theatre audiences flood the West End after curtain down.

We have to admit a bias for Great Queen Street because after the theatre we've never yearned for what is unpleasantly called 'dirty food' (burgers, fried chicken, hot dogs, and so on). What we look for are nurturing dishes we'd imagine might be served in a Thomas Hardy novel: roast shoulder of suckling pig and celeriac mash, steak-and-ale pie, seven-hour lamb and gratin dauphinois or duck cassoulet. These sharing plates are a great plus at a later hour because many are slow-cooked and benefit from an evening infusing flavours while we sit through five acts of *Hamlet*. Also, at that point in an evening, one can't be bothered with a menu that has various subplots that can't be understood without the help of your waiter.

Although we prefer plates for two as a theatre supper, Great Queen Street's menu is equally kind to the guest who just wants a bottle of Prosecco, a straw and a plate of sea-salted radishes to eat smeared with butter, or a slab of toasted sourdough groaning with white crab meat. The wine list is weighted towards bottles under £50, and the owners won't thank us for saying the house Syrah & Grenache 2012 at £17 a bottle is absolutely sensational for the price. We feel slightly churlish restricting Great Queen Street to pre- or post-theatre suppers, and we do so only because it is always top of our list after a gruesome opera or complicated play. But it is equally pleasing

> *"What we look for are nurturing dishes we'd imagine might be served in a Thomas Hardy novel …"*

for a long lunch or a spoiling midweek dinner. Our only criticism is the narrowness of the tables for two, but the solution is to hop up to the bar rather than suffer in silence.

32 Great Queen Street WC2
Tel. 020 7242 0622
Tube: Holborn
www.greatqueenstreetrestaurant.co.uk

JOE ALLEN ££ · &JS

The glamour! The camp! The beaded lashes! And that's just the waiters. Joe Allen breezed into London from New York in 1977, giving Covent Garden its first late-night, louche, brick American diner where actors, critics, stage-door johnnies and members of the audience in the know could speak easy after show time, surrounded by posters of fabulous flops. The joint still reeks of greasepaint and wig glue, and is a damned sight more fun than the Ivy, where soap stars and television presenters now hang. Every night is a cast party, and old-timers still remember evenings when the late Jimmy would tickle the upright while Liza Minnelli, Michael Feinstein, Elaine Stritch or Nathan Lane sang an impromptu eleven o'clock number. I'll never forget a New Year's Eve before the smoking ban was imposed when Patti LuPone – misted in the fug of a million Marlboro Lights – hit a piercing high C above a rousing chorus of Joe's anthem 'Somewhere Over the Rainbow'.

Joe's makes a mean Bloody Mary Sunday brunch and serves daily from noon, it's so much more amusing for a late-night supper of robust Noo Yawk classics such as Italian meatballs, chopped liver with pickles, eggs Benedict or chilli beef with sour cream, guacamole and skillet potatoes. Come 11 pm, Joe's fires a *feu de joie* of Prosecco corks like the opening number of *Mame*, although I'm with *Harry Potter* actress Miriam Margolyes, who is famed for bellowing 'House red! Lots of it!' Joe's is now under new management, and the menu has smartened up a little; sensible, one supposes, now that London is in thrall to the fad for 'dirty food' and every other door in Soho serves overpriced 'deluxe' burgers, hot dogs and fries. But the placement pecking order is still in operation, the star tables perversely being the ones closest to the open kitchen and furthest from the piano and cocktail bar. Joe's is one of the very few London restaurants that is still high-kicking at 1 am, and is particularly lively on matinee days. Be nice to the kids waiting tables: today's Joe Allen busboy is probably tomorrow's West End sensation.

13 Exeter Street WC2
Tel. 020 7836 0651
Tube: Covent Garden
www.joeallen.co.uk

POLPETTO ££

Don't you find a couture collection so much more interesting than a chain-store rail? Frankly, you're reading the wrong guide to London if you disagree. Anyway, you know our opinion of Venetian small-plate restaurant Polpo on Beak Street in Soho. It was a stroke of genius to open a Venetian-inspired kitchen in a house formerly occupied by Canaletto, but opening another four branches took the edge off the original. However, the owners, Russell Norman and Richard Beatty, had already experimented with a couture collection of their own: Polpetto, on the first floor

of the French House (see **Drinks Cabinet**), under
the direction of feisty chef Florence Knight. Polpetto
popped up and popped off, only to return on Berwick
Street, Soho, in 2014.

Knight is one of those evangelists for following
the seasons religiously, reducing ingredients to three
or four per dish, improvising with leftovers and
hammering home the message that fussy is finished
in the modern kitchen. She
also looks like one of those
cheesecake cuties painted on
the nose of a Lancaster bomber
in the 1940s, so television will
doubtless call. Berwick Street
Market is being sanitized
slightly, but there's still a great
buzz about walking the streets of Soho pre- and post-
theatre. We're particularly thrilled that the Raymond
Revuebar neon sign has been restored and winks once
more over Wardour Street.

"The wine list is so short that one would almost call it terse."

Polpetto is miniscule and minimalist. It consists
of a long red-leather banquette running the length of
a concrete wall and occasional intimate booths filled
with Soho's artists, inebriates and media miscellany.
No, it's not the kind of joint that Larry and Vivien
would sweep into to rapturous applause, but Polpetto
is a very classy dive that serves just the amount of food
one needs before or after a West End play. We like the
simplicity of sharing plates of grilled octopus, coco
beans and parsley, burrata, pumpkin and marjoram,
pork belly, chestnuts and lady's smock (the bombazine
was delicious) and darling desserts like warm jam
doughnuts and maple tart. The wine list is so short
that one would almost call it terse. But after the
theatre we always long for a garrulous red wine, and

Polpetto's Valpolicella La Giaretta 2012 (£32) was just the ticket. We do love a lick of Valpoliparrot.

11 Berwick Street W1
Tel. 020 7439 8627
Tube: Piccadilly Circus
www.polpetto.co.uk

Where to eat …
in evening dress

BRASSERIE CHAVOT ££££

Once a much grander street of bespoke tailors than Savile Row, Conduit Street is no stranger to ladies and gentlemen in evening dress dashing to theatre premieres, gala dinners on Park Lane or private parties in Mayfair town houses. We feel entirely at ease, therefore, popping in to the bar at Sketch or the Polo Bar in the Westbury (see **Drinks Cabinet**) wearing dinner jackets and floor-length dresses. Like the late couturier Charles James, Eric Chavot is acknowledged by his peers and critics as one of the true greats, but he didn't have the surname-only recognition of London's culinary superstars Ramsay, Hartnett, Wareing and Atherton. And yet the grandees of London restaurant criticism were unanimous in their belief that his ten years as head chef at the Capital hotel was worthy of three rather than the two Michelin stars he was awarded.

"… Conduit Street is no stranger to ladies and gentlemen in evening dress dashing to theatre premieres …"

Chavot inherited the dining-room interiors attached to the Westbury hotel. Although some critics reacted like the *sans-culotttes* when they first clapped eyes on the Hall of Mirrors, we don't think there's any such thing as too many chandeliers when you're dressed in black tie. The Byzantine mosaic floors, mirrored walls and generously spaced red-leather banquettes look like the set of a Jean Harlow film, even though the tables are so wide the hard of hearing (us included) might be reaching for the semaphore flags. But the glitter and the gold rather suits the posh *paysanne* menu of steak tartare, *boeuf en daube*, cassoulet and *tarte au citron*.

> *"There's an unwritten rule that the Queen will not eat shellfish on official tours abroad, the risk clearly being greater than the reward."*

There's an unwritten rule that the Queen will not eat shellfish on official tours abroad, the risk clearly being greater than the reward. We feel much the same about risking steak tartare in London restaurants. However, at Chavot the balance of tender raw beef, capers and mustard dressing laced with warm quail's egg yolk was perfection, and we regretted not ordering the dish as a main course. We can live without food served on chopping boards and in cast-iron pots (a trend that we hope will be fleeting), but admit the deep-fried soft-shelled crab petrified like a Louise Bourgeois sculpture looked striking rearing up from a slate plate. The venison, resting languidly on a bed of glazed root vegetables, was so exquisitely cooked that it was practically Schiaparelli pink, and we could have drunk neat the venison jus served on the side.

A mouthful of crab mayonnaise with avocado and gem
lettuce confirmed that Monsieur Chavot's starters
are well worth promoting to mains should you want
a dinner that doesn't strain a bias-cut gown.

41 Conduit Street W1
Tel. 020 7183 6425
Tube: Oxford Circus
www.brasseriechavot.com

FERA AT CLARIDGE'S ££££££

One could walk through the lobby at Claridge's in
white tie and full decorations accompanied by a
lady in a floor-length evening dress and a towering
fender of a family tiara, and nobody would consider
the sight peculiar. More kings and queens have dined
and slept at Claridge's than at Buckingham Palace.
Would a couple wearing white tie approve of Claridge's
relatively new dining room, Fera, decorated by Guy
Oliver and under the direction of Simon 'L'Enclume'
Rogan? The red-velvet atrium is a little perplexing
(is it regal or burlesque?), but the dining room is a
showpiece of dark wood, olive-green leather, pale gold
leaf, mirrored columns and mysterious swirling murals
like rings of tree bark. The centrepiece is a bleached,
petrified tree stripped of its bark, and the lighting is
theatrical: original deco pearl-glass screens, lanterns
and door frames warming up a rather cool interior.

Rogan is messianic about ingredients grown on
his own farm, foraged in surrounding forests and
cooked at the height of their season. As the menu
neatly puts it: 'Because Fera at Claridge's only uses
ingredients in their prime, the menus can change as
often as the weather they're grown in.' 'Fera' means
wild, and we won't be the first guests to observe that

there is absolutely nothing feral or instinctive about this restaurant. Food is served with all the care of a Japanese geisha's tea ceremony, as a succession of fiendishly complicated dishes are brought on slates, in boxes of pebbles and in vessels that look as if they were hand-thrown by Morgan le Fay. The table is kept strictly bare (presumably another caprice of the chef), and the ceremony surrounding the serving of wine makes one mischievously ask for a taster as if one is at the court of Catherine de' Medici. Should you order a bottle, it is kept not so much at arm's length but a short Tube journey away from your table, and that, quite frankly, is a bore.

However, Rogan cooked us food that we remembered far longer than the occasion for which we'd put on our glad rags. One could write a novella about every *amuse-bouche* (and some London restaurant critics have), but suffice it to say that a cloud of Winslade cheese whipped into creamed potato and topped with duck-heart ragout, chives and chive flowers was the finest balance of flavours we'd eaten all year. The beauty of the Aynsome soup made one's eye mist over: a bowl strewn with micro herbs, flower heads and touches of mustard cream, radish, truffle purée, artichoke and pickled cucumber received a bright watercress, spinach, rocket and potato soup that is in our opinion one of Rogan's masterpieces. Goosnargh duck served with a peppery watercress purée, smoked beetroot, duck sauce, berry crumble and wispy fronds of leek made

> *"Food is served with all the care of a Japanese geisha's tea ceremony, as a succession of fiendishly complicated dishes are brought on slates ..."*

us want to give a standing ovation. In Shakespearean shorthand, Fera's food is *A Midsummer Night's Dream* and the interiors pure Cleopatra's barge.

Claridge's, 49 Brook Street W1
Tel. 020 7107 8888
Tube: Bond Street
www.feraatclaridges.co.uk

THE IVY £££

The Ivy closed its doors in January 2015 to allow owner Richard Caring's decorator, Martin Brudnizki, to refurbish this West End trooper, once beloved of Noël and Gertie, the Oliviers, Ivor Novello and Alice Delysia. Opened as an unlicensed corner café in 1917 by Abel Giandellini, the Ivy earned its name when maître d' Mario Gallati decided to refurbish the dining room. When he expressed his concern that the theatrical clientele would go elsewhere, Delysia (for whom Noël Coward wrote *Poor Little Rich Girl*) told him: 'We will cling together like the ivy.' As sure as flop follows Best Actress Award, the Ivy retained the floor plan of the ground-floor restaurant, the original artworks (including Maggi Hambling's portrait of George Melly) and the multicoloured diamond-mullioned stained-glass windows that wrap around the building.

Such is the Ivy's appeal for stars of stage and screen that there will always be a paparazzo or two lurking in a bomber jacket outside its doors. This reputation is a blessing and a curse. It is of course terrific fun pretending to be fascinated by your lobster macaroni when Gillian Anderson, Benedict Cumberbatch, Jude Law or Keira Knightley make an entrance, but you're equally disappointed if the only 'people' in the house are television personalities Mary

Berry, Ant and Dec and Lorraine Kelly. We have heard whispers that the Ivy lost a lot of star power when it opened the private club next door. This is patently not the case. Respectful attention of the ilk one gets from an Ivy audience is like sunlight on a flower for the famous.

If you don't have a booking, wearing black tie and cocktail frocks will seriously raise your chances of waltzing in unannounced, although – contrary to popular belief – tables can be had if you're willing to dine after nine; that's when the stars come out, anyway. In common with all Mr Caring's restaurants, the Ivy has turned vaguely Japanese, with a selection of Shosu on the menu (beef tataki, yellow-fin tuna tataki, steamed prawn dumplings), but we tend to like slumming it along with the thesps who seem never to tire of the piquancy of having a glass of fizz in one hand and an Ivy hamburger in the other. We're partial to the aforementioned lobster macaroni, we adore the Ivy's shepherd's pie, and we could polish off the pork and leek sausages with mash and onion gravy faster than you could say *Waiting for Godot*. The wine list – divided into Classic, Exceptional and Discoveries – isn't overwritten, and if you're celebrating a BAFTA win on Sir Cameron's bill there's a super Ruinart Brut Rosé (£99). Even after the refurbishment, we will cling to the Ivy like a Bob Fosse chorus line.

1–5 West Street WC2
Tel. 020 7836 4751
Tube: Leicester Square
www.the-ivy.co.uk

THE SAVOY GRILL ££££

If you can't step out of a Bentley wearing black tie and patent-leather lace-ups at the Savoy, then where in the name of Fred Astaire can you? There are few sights that promise a night to remember in London that deliver as consistently as the green neon Savoy sign above the hotel's private driveway. The restoration of the Savoy in 2010 has not been without controversy, a fact that is hardly surprising when you consider that the hotel is historically the most important in London, if not in the world. The Savoy Grill, however, has had near universal praise. The decorator Russell Sage did a magnificent job with the dark wood banquettes, as sleek as a thoroughbred's mane, and epic Swarovski crystal chandeliers illuminating photographs of the idols who dined on this site, such as Coward and Dietrich, Callas and Onassis, Churchill and the Duff Coopers, HM Queen Elizabeth The Queen Mother and theatrical legends Binkie Beaumont, C. B. Cochran and Ivor Novello. So clever is Sage's reimagining of art deco that you'd never know it isn't the original.

The Savoy Grill was famed for its table layout, a plan of which hides in the archive, listing who favoured which place. We think the present floor plan has managed to retain that sense that every table could be the best in the house. There is no such thing as social Siberia in the Savoy Grill. Gordon Ramsay's is the name on the billboard, although the menu is designed by the head chef, Andy Cook, and is a nice balance between French and English cuisine and classic dishes reconsidered for a modern palate. It is a lovely touch to present a menu that's a tribute to the Savoy's first chef, Auguste Escoffier, who created Omelette Arnold Bennett and Peach Melba for the writer and opera singer respectively.

This being the Savoy, the menu is rich, but for every Scottish lobster bisque with poached lobster and brandy butter there is a light dish of crispy frogs' legs with parsley and garlic aioli; for every beef Wellington with horseradish cream and red wine jus there's a poached Scottish salmon. As the restaurant's name suggests, the charcoal grill rarely rests during a serving, and the Savoy has re-established its reputation as a place where Westminster MPs meet City lions and devour T-bone steaks with sautéed onions, marinated spatchcock chicken and the marvellous mixed grill. The Savoy encourages self-indulgence, and the wine list gives one plenty of opportunity. We chose a Malbec Humberto Canale 2011 (£55) to accompany chateaubriand for two, and, rather than miming exhaustion to the waiter with the pudding menu, ordered triumphant English strawberry millefeuille and pineapple soufflé with coconut ice cream.

Savoy Hotel, Strand WC2
Tel. 020 7592 1600
Tube: Charing Cross
www.gordonramsay.com/thesavoygrill

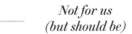

Not for us
(but should be)

BALTHAZAR £££

As Balthazar owner Keith McNally responded to the press when the London edition of his New York hottie opened in 2013, 'critics are a bunch of petty, self-regarding, back-stabbing narcissists who should be put through a meat grinder and dumped into the Indian Ocean.' We can see his point. McNally and his business partner, Richard Caring, spent £14 million replicating the Manhattan Balthazar exactly. The latter is the preferred lunch place of Anna Wintour, the editor of US *Vogue*, and in New York that's tantamount to holding a Royal Warrant. Then what do the British food press do? Mercilessly lampoon the Covent Garden Balthazar, with one unkind commentator comparing the interior to Café Rouge.

When Balthazar first opened we got in on a guest pass – and it wasn't easy – on the invitation of the head barman, Brian Silva, who had mixed us many a Dubonnet and gin at the bar upstairs at Rules (see **Drinks Cabinet**). We rather liked the screaming scarlet-leather seating, the vast raked mirrors, the mountain of shaved ice, upon which seafood is artfully draped daily, and the towering bar that looks like an Alexandrian library for booze. But when we learned that it was a carbon copy of the original Balthazar across the pond we questioned the wisdom of producing a London lookalike. Friends who know the New York Balthazar consider the London version an understudy.

We were very familiar with the old Theatre Museum, which occupied this space before a turf war broke out between Corbin and King and Mr Caring for the prime Covent Garden site. It's actually a great shame a moneybags philanthropist didn't dig deep and provide the investment to allow the museum to remain open, with the proviso that part of it could be converted into a restaurant. But, as our old grandmother used to say, 'if wishes were kisses ...' It's a pity Balthazar didn't opt for an original interior tailored to London, because the menu is pretty decent. We like the showmanship of the *plateau de fruits de mer* served as Petit, Grand and Balthazar (with lobster). We have visited more than once and thoroughly enjoyed our *côte de boeuf*, *moules frites* and duck shepherd's pie. We also have an awful lot of love for any restaurant that serves home-made profiteroles and employs such sparkling staff. Perhaps, as it did Joe Allen, in years to come London will learn to love this US import.

4–6 Russell Street WC2
Tel. 020 3301 1155
Tube: Covent Garden
www.balthazarlondon.com

THE CRITERION £££

The Criterion, which opened in 1874, hides London's most exotic and opulent restaurant interiors. The gold-mosaic domed ceiling, blind arcades with elliptical arches and octagonal columns of grey marble are reminiscent of a Byzantine prince's palace as imagined by a Victorian opium eater. This whole block on the south side of Piccadilly, incorporating restaurant, subterranean theatre and numerous private dining rooms (as well as a secret Masonic temple), is the masterpiece of the architect Thomas Verity. Unfortunately, the march of time has trampled on the Criterion. The tatty sports shop Lillywhites has spread like ivy above and around it, and Eros's island in the centre of Piccadilly Circus is now partially pedestrianized, so smartly dressed patrons must dodge delinquent rappers and street entertainers to enter.

We defy you not to gasp at the sheer scale of the Long Bar and the restaurant stretching apparently to infinity beyond floor-to-ceiling diaphanous curtains. Then we look down at the carpet – more suited to Heathrow Terminal 4 – and the tatty red-velour chairs. The bar serves a couple of cocktails from the Criterion's glory days in the 1890s designed by grand old barman Leo Engel, and they miss a trick not serving more. In its belle époque heyday, the Criterion asked ladies to leave at 8 pm, after which Engel would delight his gentlemen friends with such cocktails as the Bosom Caresser, the Corpse Reviver and the Flash of Lightning from his book *American and Other Drinks* (1878).

To bag a line from Sondheim's *Gypsy*, the Criterion has *got* to get a gimmick to bring back the beautiful crowd. It isn't enough to chalk up a cameo appearance as a location in *Downton Abbey*; that just brings in the coach tours. The Criterion's Byzantine splendour deserves better. We find the dining room too cavernous, if anything, and would send out to the hothouses at Kew Gardens for some lush, green undergrowth to give the landscape drama. We wouldn't bother with a mediocre modern European menu, either, and would suggest serving something as exotic as the interiors. Of course, it is easier to criticize than to praise, but we long to see the Criterion back where it belongs so we can make a grand entrance into London's most opulent restaurant interior.

224 Piccadilly W1
Tel. 020 7930 0488
Tube: Piccadilly Circus
www.criterionrestaurant.com

KETTNER'S ££ • &JS

How do you solve a problem like Kettner's? The Soho town-house restaurant with private dining rooms has a provenance that Heston Blumenthal could spin into gastronomic gold. Emperor Napoleon III's chef

Auguste Kettner left Paris for London in 1867, three years before his patron followed him into exile, and set the fashion for French haute cuisine thirty years before Escoffier. A twenty-first-century interpretation of quail in aspic served in High Victorian pomp would be a novelty now that every new restaurant offers South American small plates, 'dirty food' or best of British seasonal ingredients served in an ascetic fashion.

What we get at Kettner's is a rather dull brasserie with institutional chairs that attracts pre-theatre coach parties. The odd flimsy pot plant and a sprinkling of candles do not a romantic belle époque interior make. The Laurent-Perrier champagne bar on the ground floor should be firing a 62-gun salute of popping corks in honour of the fabulous 100-strong list, but the decor lets it down: its Persian carpets, sludge-green embossed wallpaper and occasional easy chairs of indeterminate vintage are more *Arsenic and Old Lace* than *French Cancan*. Why feathered Zulu hats like plates adorn the walls is a mystery, as is the burlesque-themed afternoon tea, at which performers with names like Bang-Bang-La-Desh shed ostrich feathers into your Darjeeling.

Kettner's narrowly avoided demolition in 1975 and turned the ground floor into a posh Pizza Express at one point; in 2012 the private members' club Soho House was considering a takeover. What the old girl needs is a creative like Russell Sage to redecorate the restaurant, bar and private dining rooms as a Venus flytrap for the frisky risqués who are drawn to Soho every night and have nowhere smart to go after 10 pm. A bit more research into Kettner's glory days provides inspiration. Although I don't doubt the garrulous Prince of Wales (later Edward VII) roistered in the upstairs rooms, tales of his burrowing by secret passage from the Palace Theatre to Kettner's for assignations with his mistress Lillie Langtry are balderdash. The brief affair ended in 1877, before Mrs Langtry found an alternative career on the stage, and besides, the Palace Theatre wasn't built until 1891.

29 Romilly Street W1
Tel. 020 7734 6112
Tube: Leicester Square
www.kettners.com

SUSHISAMBA £££

Heron Tower is the tallest building in the City of London. The Japanese-Brazilian-Peruvian fusion restaurant Sushisamba sprawls over the 38th and 39th floors, accessible only by a panoramic 'inside-out' glass express lift. Good luck with that to people of a nervous disposition. Prepare to change your head, because the lift leaps faster than Carlos Acosta on hot coals and transports you at warp speed to the Ginza district of Japan, where Sushisamba truly belongs. A cat's cradle of bamboo arches with lights suspended at irregular heights soars over the glass-walled dining room, which offers 180-degree views of the City.

If heaven is a disco, the Sushisamba's hypnotic music, snake-hipped waiters and small plates to soak up the pisco sours is just for you, angel. This rooftop venue definitely lends itself to the night shift; in fact, I've noticed that all the PR shots are taken after dark, because in daylight the fluoro-citrus decor of the sushi bar/reception with the flying staircase looks a little tawdry. The terrace bar isn't nearly as magical by day, when the orange-painted Singing Ringing Tree that forms the centrepiece of the circular bar is bereft of its theatrical fairy lights. Still, the masters of the financial universe still flock to Sushisamba for business lunches. They probably rather like the feeling of being kings and queens of all they survey. Or perhaps it is the frisson of feeling fashionable and daring that appeals when your closest relationship is with a handheld device.

Although it makes us sad to see the Square Mile dwarfed by the high concentration of ugly tower blocks standing shoulder to shoulder, these buildings, with their gleaming, clean concourses and glass façades, are impressive when seen from this, the highest outdoor cocktail terrace in London. One wouldn't like to be on the 38th floor in a storm, but on a clear day the topographical views of London are quite fascinating. Navigating a Japanese menu without blowing a term's school fees, on the other hand, is an art. We no more understand the nuances of Wagyu beef being grade nine (£49) than we do the intricacies of nuclear fusion, and have been stung all over London ordering small plates that add up to eye-wateringly large bills.

Heron Tower, 110 Bishopsgate EC2
Tel. 020 3640 7330
Tube: Liverpool Street
www.sushisamba.com

The Zetter Townhouse

II

Hotels

Where to stay ...
with your lover

BLAKES ££££

Blakes has class. Opened in 1978, Anouska Hempel's
pioneering boutique hotel was the first to offer as
high a level of decor and service as the big beasts
Claridge's or the Dorchester. Each suite was a
masterpiece uniquely decorated to a theme (Corfu,
Biedermeier, Empire, Africa), and the hotel proved
to be a de facto design portfolio for Lady Weinberg,
as she was titled from 1980. Lady Weinberg invented
a language of hotel interior design – Esperanto, as it
happens – that is much imitated but rarely bettered:
casually stacked vintage Vuitton trunks, low Moroccan
tables dressed with bells, books and candles, golden
Hindu gods, Japanese feathered fans and regiments
of white slipper orchids. She no longer owns Blakes,
but her influence is everywhere. In fact, waiters still
break out in a sweat when they are told the Lady
will be inspecting bento boxes in the subterranean
Chinese Room.

Blakes is a particular favourite with the fashion
industry because designers such as Karl Lagerfeld,
Valentino, Ralph Lauren and, latterly, Victoria
Beckham recognize Lady Weinberg's obsessive

attention to detail and magpie eye for sourcing and displaying original pieces from her extensive travels. Lady Weinberg knows every millimetre of Blakes. Such is her eye for proportion that she'll float a line of antique prints below a dado rail or place a ball-and-claw-foot bath directly below a natural light well, knowing her instinct is always right. I have yet to see a hotel as meticulously art-directed as Blakes or as cleverly designed.

Blakes is the perfect London hotel for lovers. The quiet South Kensington location is discretion itself. The anonymous black brick façade is a 'loose lips sink ships' wall of silence, and each suite's unique character fulfils fantasies, be it *Out of Africa*, *The Sheik*, *Gone with the Wind* or *Dangerous Liaisons*. It's a time-honoured trick. In 1876 Madame Kelly opened Paris's most infamous bordello, Le Chabanais, with rooms lavishly decorated in Pompeian, Moorish, Hindu and Louis XVI style. We are not suggesting for a moment that Blakes is furnished with love seats like that at Le Chabanais, designed by Edward VII when he was Prince of Wales. But the principle of uniquely decorated rooms is conducive to the enjoyment of those with passion and imagination.

33 Roland Gardens SW7
Tel. 020 7370 6701
Tube: South Kensington
www.blakeshotels.com

THE DORCHESTER £££££

There are few sights more pleasing on a summer's day than the yellow-and-white-striped awnings unfurled on the façade of the Dorchester. The Dorch shares the cinematic, camp glamour of its most famous resident,

Elizabeth Taylor. Old 'violet eyes' made the rooftop Harlequin Suite her own, installing the pink marble bathroom in the adjoining suite for the love of her life, Richard Burton, whom she married twice. She and Burton met on the set of *Cleopatra* (1963) and Taylor learned she'd won her $1 million contract to play the serpent of old Nile in the Harlequin Suite, hence her attachment to the eyrie overlooking Hyde Park. The Dorchester has kept the Harlequin Suite as it was when Taylor and Burton lived, loved and fought there, making it one of the most sacred places in London for lovers.

> *"The Dorchester has kept the Harlequin Suite as it was when Taylor and Burton lived, loved and fought there, making it one of the most sacred places in London for lovers."*

Admittedly there are prettier suites in the Dorchester, not least the seventh-floor suite decorated in the 1950s by the celebrated stage designer Oliver Messel, who, coincidentally, designed the stage production of *Caesar and Cleopatra*, starring Laurence Olivier and Vivien Leigh, in 1945. The Messel suite's whimsical, chintzy interiors are listed, and were restored in the 1980s under the direction of David Linley, son of Messel's nephew Lord Snowdon and Princess Margaret. Theatrical flourishes include a gilded loo seat sculpted like a Botticelli clamshell, an imperial yellow silk canopied bed and floral-painted wall panels. Marlene Dietrich and Noël Coward adored the Oliver Messel suite and stayed there often ... not together, I hasten to add.

Messel was inspired by his own set designs for *The Magic Flute* and *Sleeping Beauty* when he decorated the seventh-floor Penthouse and Pavilion private dining suites. The interiors are enchanting: a rococo fantasy of mirrored wall panels overlaid with gilded foliage and curved terrace doors framed by cardinal-red silk curtains. The terrace itself is like a stage set for *Private Lives*. A fountain gently plays at the feet of a naked stone nymph, manicured box trees stand tall in terracotta planters, and twin wrought-iron domed love seats seem to be waiting for Amanda and Elyot to recline, smoke, sulk and exchange brilliantly brittle quips.

> *"The terrace itself is like a stage set for Private Lives."*

Should you care to explore the public rooms, the Dorchester has one of London's two three-Michelin-starred restaurants – Alain Ducasse – as well as the divinely decadent China Tang and the ebulliently Scottish-themed Grill Room. One of the most thrilling aspects of the Dorchester can be seen from a seat at the Promenade Bar. This parade of richly upholstered sofas, occasional tables and hothouse plants as well as a baby grand piano seems to run the length of Park Lane. Order a Brandy Alexander and enjoy the passing show. For history buffs, the most romantic room in the Dorch is the oak-panelled Byford Room. When the Dorchester was constructed in 1931, yet another Park Lane palace, Dorchester House, was demolished. Several rooms were maintained as the hotel was built up around them, however, and of these Dorchester House interiors only the Byford Room remains.

Park Lane W1
Tel. 020 7629 8888
Tube: Hyde Park Corner
www.dorchestercollection.com

HAZLITT'S HOTEL £££

A little bit of romance died when the Sanctum Soho Hotel themed Room 404 as a *Fifty Shades of Grey* suite decorated with 'tie me up, tie me down' erotic photographs. Guests apparently pay a supplement for a Christian Grey suitcase filled with S&M accoutrements; definitely not for us on many levels, not least the pain threshold. Hazlitt's – named after the critic and essayist William Hazlitt, who died there and is buried in nearby St Anne's churchyard – is more Fanny Hill than Anastasia Steele. The hotel has been carved out of adjoining early eighteenth-century houses on Soho's Frith Street, moments away from Soho Square, where the celebrated Georgian madam Mrs Cornelys hosted lavish masquerades in Carlisle House. Hazlitt's has named its most lavish suite after Teresa Cornelys; it comes complete with gilded Cupid's bower bed, a dressing table hidden behind wood panelling and a bathing machine that promises to propel water into the most extraordinary places.

> *"Hazlitt's ... is more Fanny Hill than Anastasia Steele."*

Hazlitt's retains the aura of a richly furnished and decorated Georgian house if not of ill repute, then of many secrets. When we checked in with an American friend at a terribly late hour, we were pleased to learn that reception was open twenty-four hours, that there was an honesty bar on the ground floor and that you are known for the duration of your stay by the name of your room, which will refer to a famous or infamous denizen of Soho. When we reached the attic floor with our porter – no questions asked as to whether the two gentlemen were sharing – the stairs tilted like a tipsy chambermaid. It is all utterly charming and rather reminiscent of *Tom Jones* (Fielding's novel, that is, not the Welsh pop singer).

The most dashing suite is named after the 1st Duke of Monmouth, a resident of Soho Square and a traitor who was beheaded in 1685 for rebelling against his uncle King James II. The penthouse apartment, with a sitting room and working fireplace (a rarity in central London), has hidden treasures, such as a bath filled from the beak of a life-size bronze eagle, and a roof terrace with retractable glass roof. The terrace is made for a moonlight dance on a summer's evening. Hazlitt's is particularly precious for history buffs, because renting a room or rooms in a town house was exactly how many a young buck and his wife or mistress would set up home in Soho, Covent Garden or St James's. So, if you are a romantic of the bodice-ripping, bosom-heaving type, you will be utterly seduced by Hazlitt's.

6 Frith Street W1
Tel. 020 7434 1771
Tube: Tottenham Court Road
www.hazlittshotel.com

THE STAFFORD £££

When St James's was developed, in the early years of Charles II's reign, it became known as the place of residence for London's moneyed men about town, which is why the gentlemen's clubs were constructed there. The district is saturated with centuries of roistering and intrigue, and it still has secrets to give up. The royal vintner Berry Bros & Rudd recently discovered a Tudor well in its cellars, contemporary to nearby St James's Palace. Another secret is the

Stafford's carriage-house courtyard in Blue Bell Yard, just off St James's Street, and the 380-year-old cellars that lie beneath the cobbles. Christopher Wren lived in a house on this site; it was demolished in the early eighteenth century by Francis, 2nd Earl of Godolphin, who built the stables and galleried cottages above in 1742. These have been converted into the Stafford's twelve mews rooms and suites.

Godolphin married the daughter of the 1st Duke of Marlborough, who had rather a passion for the playwright William Congreve, so the precedent is set for a roll in the hay at the Stafford. Although the main hotel facing St James's Place is a handsome red-brick town house, the stable block is older and feels more illicit. The upper floor still has its original A-frame beams and the lower floor its hay mangers, but each room and suite is now decorated in high eighteenth-century style, with four-poster beds, Chippendale-style cabinets displaying Chinese porcelain, and circular tea tables surrounded by ribbon-back chairs. The split-level Guv'nor's Suite with minstrel's gallery, library and working fireplace is pure *Forever Amber*.

> *"The district is saturated with centuries of roistering and intrigue, and it still has secrets to give up."*

The twentieth-century history of the Stafford is heroic, and for ladies and gentlemen of the turf, Godolphin's stables offer an extra frisson. All thoroughbred racehorse bloodstock is descended from three horses, and the Earl's Godolphin Arab was one of them. As anyone who has ever turned a page of a Jilly Cooper novel will know, equestrian sport and sex

go together like Rupert Campbell-Black and Dame
Hermione Harefield. In the summer, the first-floor
balconies are planted with a cascade of bluebells,
and we can think of no more picaresque a place for
a tryst than here.

16–18 St James's Place SW1
Tel. 020 7493 0111
Tube: Green Park
www.thestaffordlondon.com

Where to stay ... in the company of beautiful people

THE BEAUMONT ££££

Jeremy King and Chris Corbin may be the only
London restaurateurs who apply the Method to
each project, creating a character and story that
influences every choice. When they successfully bid to
convert an art deco garage on the Park Lane side of
Mayfair into a hotel, they invented New York joy boy
Jimmy Beaumont. Beaumont relocated to London
to dodge Prohibition, and opened a hotel bankrolled
by his buddies Errol Flynn, Noël Coward, Tallulah
Bankhead and so forth. As someone once said of
Marilyn Monroe, there's method in this madness.
The Beaumont is entirely plausible as a meticulously
restored deco hotel that's been here since 1926,
although the entire infrastructure has been ripped
down and reconstructed.

From the moment you sweep into the forecourt
and through the revolving doors, you're in Jimmy
Beaumont's world. Dead centre is a red carpet that

rolls you through the American Bar and on into the Colony Grill Room. To the left is a private Club Room speakeasy bar reserved for guests, and to the right a pristine concierge's desk that is more like reception at Ciro's than the usual GCHQ-like tangle of telephone wires. There's a seamless mix of art deco furniture and pieces made to echo the style that prevents the Beaumont looking remotely corporate. The art collection alone – early twentieth-century figurative portraits, jazzy cartoons and vintage photographs – gives every corner of the hotel personality.

As one would expect from Corbin and King, the public rooms are already old favourites. The Colony Grill has echoes of New York's Monkey Bar and Sardi's, with sepia murals set behind half-moon banquettes and pastel portraits of Hollywood greats (some dedicated to Jimmy Beaumont). The subterranean spa is a triumph with a hammam, a plunge pool, a gleaming barber's shop and a gymnasium. Rather cleverly, artwork and photography are deployed in the spa to great effect. Who wouldn't like to exercise with Cary Grant rather than flickering CNN screens?

The Beaumont's fifty rooms, thirteen studios and ten suites are incredibly glamorous, with white marble bathrooms reminiscent of a 1930s movie queen's Beverly Hills home. The lacquered wood, mirrored walls and black-and-white photography all perpetuate the film-star aura, and the level of detail is breathtaking. One can never see the point of installing purely decorative libraries in hotel suites. Corbin and King's bookshelves reference Mayfair and the Jazz Age, and are chosen to be dipped into, with such fascinating reads as Lady Diana Cooper's letters or the Cecil Beaton diaries.

The Grosvenor Estate insists on supporting public art (with varying degrees of success), and the Beaumont has more than risen to the challenge by inviting the artist Antony Gormley to create an extraordinary cubist structure echoing the shape of a seated man that crouches above an elevation to the left of the hotel's façade. Within the Gormley 'Room' is a double-height bedroom constructed entirely from dark fumed oak. The art installation as hotel suite will doubtless be the cause of a bidding war among the international art set when the Frieze Art Fair is in town. Gormley's 'Room' is audacious, but we prefer the light-filled penthouse, with its rather smart dining room and roof terrace.

Brown Hart Gardens W1
Tel. 020 7499 1001
Tube: Bond Street
www.thebeaumont.com

DEAN STREET TOWNHOUSE £££

When the Dean Street Townhouse opened in 2008, most Londoners were unaware that it even traded as a hotel on the upper floors. The narrow street-side terrace of tables outside was (and still is) a *tableau vivant* of laughing, chaffing and flirting Soho socialites and show-offs, sending up smoke signals that the Dean Street Townhouse is 'a scene'. The restaurant, smothered as it is in BritArt and serving delicious inverted-snob dishes such as mince and potatoes, was an instant hit with the film-production and editing crews who now colonize Soho. Although Gwyneth Paltrow, Jude Law and various other pretty, conspicuous people have been spotted at the Townhouse, it isn't plagued by the paps, making it a terrific stealth address for stars who don't want to shine and attract attention.

No. 69 Dean Street was built on the corner of Meard Street and Dean Street in 1732, making a nonsense of claims that Charles II's actress/mistress, Nell Gwyn, was a resident, because she'd been dead since 1687. But should you book a top-floor bedroom from among the thirty-nine rooms and suites, you're on sacred ground as far as historians of Soho's louche life are concerned. It was here in 1928 that the Hon. David Tennant established the Gargoyle Club, where Matisse's *L'Atelier Rouge* hung on the wall, Tallulah Bankhead danced on the tables and the poet Siegfried Sassoon romanced David's aesthete brother Stephen. Today the bedrooms are classified as Tiny, Medium and Bigger (a bit glib, no?), and are tastefully if minimally decorated with white plantation shutters, free-standing baths next to well-dressed four-poster beds, Roberts Revival radios, rainforest showers and occasional pieces of antique furniture.

> *"... should you book a top-floor bedroom from among the thirty-nine rooms and suites, you're on sacred ground as far as historians of Soho's louche life are concerned."*

Much is made of the noise levels in Soho, to which we would reply sensibly that should you want a quiet life, we hear the Cotswolds are very nice at this time of year. Soho is noisy, bawdy, dirty and sexy, and one of the very few quarters in London that has kept its character, warts and all. It has been cleaned up; t'Internet and twenty-four-hour licensing have seen off many of the sex shops, gay bars and illegal drinking dens that gave it its edge of subversion and danger. But there's enough filth still in situ to provide those delicious lows that counterbalance the high of smart new hotels like the Dean Street Townhouse. One without the other would be much diminished.

69–71 Dean Street W1
Tel. 020 7434 1775
Tube: Tottenham Court Road
www.deanstreettownhouse.com

SANDERSON £££

London's beautiful people have been spoilt for choice of late with the opening of André Balazs's Chiltern Firehouse in Marylebone, the Thames-side Mondrian in Sea Containers House and Ian Schrager's London Edition collaboration with Marriott. It's curious then that Sanderson is still packing them in during London Fashion Week, Masterpiece and the Frieze Art Fair. Philippe Starck's pop-baroque millennial interiors exhilarated London's pretty people when Schrager's sister hotels St Martin's Lane and Sanderson opened in 1999 and 2001 respectively. Both are time capsules now for Starck's signature celestial white-curtained walls, mood-enhancing light installations and *Alice in Wonderland* juxtaposition of curious furniture in Jeff Koons meets Salvador Dalí fashion.

Of the two, St Martin's has the edge for location and the Sanderson – a listed late 1950s Modernist headquarters and showroom for the eponymous wallpaper factory – for architectural interest. The chequerboard glass façade hides a serene Japanese water garden quadrangle planted by Philip Hicks. St Martin's has always struck us as faintly self-conscious, and its black-clad clipboard and earpiece army goose-stepping around the lobby did not endear it to Londoners. By contrast, Sanderson's interiors greet you with a kiss. Starck's Dalí-esque Mae West's Lips sofa puckers up in the entrance hall, and the 80-foot Long Bar off the lobby draws you in with a glowing onyx catwalk counter and supermodel-tall bar stools embellished with Fornasetti eyes.

Lifts sparkling like mirrored supernovas take you to the upper floors. Unless you wish for a vast loft-like space, such as the eighth-floor penthouse, that takes up the entire tier of the hotel, or a lushly planted balcony suite, the rooms are all of a theme: white walls, diaphanous curtains, Perspex Louis Ghost chairs and bathrooms with free-standing baths divided by glass walls and blush-pink modesty curtains. All the rooms are teched-up with large flat screens, ambient lighting systems and iPod docks. The 10,000-square-foot Agua Spa in the basement is reminiscent of the Mount Olympus sets for *Clash of the Titans*: ethereal, serene and otherworldly. By contrast, the louche, low-lit Purple Bar is like being secreted inside a Fabergé amethyst cigarette box, and is a magical place for a clandestine cocktail.

50 Berners Street W1
Tel. 020 7300 1400
Tube: Tottenham Court Road
www.morganshotelgroup.com

ROSEWOOD LONDON £££

Rosewood's opening in 2013 was greeted with near-universal applause. This gleaming, sepulchral Edwardian palace on High Holborn was constructed in 1914 as the general headquarters for the Pearl Assurance Company. Built around a private courtyard, it has the beauty of a Parisian *hôtel particulier*, and doors leading from the soaring arched carriage entrance give direct public access to the restaurant and bar that sprawl across parallel wings of the building. Although not quite St Paul's Cathedral, the dome on top of the Rosewood is a landmark and looks grand now the entire building is spotlit after dark. Doubts were raised about Holborn as the location for Rosewood's London flagship, but they shouldn't have been. Although we loathe attempts to rebrand Bloomsbury and Holborn as 'Midtown' (ugh!), we recognize the area as a prime location between the West End and the City.

Rosewood is epic in scale but not overwhelming. In fact, it is rather magical. The tone is set by Tony Chi's rose-gold gallery and plush, vast reception divided by display cases filled with intriguing art, antiques, books and curios. It is all terribly modern with touches of wonder, so chapeau to Peter Millard Associates, the art consultant. We particularly like the Mirror Room, with its offset looking-glass walls and ceilings. We have oft lifted a gin Martini there and stared enviously at the floor-to-ceiling, three-dimensional origami maps of Bloomsbury and Holborn on the walls. The Rosewood's superb bar, Scarfes, has its own entry in our **Drinks Cabinet** section. The Martin Brudnizki-designed Holborn Dining Room is busy and buzzy and aspires to be a Midtown (ugh!) Wolseley, but just falls short for now. We do love the tweeds, brogues, flat caps and ties that give the staff at the Rosewood as much if not more style than the residents.

The Rosewood's rooms and suites are some of the city's largest, carved as they are from cavernous insurance offices. The original seven-storey marble

staircase, reputed to be worth in excess of £40 million,
is worthy of the Louvre, and the lower floors are
full of character; the boardroom walls and doors in
Cuban mahogany have been brought back to their
former glory. The upper floors are dark and rather
disorientating. Of the forty-four suites, we consider
the Garden House Suite the star. The Italian marble
bathroom alone is worth the buck, and the split-level
private garden beneath the dome is absolutely darling.
Holborn is still relatively low-rise, so the views over
rooftops and chimneys is uninterrupted. Considering
Rosewood is on busy High Holborn, you don't hear a
peep of the traffic from the rooms. Each is styled to
within an inch of its life, and we were amused to see a
copy of Jean-Paul Sartre's work on every bedside table.
There's nowhere like a luxurious hotel suite to remind
oneself that '*L'Enfer, c'est les autres.*'

252 High Holborn WC1
Tel. 020 7829 9888
Tube: Holborn
www.rosewoodhotels.com

Where to stay ... for grand entrances and opulent interiors

CLARIDGE'S £££££

Richard Rodney Bennett's lush, romantic theme to
Murder on the Orient Express always springs to mind
when one steps into the marbled, mirrored foyer at
Claridge's. It is not just possible but probable that a
Saudi princess and her retinue have taken an entire
floor for the season, that the in-house artist David

Downton is sketching Daphne Guinness in the Fumoir Bar, or that the editor of US *Vogue*, Anna Wintour, is dining at the next table to Prince William in the restaurant. The many different stories being told daily at Claridge's add to its lustre.

It has been so since 1860, when Queen Victoria broke precedent and visited her friend the Empress Eugenie of France at a hotel – Claridge's. The original enfilade of town houses was demolished in 1894 by Savoy impresario Richard D'Oyly Carte. His is the hotel (designed by the architect of Harrods, C. W. Stephens) you see today, with Basil Ionides's glorious art deco veneer added in the 1920s and the ingenious renovations designed by Thierry Despont in 1996, including silver-leaf columns and a chandelier by Dale Chihuly in the foyer. In short, Claridge's represents a seamless history of interior decoration.

There are many changes of key in Claridge's suites, with interiors designed by David Linley, India Mahdavi, Guy Oliver, Veere Grenney and Diane von Furstenberg. Von Furstenberg's Grand Piano Suite is the most exotic and least in keeping, although certain guests will stay nowhere else. I find the suites decorated in the grand style – such as the Davies penthouse with its roof terrace and the Prince Alexander (named for the Crown Prince of Yugoslavia, who was born in room 212) – terribly smart. The Royal Suite, with a drawing room dominated by D'Oyly Carte's baby grand piano, is a beauty, particularly the Prussian blue dining room hung with French architectural prints.

> *"The Royal Suite, with a drawing room dominated by D'Oyly Carte's baby grand piano, is a beauty ..."*

All the architects and interior designers who have contributed to Claridge's since 1894 are to be applauded for retaining a sense of intimacy and charm lost to the monoliths that line Park Lane. I adore the Fera entrance on Davies Street, with illuminated art deco archways and chequerboard marble floors, and (at the risk of sounding like Joe Orton) consider the Gents at Claridge's to be the most glamorous lavatories in London. The David Collins-designed Claridge's Bar is a classic; it was carved from the famous Causerie restaurant, which pioneered smorgasbord dining during the Second World War to get around rationing. Oliver's interiors for Simon Rogan's new dining room, Fera (see entry), continues this peerless hotel's tradition of modernizing by stealth.

Brook Street W1
Tel. 020 7629 8860
Tube: Bond Street
www.claridges.co.uk

THE CONNAUGHT £££££

Standing majestically on the curve of Carlos Place and Mount Street, the Connaught was founded in 1815 when George 'Beau' Brummell ruled fashion and the Prince Regent ruled Britain. Today the hotel has the distinction of being on the most fashionable corner of Mayfair, within walking distance of Balenciaga, Goyard, Roksanda Ilincic, Solange Azagury-Partridge, Lanvin and Roland Mouret as well as Scott's and the Kering Group's London headquarters. Bond Street looks positively tatty in comparison to serene, tree-lined Mount Street, where a water sculpture by Tadao Ando sets the tone. Originally christened the Prince of Saxe-Coburg, the hotel was renamed in 1917 when

King George V dropped the German dynastic name in favour of Windsor.

The Connaught we see today was built in 1897. The original solid mahogany staircase, which climbs five floors to a domed skylight, has survived and is much admired, not least by Ralph Lauren, who stayed here and copied it for his flagship store in New York. The Connaught and Sutherland suites look out over Carlos Place and Adam's Row respectively, and are designed by Guy Oliver in an Adam-style palette of soft pastels, reminiscent of Kenwood House in Hampstead. High ceilings with delicate plasterwork detail, silk curtains and salon chairs are coloured in Wedgwood blues, pinks, eau de Nil and ivory. Furniture is in classic English stately-home style, with the exception of beds, as anyone who has had the misfortune to sleep in an eighteenth-century four-poster will be relieved to hear.

Oliver's Terrace Suite, with its rooftop garden designed by the Chelsea Flower Show Gold Medallist Tom Stuart-Smith, is terribly pretty, but David Collins's Apartment up in the eaves of the hotel is a serene highness of London penthouse apartments. Imagine a beach house in the Hamptons transported to a rooftop in Mayfair and you have the idea.

In 2007 regular guests held their breath in case a £70 million refurbishment of the Connaught spoiled the late Victorian charm of the hotel. A new wing was built behind the hotel's façade that significantly increased occupancy, and corridors hung with black-and-white Horst. P. Horst fashion plates from next door's Hamiltons Gallery signified the shift from nineteenth to twenty-first century. The rooms in the new wing – some overlooking a Japanese water garden – don't have the character of their elders and betters, but are beyond comfortable.

A spa and swimming pool are expected in a five-star hotel, and the Connaught's Aman spa and subterranean swimming pool tick the box without taking one's breath away. Rather more impressive are the Oliver-designed ballroom, the secret Champagne Room, the Coburg Bar and the Connaught Bar (see entry). The Connaught has a great reputation for fine dining, and Michel Bourdin and Angela Hartnett have directed the kitchens in the past. Hélène Darroze at the Connaught (see entry) is a premier-league Michelin-starred chef and completely at home in the hotel's oak-panelled dining room, which dates from 1897. Although we'd rather raise a Baccarat crystal flute of vintage champagne in the aforementioned hideaway, a table for breakfast or afternoon tea in the Espelette (conservatory) overlooking Carlos Place makes one feel like an extra in Cecil Beaton's Ascot scene from *My Fair Lady*.

"... a table for breakfast or afternoon tea ... makes one feel like an extra in Cecil Beaton's Ascot scene from My Fair Lady.*"*

Carlos Place W1
Tel. 020 7499 7070
Tube: Bond Street
www.the-connaught.com

THE RITZ £££££

The Ritz keeps the promise of its illustrious name. At the Arlington Street entrance, liveried concierges, their white gloves neatly tucked into epaulettes, greet by name guests old and new, who from that moment enter a private upstairs world that has changed little since César Ritz opened his eponymous Piccadilly palace in 1906. The Louis XVI decor in the rooms and suites is uniformly light, pretty, elegant and unashamedly Old World. Just as Ritz dictated, the *boiserie* panelling is painted in the palest colours and decorated with gold leaf, and the rich brocades echo a Fragonard palette. The inevitable technology is kept in its place: largely hidden.

When the hotel was built, César Ritz asked Lord Wimborne if he could purchase the neighbouring William Kent-designed Wimborne House. The peer declined. A century later, the building's present owners, the Barclay brothers, realized Ritz's dream and restored the palatial town house to its former glory. The tourists gussied up for afternoon tea waiting in the Ritz's Louis XVI Grand Gallery are unaware that behind mirrored doors to their left are London's most exquisite eighteenth-century interiors, lavishly furnished and hung with period paintings, and available for hire as function rooms. No. 22 Arlington Street (now christened William Kent House) was Evelyn Waugh's inspiration for the Flytes' London town house in *Brideshead Revisited*. The mansion faces Green Park, has its own private garden and hides a splendidly grand entrance hall (marble pillars, sweeping gilt staircase and monumental mural) and an audacious scarlet-and-gold dining room with Italian Renaissance ceiling, gilt chandelier and wall sconces rich in romance and Medici-style glamour. If you happen to have £6,500 on the gold card to spend

"No. 22 Arlington Street ... was Evelyn Waugh's inspiration for the Flytes' London town house in Brideshead Revisited."

a night in the two William Kent House suites – the Prince of Wales and the Royal – I don't think you will find a more sumptuous set of rooms unless you're a guest of Her Majesty at Buckingham Palace.

The Ritz can justifiably call itself king of London's grand hotels. It has played host to Edward VII, Queen Marie of Romania, Edward and Mrs Simpson and, towards the end of her life, Lady Thatcher. It is a favourite of the present Queen for family parties, and was the first London hotel to be awarded Prince Charles's Royal Warrant. The Palm Court off the Grand Gallery has become a victim of its own success. Hotel guests are besieged by queues for high-tea sittings from 11.30 am to 7.30 pm (?!). But tables are always reserved for guests, who can also choose to seek refuge in the Rivoli Bar or the achingly beautiful Louis XVI dining room, with its painted ceiling reminiscent of Versailles. Set in the subterranean ballroom, the Ritz Casino is as opulent as the public rooms above and is open twenty-four hours.

150 Piccadilly W1
Tel. 020 7493 8181
Tube: Green Park
www.theritzlondon.com

THE SAVOY ££££

The legendary Savoy, one of the few hotels in the world that deserves the hyperbole of that word, opened its doors in 1889, was managed by César Ritz, introduced the French master chef Auguste Escoffier to London and is haunted by the ghosts of Nellie Melba, Oscar Wilde, Serge Diaghilev, Marilyn Monroe and Jacqueline Onassis. In 2007 the Edwardian-meets-art deco palace of the Strand closed its doors for a refurbishment that famously cost £250 million. In the parlance of previous convictions, I have 'form' with the Savoy. For its reopening on 10/10/10 I was invited to curate the Savoy Museum and to source artworks and objects for the Signature Suites, named after illustrious guests Claude Monet, Marlene Dietrich, Winston Churchill, Noël Coward, Charlie Chaplin, Frank Sinatra and Maria Callas.

The drive up Savoy Court, passing beneath the neon green sign and the golden statue of Count Peter of Savoy, has been the same since the 1930s, and is familiar from countless appearances as a film and television location. The American Bar, directed by the matinee-idol head barman Erik Lorincz, has changed little since Judy Garland and Frank Sinatra sang at the white baby grand, and the Savoy Grill retains its gravitas and glamour. The lobby is reassuringly rich and lavish, with a sweeping vista towards the Thames Foyer and its extraordinary wrought-iron birdcage in the distance. Those taking afternoon tea in the Thames Foyer cling to their seats like poison ivy when all civilized people have moved on to cocktails, but such is life in London's hotels today.

The Beaufort Bar (on the site of the Savoy's hydraulic rising dance floor/stage) is a sinfully glamorous den with gold-leaf alcoves, black-lacquer furniture gleaming like fresh caviar, and a backlit bar where the stage once stood. Cabaret has returned to the Savoy in the Beaufort, although these days it is more rhinestone and feathered burlesque than Josephine Baker or Lena Horne. The new River Restaurant failed to please, and has been reimagined as Kaspar's Seafood Bar & Grill, named in honour of the ebony cat that is traditionally commandeered when thirteen people sit down to dinner, to make up a luckier number.

Londoners do not turn down an invitation to awards, dinners or big-band dances in the Lancaster Ballroom, a gorgeous Viennese confection iced with blue-and-white stucco and dripping with chandeliers, on the Thames side of the hotel. When it comes to the 195 rooms and 73 suites, I must admit a bias. The Edwardian Thames view suites that inspired Whistler and Monet are the winners for me: particularly the Personality Suites on the upper floors, such as the gorgeous Maria Callas Suite with its soaring ceilings, soft but opulent decor and separate drawing rooms, dressing rooms and walk-in wardrobes. The spa, gym and pool above the Savoy Theatre aren't really up to snuff yet, and the hotel is missing a trick by not making the rooftop usable as a garden terrace. The Strand is as filthy as the pigeons in Trafalgar Square and needs to invest in smarter shops and services, but the Savoy rises above it.

Strand WC2
Tel. 020 7836 4343
Tube: Charing Cross
www.fairmont.com/savoy-london

Where to stay ... for charming, old-school elegance

DUKES £££

The hotelier Rosa Lewis, celebrated by Evelyn Waugh as Lottie Crump in *Vile Bodies*, was one of St James's most colourful characters. 'The Duchess of Duke

Street' ran the Cavendish hotel from 1902 until her death in 1952, entertaining kings, cads and guardsmen, including Kaiser Wilhelm (whose presentation portrait she relegated to the Gents when the Great War broke out) and King Edward VII, who allegedly stood her the lease on the premises. The Cavendish was demolished in the early 1960s and replaced by a tower block, but its spirit lives on at Dukes, an Edwardian beauty hidden in its own private courtyard off St James's Place.

Dukes is not quaint, you understand, but it is run with the quiet efficiency of a fully staffed private town house. Turning into the courtyard, you see the Union flag flying high above the front door and doormen ready to greet you with just the right amount of formality and friendliness. The public rooms in Dukes are decorated with artworks and antiques that look like a family collection, and because there are fewer than 100 rooms and suites, it does feel as if one owns the place. We have never seen guests waiting at reception, except at Christmas, when seats in Dukes Bar become more coveted than a Tiffany blue box under the tree. Dukes Bar is to the Martini what Vatican City is to Roman Catholicism, and laurels are laid at

"Dukes Bar is to the Martini what Vatican City is to Roman Catholicism ..."

its feet in our **Drinks Cabinet** section. Londoners and guests collude in keeping Dukes as secret as possible, and we all have our favourite corners, whether it's the Turkish bath in the basement spa (a last echo of Jermyn Street's Grand Hammam at No. 76) or the Ottoman tented Cognac & Cigar courtyard garden at the heart of the hotel.

The rooms and suites at Dukes are decorated for tranquillity and comfort rather than show – a distinct plus in our book – and there is something intimate about the rooms that look over the courtyard. The penthouse suite, the Duke of Clarence, is so named because its private terrace overlooks Green Park and Clarence House (built for King William IV and now the Prince of Wales's London home). The suite is decorated with antiques and – rather charmingly – a collection of fine china from the Royal Warrant-holding Mayfair maker Thomas Goode, which designed dinner services for Tsar Nicholas II of Russia and Queen Victoria.

The Drawing Room and Conservatory are aptly named ground-floor salons that are generally less hugger-mugger than Dukes Bar, and are a delight for a light lunch or afternoon tea served with a gin and tonic. We confess to being less enamoured of the PJ Champagne room in the basement. The decor – all raspberry pink and minty green – is charming but a bit Cath Kidston compared to the rest of the hotel's understated, aristocratic demeanour. The Thirty-Six restaurant is not for us, either. We'd much prefer to take up the Dukes picnic service instead, whereby your butler prepares toasty blankets, hot-water bottles, lashings of booze and a feast in a hamper, then sets the whole kit and caboodle up for you in Green Park.

35–36 St James's Place SW1
Tel. 020 7491 4840
Tube: Green Park
www.dukeshotel.com

THE GORING ££££

In 2011 this fourth-generation family-owned and -run hotel made headlines worldwide when the then Kate

Middleton and her family chose to stay there during the days before her wedding to Prince William. The future queen was driven to Westminster Abbey from the Goring's doorstep. An annex to Buckingham Palace in all but name, the Goring has enjoyed royal patronage since it was built, in 1910. The reason is rather prosaic: it was the first hotel in the world to furnish each of its sixty-nine rooms with en suite bathrooms. As Norway's Crown Prince put it when he visited London for the coronation of George VI in 1936: 'At the Palace I have to share a bath with five people. Here I have one to myself.' The Goring has since hosted visiting royal families from Denmark, Sweden, Liechtenstein and Greece.

The Goring is the only hotel in London to hold Her Majesty The Queen's Royal Warrant (for hospitality and services). As a girl, Queen Elizabeth and her sister, Princess Margaret Rose, were treated to sausages and scrambled eggs at the Goring by their parents, King George VI and Queen Elizabeth. It was 1945, and Russia's Grand Duchess Xenia was in residence at the time. Art and ephemera of royal provenance are now on display in the Goring's Royal Suite, where Miss Middleton spent her last night as a commoner. The keynote of the Goring's interior decoration is reassuringly rich comfort. Walls are hung with patterned Gainsborough silk, plump leather club chairs positively gleam and lighting is kept to a deliciously low glow.

The rooms and suites that overlook the private garden (bought from the Duke of Westminster and apparently the size of Centre Court at Wimbledon) are the treasures, particularly those with balconies. It is worth noting that it is for good reason that the Goring says its windows actually open: it is a rarity these days, since health and safety regulations have hermetically sealed many a London hotel bedroom window above the second floor. The Goring Dining Room, beloved by Queen Elizabeth The Queen Mother (and decorated in 2005 by her grandson Lord Linley), is discussed in our **Restaurants** section. A bronze of the Queen Mother stands at the entrance to the Goring Bar, which is one of the very few hotel bars to stock Dubonnet (Her Majesty's favourite drink, when cut with equal parts gin). The raised terrace overlooking the Goring's gardens is a delightful spot for afternoon tea or champagne cocktails. Stories of Prince Harry vaulting from the Goring's terrace in the small hours before the wedding day, en route home to Clarence House, only enhance the hotel's royals-at-play provenance. To their great credit, the staff at the Goring remain tight-lipped about the royal wedding. Anything else would be treason.

Beeston Place SW1
Tel. 020 7396 9000
Tube: Victoria
www.thegoring.com

THE LANGHAM ££££

In 1767 Lord Foley built a mansion on the site of the present-day Langham hotel, securing a guarantee from his landlord, the Duke of Portland, that nothing could be built to impair his view north towards Hampstead. This ancient agreement is why Portland Place – the grand, unusually broad thoroughfare that leads from the Langham to Regent's Park – is 125 feet wide: that is the exact width of Foley House. The Langham was London's first grand hotel. It was purpose-built in 1864–65 in the style of a Florentine palazzo, with 600 rooms on seven floors. Hotel lore says that afternoon tea was first served in the Langham's Palm Court. In the 1840s Anna, 7th Duchess of Bedford, had set the fashion for taking a 'low tea' on occasional tables in her drawing room, to combat 'the sinking feeling' that occurred mid-afternoon as the dinner hour became later and later. Perhaps the Langham patented 'high tea' at dining tables in the Palm Court.

It was in the Palm Court of the Langham that both Arthur Conan Doyle and Oscar Wilde were commissioned to write for *Lippincott's Magazine*. Wilde wrote *The Picture of Dorian Gray* and Conan Doyle the second Sherlock Holmes mystery, *The Sign of Four*. Writers and musicians such as Mark Twain, Arturo Toscanini, Arnold Bennett and Antonín Dvořák have stayed here, as have the exiled emperors Napoleon III of France and Haile Selassie of Ethiopia. Today the Langham is popular with guests of neighbouring BBC Broadcasting House (the corporation used to own the building), and with Lady Gaga, who stopped traffic on Portland Place to greet her 'little monsters'.

"Today the Langham is popular with guests of neighbouring BBC Broadcasting House ... and with Lady Gaga, who stopped traffic on Portland Place to greet her 'little monsters'."

The Langham is vast, even though the number of bedrooms has been reduced significantly (to 380). Ceilings soar on every floor, and the decor of the rooms and suites is traditional – dark wood, chandeliers and swagged silk curtains – with technology provided but largely kept out of sight. The two-bedroom Infinity Suite is the star, with a bay of windows looking towards the spire of All Souls Church opposite, and a vast sarcophagus of a marble infinity bath in the master bathroom. In February 2015 the Langham unlocked forty newly decorated rooms in the Regency Wing, with a private door leading out on to Regent Street. Service at the Langham is in the grand tradition, and it does feel as though there are five members of staff to every guest.

With the luxury of space, the Langham has a decent swimming pool and health club, a ballroom and a private rose garden to the side of the hotel. The Palm Court – denuded of palms – is faintly disappointing, but the superlative Artesian bar (see **Drinks Cabinet**) is world class, and Roux at the Landau is one of the prettiest dining rooms in London.

1c Portland Place, Regent Street W1
Tel. 020 7636 1000
Tube Oxford Circus
www.london.langhamhotels.co.uk

THE PORTOBELLO HOTEL ££

Opened in 1971, the Portobello Hotel, with its twenty-one bedrooms reclining languidly on the upper floors of two neoclassical Victorian town houses, was one of London's first fashionable boutique hotels. Each room was uniquely decorated with sleigh beds or four-posters, crystal decanters, antique prints and nice bits of brown furniture bought from Portobello Market. It has a reputation for giving sanctuary to rock, fashion and film stars such as Tina Turner, Mick Jagger, Gwyneth Paltrow, Robbie Williams and Naomi Campbell. But banish any thought of giggling groupies or of televisions being hurled into

Stanley Gardens. That parade has long since passed by, and the Portobello has settled into a more refined middle age. What would have been considered wildly bohemian in the 1970s and '80s – mismatched Royal Doulton china, Victorian bathing machines, well-loved sofas in the scarlet drawing room – is today as comfortable and reassuring as an old pair of velvet slippers.

We're not entirely sure classifying the bedrooms as Single, Good, Better, Great and Exceptional is appropriate. Who would settle for Better when Greatness calls? And shouldn't it be up to the guest to decide which is their favourite room without a pre-ordained pecking order? But what we do like about the Portobello's rooms and suites is the faintly eccentric choice of furniture, as if a bachelor uncle with a very good eye has spent a lifetime ferreting around in London's markets and auction rooms. If your idea of luxury is a pointless strip of cashmere draped across the bottom of a bed and a marble wet room like a mausoleum, the Portobello is definitely not for you. For us, however, luxury is being able to order gravadlax and creamy scrambled eggs with a bottle of Pol Roger at 4 am, knowing the hotel will not think ill of us. We rather like threadbare sofas, open fires and well-worn antique chess sets, thank you very much.

Room 16 earned a degree of infamy when it became an urban myth that Kate Moss and Johnny Depp had spent nights of passion there, and allegedly requested that the free-standing bath next to the muslin-draped circular bed be filled with champagne. It's not quite Elizabeth Taylor and Richard Burton at the Dorchester, is it? Besides, Taylor and Burton would consider that a waste of champagne. But circular beds and supermodel shenanigans aside, the rooms and suites with views over Stanley Gardens are the loveliest. The Portobello doesn't have a restaurant on site, but nearby Julie's, opened by the Portobello hotel's former owners, Tim and Cathy Herring, is a much-loved Notting Hill institution.

22 Stanley Gardens W11
Tel. 020 7727 2777
Tube: Notting Hill Gate
www.portobellohotel.com

Where to stay ... for two gentlemen sharing

11 CADOGAN GARDENS £££

At 6.20 pm on 5 April 1895, the celebrated Irish playwright and society darling Oscar Wilde was arrested in Room 118 of the Cadogan Hotel. His lover Lord Alfred's father, the Marquess of Queensbury, had accused Wilde in writing of 'posing as a somdomite [*sic*]'. Wilde's libel case had collapsed, and he was found guilty of indiscretions with gentlemen for hire at the Savoy. Drowning his sorrows with hock and seltzer at the Cadogan, Wilde awaited his captors with the devoted Robbie Ross, a vigil celebrated by John Betjeman in 1937 with the poem 'The Arrest of Oscar Wilde at the Cadogan Hotel', and by David Hare's play *The Judas Kiss* (1998).

The Cadogan has been acquired by Belmond (formerly Orient Express Hotels), and will not reopen until 2016. Fortunately, Wildean opulence and amusement are to be found not five minutes away, at 11 Cadogan Gardens: four late Victorian red-brick town houses converted into an extravagantly decorated hotel by the interior designer Paul Davis. It's hard to know how to describe it. Imagine a cocktail mixed from equal measures of Colefax and Fowler and Palazzo Versace, with a dash of Castle Dracula to taste. The interiors remind us of Lord Berners's country house, Faringdon in Oxfordshire, where cases of antiquarian books, long-case clocks and four-poster beds live cheek-by-jowl with mad scarlet Murano chandeliers, humbug-striped silk salon chairs and a white baby grand piano.

We have all stayed in hotels where the staterooms are show-stoppers but the bedrooms are understudies. The rooms and suites at 11 Cadogan Gardens do not disappoint. The Sloane Suite is a Second Empire symphony of gold, black and white with a canopied four-poster bed and curtains made from enough silk to cut a Worth crinoline. The curtains frame huge bay windows overlooking Cadogan Gardens. It is a rare pleasure in London to have the luxury of space in a bedroom, and not to be constantly bumping into the tightly packed furniture. We also love the bedroom with claret-velvet-and-gold-embroidered curtains puddling on the floor around a four-poster, matching the curtains at the window; it can only be a tribute to the Royal Opera House, Covent Garden. With its drama and lavish interiors, and running to the traditional rhythms of a London town house in the belle époque, 11 Cadogan Gardens reminds us of one of Wilde's most prescient

> *"It is a rare pleasure in London to have the luxury of space in a bedroom, and not to be constantly bumping into the tightly packed furniture."*

aphorisms from *An Ideal Husband*: 'Nothing is so dangerous as being too modern. One is apt to grow old-fashioned quite suddenly.'

11 Cadogan Gardens SW3
Tel. 020 7730 7000
Tube: Sloane Square
www.no11cadogangardens.com

COVENT GARDEN HOTEL £££

Tim and Kit Kemp's Firmdale Hotels group has cast its net wide over central London, and we could legitimately recommend all eight sites because, like the Kennedys, each hotel has a distinctive personality while being unmistakably part of the same family. Why do gentlemen prefer the Covent Garden Hotel? Well, the quaint and pretty cobbled streets that emanate from Seven Dials are Greenwich Village cute, but they have a past as dark as that of Defoe's Moll Flanders. In the late seventeenth century the developer Thomas Neale thought he would make more money building a series of triangular 'Flatiron' properties with house fronts on three sides, meeting at Seven Dials, rather than a fashionable open square. The development failed abysmally, and Seven Dials became one of the most notorious slums in London. The poet Keats wrote of it: 'Misery clings to misery for a little warmth.'

Of course the whiff of bohemia – or is it incense puthering from the astrology shop across the road? – is window dressing. Today Seven Dials is an incredibly smart shopping and residential area, and the Covent Garden Hotel is its most luxurious billet. The hotel's long, grand façade gives a view of the bar and restaurant Brasserie Max within, filled from breakfast to nightcap with 'people like us' who dress as if every day is a scene from *The September Issue*. Non-residents aren't encouraged to mill around reception, and may not drift up to the first-floor drawing room and library, where you might be sharing an honesty bar with Tom Cruise, Kirsten Dunst, Amy Adams or Daniel Day-Lewis.

The rooms and suites in the Covent Garden Hotel are Kit Kemp's most subdued designs. What we love is the absence of show furniture and the emphasis on easy chairs and low sofas into which you want to sink, velvet slippers in the air, a copy of *Vanity Fair* in one hand and a glass of Chablis in the other. The bathrooms are of dramatic black-and-white-flecked granite with rainforest showers, double basins and sunken baths. A few bedrooms have working fireplaces. For those who feel like audience participation, there is a screening room in the hotel (as in most Firmdale hotels), but we much prefer snuggling into a snowy towelling robe under the duvet with a DVD, room service ordered and a loved one.

10 Monmouth Street W1
Tel. 020 7806 1000
Tube: Tottenham Court Road
www.firmdalehotels.com

THE FOX & ANCHOR ££

Equidistant between Smithfield Market and Charterhouse Square, the Fox & Anchor is a delightful late Victorian public house with mahogany saloon doors, tall tiled façade, mullioned windows and hanging baskets worthy of a Gold Medal at Chelsea. It was bought as a rundown meatpackers' pub and restored by Richard Balfour-Lynn in 2008. At the time Balfour-Lynn owned the Malmaison group, including

the London flagship in Charterhouse Square. The Fox
& Anchor is more *Oliver!* the Lionel Bart musical than
Charles Dickens's original of 1837, and advertises itself
as 'hops & chops, cuvees & duvets' – nothing camp
about that! – in coy reference to six smartly decorated
rooms above the pub and Fox's Den dining room.

The posh pub act is rather marvellous for anyone
who adores Victorian architecture but can't stand the
smell of stale beer, execrable food and unspeakable
lavatories. We love pressed iron
ceilings, pewter tankards, and
oysters and champagne shared in
private wooden booths. We love
the bedrooms above the Fox &
Anchor even more. The design
is masculine, contemporary
and nicely in keeping with the
area. Each room is hung with
blown-up architectural studies
of local buildings such as
Smithfield Market, the church of
St Bartholomew the Great and

> *"The posh pub
> act is rather
> marvellous for
> anyone who
> adores Victorian
> architecture but
> can't stand the
> smell of stale
> beer ..."*

the Barbican. Bathrooms are furnished with copper
his and his basins and free-standing copper or hand-
painted ball-and-claw baths. The palette is dark and
rich, there's a refreshing lack of clutter and all the
requisite technology is provided for those who travel
with multiple devices and still need more.

We do like 'rooms at the inn' because they provide
all the comforts that are lacking when staying with
friends (room service, heavenly bathrooms, maids, total
privacy, total autonomy) and none of the inconveniences
of large hotel life, such as over-solicitous staff, endless
tipping and a feeling that one is being watched. Mr
Balfour-Lynn has another such concern near Liverpool

Street – the Bull on Devonshire Row – but that area isn't half as romantic as Clerkenwell, or as amusing at the weekend. If you do one thing while staying at the Fox & Anchor, do drift into Clerkenwell Square and have a look at the art deco apartment block where David Suchet's *Poirot* was filmed, then blag your way on to a tour of what is left of the medieval Charterhouse monastery and Tudor almshouses. Fans of C. J. Sansom's *Shardlake* novels will feel at home.

115 Charterhouse Street EC1
Tel. 020 7250 1300
Tube: Farringdon
www.foxandanchor.com

THE WELLESLEY ££££

Should you wish to reside in that sweet spot equidistant on foot between Mayfair and Knightsbridge, then the Wellesley will be the picture in your locket. The naysayers questioned the wisdom of converting the former Pizza on the Park jazz club into a hotel because of the busy road outside. Tell that to the Lanesborough next door. That palatial hotel (currently under refurbishment) certainly hasn't been held back by the traffic. The Wellesley has thirty-six bedrooms and suites glamorously decorated by Fox Linton Associates in an homage to 1930s film-star style. Although the duplex penthouse on the sixth and seventh floors, with its private staircase, is a wow, two gentlemen sharing might prefer the suites on the lower floors, with half-moon windows overlooking the rose garden in Hyde Park and decorated in Syrie Maugham tones of champagne, cream and Dior grey, with acres of mirror, marble and glossy macassar ebony.

On the upper floors, photography from the *Vogue* and *Vanity Fair* archives of Hollywood beauties shot by Erwin Blumenthal, George Hurrell and Clarence Sinclair Bull sets a tone of high-voltage va-va-voom that puts any boy worth his pout in the mood for dinner in the devastatingly chic Oval dining room. An interior like that would perfectly frame platinum-blonde Jean Harlow in a slipper-satin bias-cut gown dripping in Cartier art deco diamonds, and the lighting could have been set by the legendary Hollywood cinematographer Jack Cardiff to flatter and soothe. The Wellesley's Crystal bar with its mirrored wall of whiskies and cognacs is the perfect obbligato to late-night cocktails and cabaret in the Jazz Lounge.

Those of us of a certain vintage will remember stars such as Liza Minnelli, Marion Montgomery and Barbara Cook performing at Pizza on the Park. The Wellesley has been smart to nurture a new generation of cabaret artists, including the lovely Rebecca Poole, Orli Nyles, Theo Jackson and Darren Reeves. The hotel has old-school MGM glamour down to a fine art, and treats its guests like the stars they are (or think they are), even twenty-first-century divas who require twenty-four-hour room service and a complimentary Rolls-Royce chauffeur service within a 1.5-mile radius. The smart humidor and cigar terrace with roaring fire and underfloor heating, shielded from prying eyes (and the admittedly busy road) with high box hedging, is a terrific hideaway.

11 Knightsbridge SW1
Tel. 020 7235 3535
Tube: Hyde Park Corner
www.thewellesley.co.uk

Where to stay ...
on business

THE CORINTHIA ££££

When beauty editors lumber towards the elephant's graveyard, it is their dearest hope that Heaven is the Corinthia hotel's Elemis spa: four storeys of black marble and gold mosaic, saunas as monolithic as Roman amphitheatres and invigorating pools that dance with fountains, waterfalls and submerged jets that put a smile on even the most Botox-tight faces. Fortunately, the rest of the hotel is equally cerebral and decorated to make one swank like a visiting head of state. The façade of the Corinthia has all the gleaming, sepulchral grandeur of the Quirinal presidential palace in Rome. Opened in 1885 as the Métropole hotel, the building was commandeered by the Ministry of Defence for the best part of a century until it reopened in 2011 as Whitehall's answer to the Savoy, Connaught and Lanesborough.

There is nothing antiquated about the hotel's interior, except for the stucco-and-gold-leaf ballroom that was graced by King Edward VII when he was the Prince of Wales. The Corinthia has been eviscerated by developers, and what was a 600-room Edwardian hotel has been reimagined as a 294-room concern with 43 suites, including the largest set of staterooms (the Royal Suite) in London. Spectacle is the key to the Corinthia's success, from the 2-ton, 1001-crystal Baccarat full-moon chandelier in the lobby to the specially commissioned pressed-bronze lift doors reminiscent of a Jazz Age Aztec temple. The public rooms are an adagio of vast, plush, white Olympian hallways and darker, sexier spaces such as the low-lit Bassoon bar with its black veneered top that curves into a custom-built baby grand piano.

The Corinthia has its show-stopping suites, such as the Royal with its 180-degree views encompassing Nelson's Column and Big Ben, not to mention the Musician's penthouse, complete with Steinway and cocktail bar in homage to the Métropole's resident conductor, Mantovani. But the hotel is popular with alpha males on business, many of whom are billeted there for months on end, for its discreet Whitehall location, generously sized rooms and palatial Italian marble bathrooms with underfloor heating, rainforest showers and baths that you could drown a hippo in. Epic poems have been written about the deco decadent restaurant Massimo, which has a private dining room complete with kitchen counter for a private chef to perform. On a busy night Massimo is grandiose and glamorous. When quiet, it feels as though you're the last man standing on board RMS *Titanic*.

Whitehall Place SW1
Tel. 020 7930 8181
Tube: Charing Cross
www.corinthia.com

THE SOHO HOTEL £££

Ambitious as it might be for hoteliers to take on historic buildings like the Port of London Authority Building at 10 Trinity Square, Regent Street's Café Royal or Sea Containers House, it takes moxie to transform an NCP car park in a dingy Soho cul-de-sac into a funky hotel headquarters for film, media and fashion folk. Kit Kemp, who owns the Firmdale Hotels group with her husband, Tim, decorates with attack: no minimalist she. Her public rooms are as effervescent as a Steradent tablet but never descend into kitsch, and the whole place is hung with an impressive collection of contemporary art. A smiling black bronze cat sculpted by Fernando Botero stands guard in the lobby, and the buzzy Refuel restaurant and zinc-topped long bar visible through conservatory-style windows promise that the joint is jumping. You can't really avoid being seen at Refuel, so it is a popular location for lone wolves who mean business to nurse a Soho Sensation and schedule the casting calls.

Soho was lacking a luxury hotel before the Kemps had the vision to transform this tasty slice of real estate off Wardour Street. The approach isn't particularly inviting, but Soho is deceptive. Back in the day, the closed doors of low-rise terraces would conceal ladies of the night and crack dens. Now Soho is a community of film-editing suites, recording studios, television production companies and private clubs, including Soho House, the Groucho Club and Blacks. Soho is second only to Clerkenwell for lateral loft conversions, and the Kemps have obliged with open-plan apartment-style rooms and suites with a New York state of mind. The hotel has all the polish of the Park Lane Four Seasons but is fortunately in a much more fascinating location.

We can't tell you how many fashion PRs have hosted press days in the 180-square-foot fifth-floor terrace suite with wraparound balconies and Mary Poppins views over the roofs of London. Kit Kemp's are the kind of suite that you walk into and know where to sling your Birkin, kick off your Manolos and park your laptop: it's a practical magic that makes a lot of hotels look Muggle in comparison. I have stayed at the Soho Hotel once, after a particularly lively, cocktail-fuelled film screening, and for those without a penthouse budget, the Deluxe rooms on the fifth floor have equally lovely if more modest terraces and just the same views. As a postscript, live performances of opera and ballet from the Royal Opera House have proved incredibly popular in cinemas throughout the UK. Firmdale has cleverly struck a deal to show 'live from the Garden' performances in its Soho Hotel screening room.

4 Richmond Mews W1
Tel. 020 7559 3000
Tube: Tottenham Court Road
www.firmdalehotels.com

ONE ALDWYCH ££££

Whether clients visit you or not, you will inevitably be judged by the hotel you choose when in London on business. What, for example, does a room at the London Edition, with its identikit Scandinavian shag-pad bedrooms and secret nightclub in the basement, say about you? Will you earn respect or ridicule booking into the Tom Dixon-designed monolith the Mondrian? Dignity is not a dirty word when you're looking for a hotel that means business, and when in doubt we always recommend the silver fox that is One Aldwych. The location is Switzerland (i.e. neutral) and the building was designed by the same architect as the London Ritz (Mewès & Davis). The meet and greet is slick and professional, as is the first glimpse of the pristine Lobby Bar, decorated with important contemporary sculpture from the collection of the hotel's owner, Gordon Campbell Gray.

One Aldwych is basically George Clooney rendered in bricks and mortar. Requests are fulfilled in a suave, understated manner, if indeed they haven't been anticipated. For longer stays, there are executive suites with private kitchens, triple-glazed windows and beds dressed with Frette linen sheets. The briskly smart circular Studio Suites on the top floor have Thames views that clear the head and please the soul. Each of the 105 rooms and suites is hung with original artworks, although only the Deluxe Suite is furnished with its own gym. Still, one can spend too much time alone, and we'd much rather descend to the subterranean gym, sauna, steam room and miraculous 60-foot chlorine-free swimming pool with its ambient light and underwater mood music.

Even if we are fortunate enough to have been booked into a suite the size of Luxembourg, we do find that too much time in a hotel room can make one stir-crazy. One Aldwych has anticipated this with a Fox Linton Associates VIP Lounge, where one can read the newspapers or a collection of Rizzoli books 'curated' (how we loathe the misuse of that word) by Sir Paul Smith; although, knowing Sir Paul, the choice could be anything from *Pushbikes of the Kalahari* to *Etruscan Beads Made Easy*. The soaring ceiling of the aforementioned Lobby Bar makes it one of the most imposing and impressive hotel bars in London. Restaurants Indigo (upstairs and informal) and Axis (downstairs and grand) cover all bases for clients, friends and new acquaintances.

1 Aldwych WC2
Tel. 020 7300 1000
Tube: Holborn
www.onealdwych.com

ST PANCRAS RENAISSANCE £££££

As a matter of urgency, please pay no heed to Marriott Hotels' woefully corporate website. It makes George Gilbert Scott's High Victorian Gothic masterpiece look about as appealing as a Premier Inn. The red-brick St Pancras station hotel, with its turrets, towers and spires reminiscent of Mervyn Peake's Gormenghast, is a glorious folly. Built in 1873 and originally christened the Midland Grand, the hotel closed its doors in 1935 and, like a Sleeping Beauty, was left nearly derelict until 2011, when a restoration costing £150 million brought the Grade I-listed interiors back to life. The Poet Laureate John Betjeman, whose statue stands on the Eurostar concourse behind the hotel, helped to save the building that he once deemed 'too beautiful and too romantic to survive'.

> *"The red-brick St Pancras station hotel, with its turrets, towers and spires reminiscent of Mervyn Peake's Gormenghast, is a glorious folly."*

The Grand Staircase, papered with scarlet and gold leaf, rising three floors to a vaulted 'star chamber' ceiling and backlit by towering arched windows, is roped off for the use of guests, and public rooms – such as the old Ladies' Smoking Room above the original entrance to the hotel – are similarly closed to curious interlopers. Thirty-eight Chamber Suites on the *piano nobile*, with 16-foot ceilings and floor-to-ceiling windows, are individually decorated, some with re-creations of wildly patterned wallpapers rediscovered beneath layers of dreary paint. The London-based architect RHWL has shown ingenuity in finding spaces behind new wall panels for state-of-the-art bathrooms.

Housed in the former Venetian Ballroom, the Royal Suite is more than 3,000 square feet of bliss, with two bedrooms, walk-in wardrobes, a study, a vast drawing room and a dining table for intimate parties of up to twenty. The bathrooms are fit for a Victorian courtesan, with romantic free-standing ball-and-claw-foot roll-top tubs.

The most successful of the Grade I-listed Chambers suites face the hotel concourse, although smaller suites facing the Eurostar platform also have charm. However, the lion's share of hotel rooms are housed in the newly built Barlow House wing, and, as the name suggests, there is little magic in being banished from the Gothic splendour next door. It's rather like being invited to dine and sleep at Downton Abbey and being billeted in the servants' wing.

The monolithic Booking Office bar with its terrace on the station concourse is splendid and deserves a solo spot in our **Drinks Cabinet** list. It was a coup for the St Pancras Renaissance to secure the services of Marcus Wareing to headline the Gilbert Scott restaurant, which is set in one of the prettiest, most serene dining rooms in London, designed by the late David Collins. But Wareing's residency at the Berkeley eclipses it. Similarly, there are more luxurious and central subterranean spas than that in the St Pancras Renaissance, although it is a terrific reviver for those who have stepped off the Eurostar.

Euston Road NW1
Tel. 020 7841 3540
Tube: King's Cross St Pancras
www.marriott.co.uk

Where to stay ... for dedicated followers of fashion

BOUNDARY £££

Hip hotels fall like confetti on London's East End, and the latest at the time of writing is the New York import Ace Hotel. In its own words, Ace's 'hood', Spitalfields, is 'a place where art, design, culinary innovation, culture and tech gather and phosphoresce from the heat of collaboration, inspiration and a soft spot for the future'. It was also the home of London's Huguenot silk weavers from the early seventeenth century, the birthplace of the father of the modern novel, Daniel Defoe, and the scene of the nineteenth century's most infamous serial killings. But fashionable hotels don't tend to have much of a soft spot for the past. When it comes to the vagaries of being à la mode, we agree with George Santayana, who wrote: 'Fashion is something barbarous for it produces innovation without reason and imitation without benefit.' That is why we ignore Ace and admire Terence Conran's Boundary: a multitasking collection of restaurants, hotel rooms, a delicatessen, a bakery and an art space, opened in 2008.

Conran is a walking compendium of contemporary design – not to mention the patriarch of a dynasty that is to creative London what the Borgias were to Rome – and he was smart to decorate the Boundary's twelve rooms as homages to his heroes, including Andrée Putman, Eileen Gray, Ludwig Mies van der Rohe, Le Corbusier and Charles and Ray Eames, as well as the design movements Bauhaus, Werkstätte and Shaker. The five duplex suites on the third and fourth floors are basically East End apartments, and although design purists will find us crass, we absolutely adore the Modern Chinoiserie Suite, designed by David Tang with painted silk wallpaper snaking up the walls and on to the ceiling.

Of course, dedicated followers of fashion know that Redchurch Street is one of the most relevant byways for British fashion in the East End. Even though it looks rundown and grungy, any brand that is seeking credibility will be looking for real estate next to Aubin & Wills, Caravan and Hostem. Somehow we never find ourselves near Redchurch Street in the evening to enjoy dinner at Boundary's Albion restaurant, but we have on more than one occasion conspired to be visiting the tailor Timothy Everest on a summer's day, only to find ourselves miraculously at Boundary's Bar & Grill on its rooftop terrace. There, enough time could pass for hemlines to rise and fall several times, and frankly, my dear, we wouldn't give a damn.

2–4 Boundary Street E2
Tel. 020 7729 1051
Tube: Liverpool Street
www.theboundary.co.uk

HOXTON HOLBORN ££

There is no better vantage point for studying self-consciously cool London behaviourism than the lobby of the Hoxton Holborn. The loafers, hot-deskers and freelancers posing on the battered, slightly pikey 1970s comprehensive-school staffroom furniture look like the cast of a suspiciously well-dressed appeal for Help the Homeless. Is there perhaps a stylist on the door denying entry if a chap isn't wearing True Religion

raw denim, Grenson Archie brogues and a beanie hat?
Dedicated Followers of Fashion do tend to flourish
in crowds; their endorphins rush in proportion to
the number of Apple handheld devices and Ed
Sheeran lookalikes in the room. The hotel's all-day
Hubbard & Bell canteen on the ground floor is a
scene, and goes some way to redressing WC1's dearth
of decent restaurants.

The entire façade of Hoxton Holborn is a shop
window for how Generation Dr Dre Headphones rolls.
The open-plan reception is flanked by the Holborn
Grind coffee shop – another
window full of caffeinated beards
staring into their laptops – and
a nail bar called (what else?)
Cheeky, where ladies in bright-
red lipstick and Land Girl
headscarves sit beneath neon
signs enjoying the attention of
a tattooed pedicurist. It takes
chutzpah to feign indifference
while someone is painting your
toenails in clear view of passers-
by, but Dedicated Followers
of Fashion are nothing if not
exhibitionists. The hotel also has a chicken shack in
the basement, single-foodstuff eateries – for burgers,
lobsters, steaks or chooks, for example – being all the
rage at the time of writing.

Sleep is not high on the 'to do' list for DFoFs,
and Hoxton Holborn's 174 bedrooms are classified
as 'shoebox, snug, comfy and roomy', rather cleverly
making a virtue out of a potential drawback. Each
room is decorated in a vaguely Scandi minimalist
style, with retro wallpaper and Penguin Classics, and

> *"... ladies in
> bright-red lipstick
> and Land Girl
> headscarves sit
> beneath neon
> signs enjoying
> the attention
> of a tattooed
> pedicurist."*

equipped with a nosebag containing orange juice and granola plus fresh milk. We have to say that that lactic little detail is reason enough to love the Hoxton Holborn, since the infernal plastic cartons of gloop supplied in most hotel bedrooms have been the ruin of many a Dockers chino. The Hoxton Holborn is always 'in character', hence references to its food as 'nosh' and to sleep as 'catching some zzzzzs'. Haute fashionistas might find it a little basic, but then again, the style police in the lobby might find them overdressed and over the hill.

199–206 High Holborn WC1
Tel. 020 7661 3000
Tube: Holborn
www.thehoxton.com/london/holborn

TOWN HALL HOTEL & APARTMENTS ££

If the moneybags developers of Mayfair, Piccadilly and St James's showed a fraction of the creativity, integrity and respect that have been lovingly given to Bethnal Green's Edwardian Town Hall hotel conversion, they'd pulverize the competition. The building, constructed in 1910 and with a dash of deco added to the interiors in the 1930s, was on the 'at risk' register when the Singaporean hotelier Peng Loh commissioned RARE architects to give the structure a third age. The firm added an elevation and an extension sheathed in laser-cut aluminium. With minimum intervention, a grand municipal building gleaming with white and green marble and polished mahogany panelling and decorated with high stucco ceilings has become a hotel with ninety-eight rooms and suites. It is all quite brilliant and rather like a time machine of twentieth- to twenty-first-century design. We adore the

De Montford Suite (formerly the Council Room), with its triple-height barrel-vaulted ceilings. To retain the drama, RARE divided the vast room with glass panels and a mezzanine.

Equally smart are the rooms built up into the eaves of these soaring ceilings, in which contemporary design harmonizes with lovingly restored original features. Imagine a perfect marriage between Edwin Lutyens and Carlo Silvestrin and you have the idea. The interior design demonstrates great taste – 1970s furniture placed around the Edwardian marble staircase beneath a geometric art deco clock – but also an appreciation of design for living, not just looking. The east London practice Artsadmin was asked to commission original, site-specific art. Our favourite piece is Debbie Lawson's mad wall-mounted *Persian Moose* carpet. The Town Hall Hotel does not have a spa, but there is a slim, sleek swimming pool naturally lit by a skylight and surrounded by white, sculpted loungers that are more Art Basel Miami than east London.

Bethnal Green may be fashionable, but it isn't fabulous, and it is the devil to get to. For that reason, Town Hall offers a morning shuttle service to Liverpool Street and Bank stations. That said, it's smart to have a restaurant that foodies and fashionables would walk over hot coals to reach. Town Hall's former guest chef Nuno Mendes dazzled us with his Viajante before decamping to the Chiltern Firehouse kitchen. At the Town Hall, the newly christened Typing Room's leading man is Lee Westcott, under the direction of Jason Atherton. Typing Room belongs in our **Restaurants** section, and is absent only because Mr Atherton's City Social got our gold medal. Mr Westcott's dishes at Typing Room are some of the prettiest you'll ever see, with delicate flowers, fragile fronds and heart-melting drifts of colour comparable to Monet's garden at Giverny.

Patriot Square E2
Tel. 020 7871 0460
Tube: Bethnal Green
www.townhallhotel.com

THE ZETTER TOWNHOUSE £££

Clerkenwell is one of London's most visceral boroughs, built as it was around Smithfield meat market, which has traded on the same site for more than 1,000 years. Recently the area's Victorian warehouses and factories have been converted into loft apartments and its taverns, cellars and shops into establishments that make it one of the city's most dynamic gastronomic quarters. When Michael Benyan and Mark Sainsbury opened the Zetter boutique hotel in 2004, they created an ironic Austin Powers-like antidote to the overblown luxury of the West End, with Timorous Beasties wallpaper, Eley Kishimoto textiles, roof terraces and vending machines offering everything from champagne and condoms to deodorant and Berocca. The opening of Bistrot Bruno Loubet, with its floor-to-ceiling windows facing St John's Church across the square, made the Zetter a major player on the city's restaurant scene.

In 2011 Zetter annexed a brace of Georgian town houses behind the hotel in the newly cobbled St John Square, and created the whimsical, eccentric wonderland that is Zetter Townhouse. The infernal cocktail lounge by the interior designer Russell Sage, stuffed to the rafters with flea-market oil paintings, mad taxidermy, reclaimed antique furniture and a library of dusty vellum-bound books, doubles as reception. The owners invented a character called Great Aunt Wilhelmina (London loves a little method acting), whom they had in mind when they created this High Victoriana meets *Rocky Horror* cocktail lounge directed by Tony '69 Colebrooke Row' Conigliaro, with sharing plates from Monsieur Loubet's kitchen across the courtyard.

The Zetter Townhouse's thirteen rooms and suites are furnished with figured-oak four-poster beds hung with Union flags, circus beds reminiscent of Cecil Beaton, marble-panelled baths in alcoves lined with mosaics of Byzantine gold, Roberts Revival radios, antique telephones, carriage clocks, artworks and textiles that clash like cymbals at the climax of *Carmina Burana*. How marvellous it would be to commandeer all thirteen rooms for a bacchanalian house-party weekend, with parlour japes in the basement games room, raucous epicurean nights in the company of the stuffed boxing kangaroo in the dining room, assignations by the open fire in the Cocktail Lounge and bed-hopping aplenty. We can think of few more romantic sights to wake up to with a crashing hangover than the view of the early Tudor St John's Gate. Although the façade of St John's Church looks undistinguished, below it is a twelfth-century crypt that we urge disciples of *The Da Vinci Code* to see. It is so much more magical than the Temple church, where the film was made.

49–50 St John's Square EC1
Tel. 020 7324 4567
Tube: Farringdon
www.thezettertownhouse.com

Where to stay ...
for low-key luxury

THE BERKELEY ££££

We always think of Grace Kelly when we enter
the classy, low-key lobby of the Berkeley. Behind a
calm, honey-hued façade lies a hotel that is swan-like
in its quest for perfection. Even the royal family
of London hotels are satisfied with one star chef,
but the Berkeley has two: Pierre Koffmann (see
Restaurants) and Marcus Wareing. Belgravia's ladies
who lunch still talk about the day the Duchess of
Cornwall chose Koffmann's for a pre-wedding pep-
talk lunch for the then Miss Kate Middleton. It is
a rare occurrence even these days for senior royals to
eat in public, so the Duchess's choice of the Berkeley
is praise indeed.

The hotel's Blue Bar is the magnum opus of the
David Collins Studio, with its white onyx counter,
black crocodile-embossed leather bar and 'Lutyens
blue' lacquered walls reflecting the kindest light on
the complexion of the cocktail drinker. The convex
mirror in the Blue Bar was taken from the Lutyens-
designed old Berkeley next to Devonshire House on
Piccadilly, before both were demolished. To call the
late David Collins a 'fashionable decorator' is rather
faint praise. In the two decades around the turn of the
millennium he was the *only* decorator with the finesse
to give new life to listed London interiors. When he
was interviewed for *The World of Interiors*, Collins
said his choice of Lutyens blue promised 'endless
possibilities'. One could say much the same thing
about an evening at the Berkeley.

The Berkeley knows its clients. Every new guest is greeted by name and, whether it's transmitted by voodoo or earpiece, this is a lovely touch. You're not going to find a disappointing room or suite, although the Hyde Park view from the upper two floors and the Wilton Place aspect from the lower are preferable. The Berkeley Suites decorated by Helen Green and Robert Angell are in a billionaire classic-car-collector palette of silver, anthracite grey, bronze, cream and black. The Berkeley is not theatrical, preferring instead that relatively anonymous but rich decoration that reassures Saudi prince and Brazilian minerals heiress alike. We had a peek at the aptly named Opus Suite, which is roughly a quarter of the size of Trafalgar Square, but we infinitely prefer the fabulous Pavilion Conservatory Suite. As its name suggests, the Pavilion has a vast terrace, dotted with box hedging, that overlooks the spire of St Paul's Church next door. Secret outdoor spaces in London are to be treasured, and the Berkeley's rooftop swimming pool with retractable ceiling and gorgeous solarium gardens planted with white hydrangeas remind one of a Tuscan terrace in high summer.

Wilton Place SW1
Tel. 020 7235 6000
Tube: Hyde Park Corner/Knightsbridge
www.the-berkeley.co.uk

BROWN'S HOTEL £££££

The world's best-selling crime novelist, Dame Agatha Christie, stayed at Brown's and based her novel *At Bertram's Hotel* (1965) on the Georgian terraced hotel, which had been opened by James and Sarah Brown in 1837. Or did she? Dame Agatha's estate also names the neighbouring hotel Fleming's as a model for Bertram's. Either way, Christie's Bertram's Hotel was frozen in aspic. By contrast, Brown's has benefitted from a multimillion-pound makeover courtesy of Olga Polizzi, the sister of its owner, Rocco Forte. This has rendered the rooms and suites sufficiently swish and bland not to panic those who mistake character for decrepitude.

Brown's is the oldest London hotel that is still trading, although it wasn't until 1889 that the original hotel on Dover Street annexed the adjacent St George's Hotel, with its doorway on Albemarle Street. The Edwardian public rooms are to be treasured, because they have somehow smuggled the charm of town-house living into the twenty-first century. Top-hatted doormen welcome one into a discreetly grand reception that doesn't need soaring atriums or Dale Chihuly chandeliers to impress. The dining room, now hosted by Mark Hix, has gravitas despite the occasional Tracey Emin neon that can go back to Sotheby's when figurative art comes back into fashion. The ladies and gentlemen who make Mayfair tick practically live in the Donovan Bar at Brown's.

Hotel lore maintains that Queen Victoria 'loved to take tea' at Brown's. The Widow Windsor might – just might – have called on resident ex-Emperor Napoleon III and Empress Eugenie in 1871, but Her Majesty was rarely seen in public, let alone in a public place. Perhaps the hotel could make more of its literary history: it was a favourite of Arthur Conan Doyle, Oscar Wilde, J. M. Barrie and Bram Stoker. Still, there is a Kipling Suite, named after the author who, according to the Rudyard Kipling Society, wrote *The Jungle Book* while living, not at Brown's hotel, but in Vermont.

33 Albemarle Street W1
Tel. 020 7493 6020
Tube: Green Park
www.roccofortehotels.com

THE ROOKERY £££

Equidistant between the City, the East End and
Bloomsbury, Clerkenwell is a district with a distinctly
seditious history. The Peasant's Revolt against
King Richard II in 1381 was crushed on the site of
Clerkenwell Green; that spot was also the *mise-en-scène*
for Charles Dickens's Artful Dodger teaching Oliver
Twist to pick a pocket or two. The Rookery nods to
the district's past, with thirty-three rooms and suites
named after local saints and sinners; the top-storey
Rook's Nest duplex piquantly offers views of the
dome of St Paul's and the golden statue of Justice
atop the Old Bailey. The Rookery comprises a terrace
of crooked brick Georgian houses dating from 1764,
entered via a lantern-lit pedestrian alley that gives
a frisson of Fagin's den. The oak-panelled interiors,
with decent period paintings, furniture and plush
silk curtains that rustle like a dowager duchess's
court train, are bathed in warm but reassuringly
low light that makes one feel like dipping a curtsey
to fellow guests.

The Rookery retains the mood of a Georgian
town house, with library, conservatory, charming
ivy-clad city courtyard and dining-cum-boardroom
with a fourteen-seater mahogany table. Once handed
their keys – yes, keys – guests are greeted with rooms
containing seventeenth-century carved-oak four-
poster beds and restored Victorian bathroom suites
with free-standing baths and copper shower heads the
size of Wedgwood dinner plates. The Rook's Nest is a

bower of bliss for a gentleman and his doxy or perhaps a countess with her highwayman, depending on the way one's fantasies incline. Four carved blackamoors stand sentinel at each corner of the bed, and a dog-leg staircase leads to a top-floor drawing room-cum-study beneath a 40-foot spire. For those who desire more than a bottle of fizz and an *amuse-bouche* delivered to the suite, Clerkenwell is one of London's erogenous zones for fine dining, with St John, Hix, Polpetto and Bistrot Bruno Loubet within walking distance.

12 Peter's Lane, Cowcross Street EC1
Tel. 020 7336 0931
Tube: Farringdon
www.rookeryhotel.com

Z HOTEL SOHO £

Doubtless a few new facelifts will ache as eyebrows shoot heavenward on seeing the Berkeley in the same genus of *Discriminating Guide* hotels as Z Soho. Z Soho might not be for us, but the Berkeley and Brown's would be wasted on the godchild we alluded to in our **Restaurants** section, hence the mention. For Generation *Hunger Games*, Z Soho is an acceptably cool brand of low-key and luxurious. Although it has adopted the unfortunate word 'Urbanite' for its prospective guests, the concept of bijou but luxe bedrooms is a smart one for dirty flirties planning a wild weekend in London. Let's face it, you're not going to choose a hotel in the middle of Soho for a godchild who is planning early nights with a green tea, Neal's Yard face pack and Kindle.

Z Soho has sensibly kept the Georgian façade of this triangular island of former dive bars and brothels between Charing Cross Road and the gay catwalk that is Old Compton Street. The interiors of all twelve houses have been gutted, and the hotel is as stark and modern as a person who doesn't know the meaning of 'reverse charges' could wish for. Within the Georgian walls is a cat's cradle of steel gantries and spiral staircases constructed around a light well. We cannot see the point of a single bedroom – albeit with high-thread-count sheets, a flatscreen television, free WiFi and a walk-in wet room – if we're booking a room in Soho for a young person who has access to Tinder, Grindr and God only knows what other dating apps are in vogue.

The largest beds in the Z are queen size (natch!), and of those the best face the pedestrianized Moor Street, even though Z Soho had the foresight to triple-glaze all the windows. The Inside Doubles have no windows at all, which might be unsettling for some, but full marks to Z for its marketing: 'Who needs windows when you're young, smokin' hot, ripped and up for it?' Z now has outposts on Orange Street in Piccadilly and Lower Belgrave Street in Victoria, but Soho is preferable for the young. It sits on top of one of London's hottest restaurants, La Bodega Negra (the basement club, not the street-level café), and is only a tipsy drag queen's totter to the bars, clubs and speakeasies that make Soho sin central. It might not be for those of us who remember when Madonna was queen of clubbing and Lady Thatcher was prime minister, but the Z Soho is a treasure for your teens.

17 Moor Street W1
Tel. 020 3551 3700
Tube: Leicester Square
www.thezhotels.com/z-soho

Not for us (but should be)

BULGARI HOTEL £££££

The tone in Knightsbridge was changed when the Candy brothers built their monstrous concrete and smoked-glass towers at One Hyde Park: the development cast a dark shadow over the neighbourhood and set a world record for its penthouse flat, which was sold to the eastern European gentleman in the dodgy Ray-Bans for £140 million. The nearby Bulgari Hotel is as stark and anonymous as One Hyde Park, and the subterranean excavations six storeys down are reminiscent of a Bond villain's bunker. The public rooms, with their polished steel, black-granite flagstones and smoked glass, make one feel that the only suitable conversation should involve an Arab sheikh and a Thierry Mugler-clad Baltic blonde in dark glasses muttering darkly about the microfilm being in a locked box in Belgrade.

There is, of course, the requisite screening room, spa and swimming pool on the lower floors, as well as the imaginatively named Il Bar, where you'll feel out of place without a burka, fat-cat banker's bonus or pneumatic date with Zeppelin bosoms and a face that is not first edition. This being a new building, the Bulgari's eighty-five guest rooms and suites – sleekly modern and suitably plush in silver, brocade and grey velvet – are deliciously luxurious, and the black-marble bathrooms are to die for. But with rooms at a minimum of £850 per night, rising to £14,400 for the penthouse, the Bulgari is not for us.

The subterranean restaurant, named (drumroll) Il Ristorante, didn't set the world on fire – it didn't even light the match – and so Alain Ducasse was called in to rebrand the carousel as Rivea London and redecorate with a lighter touch. Rivea is inspired by Mediterranean *cuisine du soleil* from Monsieur Ducasse's childhood, and there lies its Achilles heel. Small plates inspired by St Tropez and Portofino taste glorious al fresco under a white canvas sunshade, but the concept doesn't really travel to a basement in Knightsbridge. Should the Bulgari's clientele fancy *cuisine du soleil*, they could probably hop on a private jet to Nice as easily as the rest of us would take a No. 38 bus.

171 Knightsbridge SW7
Tel. 020 7151 1010
Tube: Knightsbridge
www.bulgarihotels.com

HOTEL CAFÉ ROYAL ££££££

Opened by the French émigré Daniel Thévenon in 1863, the Café Royal on the curve of Nash's Regent Street was the most elegant, intriguing palace of pleasure for London's café society. Celebrated couples – such as Oscar Wilde and Lord Alfred 'Bosie' Douglas, Noël Coward and Gertrude Lawrence, and Elizabeth Taylor and Richard Burton – graced its opulent interior, a Francophile waltz of Louis XVI and First Empire. We toured the Café Royal with Bonhams auctioneers when the café closed its doors in 2008, before a multimillion-pound facelift courtesy of the Israeli hoteliers the Cut and David Chipperfield Architects, and it was a sorry sight.

One cannot fault the ambition of the investors. The Cut acquired the neighbouring County Fire Office facing Piccadilly Circus; it had been boarded up for years and now serves as a new wing. Such important historic features of the belle époque Café as the gilded, mirrored Grill Room, the Pompadour Room with its painted ceilings, and the horseshoe-shaped grand staircase have been preserved. The contemporary interventions, however, are soulless and – rather ironically, given the Café's past – lacking in character. With the exception of six signature suites, including the wood-panelled Tudor Suite with its listed interior, the hotel rooms are bordering on ascetic, clad in either fumed oak or sepulchral rusticated Portland stone. Also, we didn't see a single picture on the walls of the public or guest rooms, a fact that made the hotel feel lonely and lacking in wit and flair.

The world-famous Café Royal cellars, which hid a clandestine Masonic temple, have been gutted and replaced with the Zen-like Akasha Holistic Wellbeing Centre and a swimming pool. We feel it would have been more in character to re-create a palatial Victorian Turkish Hammam, considering St James's and Piccadilly were once famous for them. Renaming the Grill Room Oscar Wilde's Bar is like the Savoy rebranding its American Bar 'Sinatra's' or some such. Hope is to be had in the eccentric, sprawling signature suites, such as the glam circular Dome Suite atop the old County Fire Offices, with a roof terrace that makes one think of Talitha Getty in Tangier. London may love the Café more when new stories have been added to those of its scandalous past.

68 Regent Street W1
Tel. 020 7406 3333
Tube: Piccadilly Circus
www.hotelcaferoyal.com

MONDRIAN £££

If we may attempt to accentuate the positive, the opening in 2014 of Mondrian London finally restored Warren Platner's hulking 1970s Thames-side structure to its original purpose. For decades Sea Containers House was the London office of this author's namesake. Although not punching at the architectural weight of Tate Modern, Mondrian London is a brute and stands even taller than the former Bankside power station, thanks to its fabulous glass-box penthouse, which houses the Rumble Room champagne bar. But Tom Dixon's monumental interiors are terribly hard to warm to. Reception echoes a giant copper ship's hull that is both discombobulating and rather intimidating. The giant tubular-metal sculptures and random objects (is it art? is it lost property?) that are the speciality of Morgans hotels litter the public rooms. We prefer the proportions of the Group's much more central Sanderson.

We like the portholes, the waiters in sailor stripes and the model ships on display (although we do think Dixon missed a trick by not showing an empty glass case bearing the legend 'the Marie Celeste'), but we don't like being on display ourselves. A ground-floor façade of sheet glass means you're on show to every Tom, Dick and Harriet walking the Thames Path. Like people who try to be funny, Mondrian's desperation to be hip becomes grating on the nerves. Once you've shared a lift with murals of Queen Elizabeth I, a pearly king and a spaceman, the artistry becomes an irritant. The views from rooms and suites on the river side, overlooking St Paul's, are tremendously romantic, although we'd probably prefer to look the other way from a suite at the Savoy. The pink-and-black bed throws in some of the otherwise grey rooms remind us of a MyHotel, and that is not a compliment.

Dixon modelled Mondrian London on a cruise liner. The good ship Mondrian has 359 berths, a Curzon cinema showing new releases (open to the public), numerous bars and restaurants, an art gallery and a major subterranean spa complex that reminded us of a Dignitas clinic. The damned thing is far too big to feel exclusive. There's nowhere other than one's room to get away from fellow passengers. For Londoners, the Mondrian is terribly good news: an ugly, unloved building has been spruced up and converted into a shiny new public entertainment complex. But visitors to London not keen to see and be seen should go elsewhere.

20 Upper Ground SE1
Tel. 0800 3747 1000
Tube: Waterloo
www.mondrianlondon.com

SHANGRI-LA AT THE SHARD £££££

Renzo Piano's Shard, the tallest building in Europe, is divisive. It can be seen from practically any point in Greater London, and is a totem for the relentless successful planning applications for skyscrapers in the City and on the South Bank that are, quite frankly, waging war with our historic skyline. Rather worryingly, more than 200 applications to build skyscrapers in London have been approved. It seems money can conquer all. We attended the first private party on the upper observation deck of the Shard and could not deny feeling the urge to give a diabolical Dr Evil laugh standing astride the city, with lights sprawled like a diamond-encrusted carpet below. Then the vertigo kicked in and the novelty wore off.

For those of us born in the 1970s, skyscrapers mean one thing: *The Towering Inferno*. We could not wait to be back on terra firma. Personal phobias and foibles aside, the Shard sets a dangerous precedent. As Uncle Matthew would say in Nancy Mitford's *Love in a Cold Climate*, the Shard is the thin end of the wedge. Is it the first step towards turning London into Dubai? The Shangri-La hotel occupies the 34th to the 52nd floors of the glass stiletto and boasts floor-to-ceiling glass walls that give impressive views of the city below and, apparently, the bathrooms of your fellow guests, so do pack your binoculars or your best La Perla negligee. Of course, blinds can be drawn, but that rather defeats the object, no?

The interiors of the Shard can best be described as a blind date between Kelly Hoppen and Suzy Wong: sleek, contemporary, could be anywhere in the world. The infinity pool on Level 52 sounds like fun, but – despite all the hoopla about unprecedented levels of luxury (boom boom) – the Shard may have its head in the clouds but its feet are planted in rather a tatty part of town. The grand entrance is on the concourse of London Bridge station, a joy come rush hour and a conduit for Bart's Hospital, hence the carnival of people on crutches and in wheelchairs smoking cigarettes. Parking is the very devil, the streets surrounding the Shard are a rabbit warren of dark railway arches and cul-de-sacs, and it can take forever to cross the Thames to the City or the West End. Other than that, what's not to like?

31 St Thomas Street SE1
Tel. 020 7234 8000
Tube: London Bridge
www.shangri-la.com

Radio Rooftop Bar

III

Drinks Cabinet

Where to drink …
champagne

CHAMPAGNE & FROMAGE £££

There is arguably no place in London more *soigné* to
quaff Ruinart than the Champagne Bar in the Royal
Opera House's Paul Hamlyn Hall. That said, theatre
bars aren't known for being easy on the wallet, and
we prefer a pre-theatre snifter at Champagne &
Fromage, a sensational little *boîte* a brisk trot from the
Garden. As its name suggests, this charming shop-
meets-bistro serves and sells a list of champagnes
made by award-winning family-owned French
producers and a smorgasbord of gorgeous Gallic
rustic cheeses, charcuterie and foie gras chosen to
complement the wine.

    The few café tables and chairs are dotted between
the deli counters, and the walls are stacked with
jars, bottles and pots containing terrines, preserves,
rillettes and confits. Licensing laws dictate that one
must order food with a glass of champagne, but this
is no chore. Eating a full meal before curtain up is
always a bore, and drinking on an empty stomach
is fraught with difficulty … particularly if you've got

three acts of *Tristan und Isolde* to sit through. A rough-hewn slice of Poilâne sourdough slathered with Bleu d'Auvergne or topped with slivers of salmon gravadlax is the perfect pre-theatre light bite with a glass of Champagne Paul Lebrun or Lacroix Demi-Sec.

A word of caution about being too clever and booking interval drinks at Champagne & Fromage. If you're at the Drury Lane Theatre, this could be a smart move. But unless you're Usain Bolt we wouldn't recommend it for the Royal Opera House.

Champagne & Fromage is open daily and is a super treat for a reviver and a plate of cured meat any time after the sun is over the yardarm (noon). Afternoon tea served with champagne and raspberry macaroons sounds divine. The owners, Maud Fierobe and Stefano Frigerio, opened a branch of Champagne & Fromage in Brixton Village; it didn't go down too well with the locals, being somewhat akin to the *Socialist Worker* opening a drop-in centre in Belgravia. But Champagne & Fromage and Covent Garden go together like Nureyev and Fonteyn.

22 Wellington Street WC2
Tel. 020 7240 1604
Tube: Covent Garden
www.frenchbubbles.co.uk

GALVIN AT WINDOWS ££££

The Park Lane Hilton, a towering concrete monstrosity built in 1963 by the architect William B. Tabler, is one of the few high-rises approved for construction in the West End. It is all the more inexplicable because the Queen's garden behind Buckingham Palace is visible from the upper floors; for that reason, Her Majesty has not attended a function there since it went up. One can almost forgive the Hilton for the kitsch basement bar, Trader Vic's, and the Galvin at Windows bar on the 28th floor. The pull of gravity and a toxic Mai Tai are both hard to resist, but the Windows bar has its own rewards.

Galvin at Windows has spectacular 360-degree views over London, and the bar itself offers a crow's-nest view towards the City. The Hilton's Brutalist exterior belies the beauty and cool 1930s sophistication of the Windows bar interiors. One could almost imagine Clark Gable and Carole Lombard draped across a silver banquette, sipping unspeakably dry Martinis beneath the softly lit rondel on the ceiling. Although the City's skyscrapers have increased the number of 'treetop bars' in town, Windows is the tallest drink in the West End, and the service is as smooth as that of the Michelin-starred restaurant next door.

We don't find the Windows bar a place for large parties or boisterous celebrations; it is rather for drinking a glass of the Widow (£15) with the one you love up in the stars over London. Windows is also a winner when the witching hour is approaching and one wants somewhere civilized to have a nightcap. Later in the week, last orders is at 1.15 am. Should we have been punishing the parquet at a nightclub and be in need of sustenance, the Windows bar offers a chic little menu of lifesaving treats such as devilled Toulouse sausages, cod crackling, Galvin's burger and – perfect with champers – Eton Mess.

Hilton, 22 Park Lane W1
Tel. 020 7208 4021
Tube: Hyde Park Corner
www.galvinatwindows.com

THE OSCAR WILDE BAR ££££

The former Grill Room at the Café Royal – now
rechristened the Oscar Wilde Bar – is sacred ground
in the history of the bohemian West End. The artists
James Abbott McNeill Whistler, Aubrey Beardsley
and Augustus John treated the Café (now a hotel; see
entry) as their clubrooms. It was at the Grill Room
that the 9th Marquess of Queensberry witnessed
his son Lord Alfred and Oscar Wilde dining à deux,
proving that absinthe makes the heart grow fonder.
The sight of the lovers precipitated the trials that
saw Wilde disgraced and imprisoned. Although the
newly restored gilded, mirrored salon with seaside-
postcard Bouchers on the painted ceilings is described
as Louis XVI, the style is really rococo bordello, an
infernally glamorous hall of mirrors.

The Oscar Wilde is reserved for afternoon
tea, champagne and cocktails, and (on Friday and
Saturday) the Black Cat Cabaret's Salon des Artistes.
When we first visited at the tail end of afternoon
tea, throats screaming for a cocktail, there was a
distinct feeling that the transfer between Earl Grey
and bubbly hour was anything but smooth. We were
almost reluctantly served a glass of Veuve Clicquot
Yellow Label (£15 a glass and £70 a bottle), and this
seemed to contradict the 'be our guest' attitude that
is imperative for a smart hotel. On our next visit we
waited until after dark and the old Grill Room began
to work its magic.

We are great believers in dress codes, and
although 'celebrative and sophisticated' is terribly
subjective – suggesting balloons and a party hat – we
applaud the fact that one has to make an effort for
an evening at the Café Royal. The glitter of gold in
mirrored glass, the tinkling of the ivories, the crisp

efficiency of the waiters and an absolutely first-class champagne cocktail remind one of the days when Fanny was by gaslight and Oscar held the entire Grill Room in raptures by dropping perfectly crafted (and rehearsed) aphorisms such as 'I have the simplest tastes. I am always satisfied with the best.' The bar that bears his name is undeniably camp, and lends itself to cabaret. We prefer our artistes on stage or on top of a piano, rather than at large working the tables, so have not had the pleasure of the Salon des Artistes. But the £69 dinner and show ticket does sound tempting, and – like Wilde – we can resist anything but temptation.

> *"The glitter of gold in mirrored glass, the tinkling of the ivories, the crisp efficiency of the waiters ..."*

Café Royal, 68 Regent Street W1
Tel. 020 7406 3310
Tube: Piccadilly Circus
www.hotelcaferoyal.com

Where to drink ... in the company of beautiful people

ARTESIAN £££££

The Langham's Artesian bar is one of the prettiest interiors designed by the late David Collins. The pagoda bar, like a Forbidden City in miniature, is echoed in the chandeliers, and low clamshell-shaped sofas upholstered in lavender leather are a charming counterpoint to silver-leaf *boiserie* and pale, wafting

curtains. It is the perfect meeting point for Soho
and Mayfair, and is the unofficial green room for
Broadcasting House next door. Artesian is the domain
of world-class mixologists Alex Kratena and Simone
Caporale, who have earned *Drinks International*
magazine's 'World's Best Bar' laurels for three
years running.

You don't need Paris to tell you that judgement
comes with consequences. Artesian has earned its
spurs by pushing cocktails far
beyond the confines of
the conventional highball.
The Dorian Gray-inspired
Forever Young is served in a
tumbler concealed by a looking
glass, forcing one to kiss one's
reflection with each sip. The
Above & Beyond is perhaps
the most Heath Robinson
of Kratena and Caporale's
inventions, a cocktail of rum,
Fernet-Branca, crème de
banana and mandarin bitters served with a large
inflatable plastic pillow that pops to release a cloud of
eucalyptus. Further olfactory tricks are served up in a
paper panda-head lantern, a skull wearing a sombrero
and a test tube with sprigs of seasonal herbs.

The question is how far Artesian will have to go
in the pursuit of cocktail-as-performance-art to keep
winning awards. What next: waitresses being forced to
dance a mad voodoo shimmy shawobble while spraying
clouds of Mitsouko? We'd recommend putting the bag
of tricks away. Our senses are perfectly satisfied by a
classic Between the Sheets and a complex Morning
Glory Fizz served the old-fashioned way: in a glass.

> *"The Dorian
> Gray-inspired
> Forever Young
> is served in a
> tumbler concealed
> by a looking glass,
> forcing one to kiss
> one's reflection
> with each sip."*

We very much like the bar's large single balls of ice and exotic touches, such as a passion-fruit island floating in a Martini glass. But producing props like a demented magician's assistant is superfluous to the requirements of a seasoned cocktail drinker. And because solids are supposed to be good for us, we recommend Artesian's club sandwich, lobster BLT and pastrami, sauerkraut and Gruyère on rye.

The Langham, Portland Place W1
Tel. 020 7636 1000
Tube: Oxford Circus
www.artesian-bar.co.uk

BEAUFORT BAR ££££

We have a great fondness for the Savoy's American Bar when we want our liquor hard and our conversation to be heard without bellowing like a fishwife. The ghost of Harry Craddock, who wrote the *Savoy Cocktail Book* in 1930, hovers, and Terry O'Neill's black-and-white portraits of Savoy legends are a pleasing *mise-en-scène* for a Hanky Panky, first concocted by London's first female bar chief, Ada Coleman, in 1903. But for sheer Gershwin glamour, the low-lit, mirrored Beaufort Bar with its dark deco furniture and gold-leaf alcoves is a triumph. Unveiled in 2010, when the Savoy reawakened after an extreme makeover, the Beaufort is on the site of the hotel's famous rising cabaret stage, on which Carroll Gibbons and the Savoy Orpheans performed, Josephine Baker sang and George Gershwin's *Rhapsody in Blue* was introduced to London.

The Beaufort is a masterclass in dramatic lighting. Tables and banquettes are arranged to face a dramatically backlit bar that leaves the rest of the room so dark you can barely see the bill in front of your face ... a mercy, as it happens, when the first cocktail on the list is a £50 Blue Angel, named in honour of Savoy guest Marlene Dietrich, mixed with gin, Martini, Dom Perignon 2006, lemon sorbet and gold leaf. But this is the Savoy. We'd be disappointed if it didn't feature such 'vintage standard' cocktails as Craddock's Satan's Whiskers, mixed with the cache of spirits previously undiscovered in the old cellars. The champagne list is as long as the Gutenberg Bible, rising to a £21,000 climax for a methuselah of Louis Roederer Cristal 2006.

The Beaufort Bar has kept its promise to the Savoy's glorious history. Themed cocktails can be terribly naff, but not when they are those originally mixed at the hotel for Hemingway, Churchill or Sinatra. There isn't enough magic in London, and the Savoy can get away with the Impressionist (served with a red rose and billowing dry ice) because it was Monet's alma mater. Entertainment in the Beaufort can be a little intrusive, and the smart-casual dress code – that ineffable contradiction in terms – is a little too open to interpretation, but the monthly burlesque evenings are an absolute riot. If you can't waft ostrich-feather fans and twinkle a rhinestone G-string at the Savoy, then where in the name of Dita von Teese (who loves the Beaufort Bar) can you?

"... the monthly burlesque evenings are an absolute riot."

The Savoy, Strand, WC2
Tel. 020 7836 4343
Tube: Charing Cross
www.fairmont.com/savoy

EXPERIMENTAL COCKTAIL CLUB £££

In the 1920s Kate Meyrick's 43 Club on Gerrard Street
in Soho was the Charleston and cocaine den of choice
for London's patron saint of hedonism, Tallulah
Bankhead. An element of menace still stalks the
street – the carotid artery of Chinatown – making it
a suitable haunt for a twenty-first-century speakeasy.
Speakeasy-themed bars have come and gone, but
the Experimental Cocktail Club sprawling over a
three-storey town house above no. 13 has survived
and remained in character. The scuffed doorway isn't
signed and a sinister doorman lurks after dark. In
the early days the door policy was brutal, and the
doorman sometimes denied there was anything to see
and moved people on. This is taking the 'knock three
times and ask for Ada' role play a tad too far; it is
acceptable for a private club but not for a cocktail bar,
however clandestine.

We remember this joint with the half-moon
window on the first floor when it served cheap booze
all night and a man was shot dead in the Gents, so
we're not afraid of big bad wolves on the door. On
our last visit to Gerrard Street we breezed past the
doormen unchallenged in a 'king of the monkeys'
fashion after a late supper, remembering why we
first fell in love with it and persevering despite
the bad Edward G. Robinson act on the door. The
Experimental Cocktail Club is licensed until 3 am,
so it's perfect for late-night slumming in Soho. The
first floor is decorated as a cross between a Victorian
pub and an opium den, with exposed brick walls,
exotic Chinese tapestries, a gilded ceiling and a dark
wood bar. We adore candlelight, and wanted to adopt
the moustachioed barmen dressed like extras in *The
Sting*, who recommended a velvety Havana made with

cigar-infused bourbon, marsala and single malt as
a soothing soporific.

The Experimental Cocktail Club was born in
Paris and – low blow alert – that might explain the
flashes of contrary surliness on the door. But now
the heat is off, it has matured into a deliciously shady
joint in which to drink like a grown-up. It works
where other wannabe speakeasies failed because
it is modelled on the real thing, not an am-dram
production of *Bugsy Malone*. A few words on using
vintage spirits from the 1950s and '60s to mix veteran
cocktails: Cannot. See. The. Point. Ladies and
gentlemen, there's a new artisan gin produced every
week in some trendy London distillery or other,
and it's your duty as a serious drinker to support
young enterprise.

13a Gerrard Street W1
Tel. Bookings by email only
Tube: Leicester Square
www.chinatownecc.com

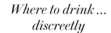

Where to drink ...
discreetly

THE WINE BAR ££

Mayfair might call Fortnum's 'the Queen's grocer'
(as it has been since 1707, when Queen Anne was on
the throne), but we always think of it as a magical
emporium for luxurious, whimsical gifts. We also hold
its below-ground Wine Bar in high esteem because it
was the first place in London that we encountered the
joys of the Wine Flight. Admittedly, the David Collins

interior is an odd one. The walls are lined with planks
of blonde wood, the vaulted ceilings are whitewashed
and a glass wine cooler-cum-workstation flanks the
high marble counter in the centre of the room. Collins
was known for neither minimalism nor parsimony, but
this stripped-back interior works.

In fact, the Wine Bar is as nearly perfect a
subterranean hideaway as it is possible to get should
you require a wine bar that is smart, discreet and
incredibly cosy. We have never yet tested the offer
to buy any bottle from Fortnum's wine department
and drink it in the Wine Bar for a £10 corkage fee,
but have on numerous occasions taken a Wine Flight
... with not a few crash landings. It comprises three
glasses grouped by region or type (reds, whites,
Riesling, rosé, Bordeaux, Pinot Noir, and so on); the
champagne flight is changed monthly. On our last visit
it was Pol Roger (£42) for Vintage 2004, Rich NV and
White Foil Brut NV.

However, we particularly enjoy bunking off work
on a winter's afternoon, ordering a Pinot Noir flight
and making an afternoon of it
while grazing on small plates
devised by chef Shaun Hill from
produce sold in the Fortnum's
food hall. The chorizo with grain
mustard and honey, grilled tiger
prawns and chorizo, patatas
bravas and chicken-liver parfait
are particular favourites and
perennials on a fluid bar menu.
Stay long enough and you may

*"Stay long enough
and you may be
rewarded with an
acoustic guitarist
who plays – quietly
I might add – into
the evening."*

be rewarded with an acoustic guitarist who plays –
quietly I might add – into the evening. Although we
thoroughly enjoy sweeping down to the Wine Bar on

the marble circular staircase, we're often grateful
for the secret staircase that takes one out on to
Jermyn Street via the Fountain restaurant.

Fortnum & Mason, 181 Piccadilly W1
Tel. 020 7734 8040
Tube: Piccadilly Circus
www.fortnumandmason.com

BOOKING OFFICE £££

Was it Patricia Highsmith or Jason Bourne who
famously said that the best place to hide is in public?
W. H. Auden's lines 'Private faces in public places/ Are
wiser and nicer/ Than public faces in private places'
always resonate when we organize an assignation in
a railway station. Sadly, London's main stations are
by and large as grubby, smelly and crowded as the
Jemaa el Fna in Marrakech. Waterloo? My dear!
It's more *Trainspotting* than *Brief Encounter*. But
St Pancras, the cathedral of London stations, is a
true beauty, having had an £800-million facelift
between 2001 and 2007, not to mention the exquisite
restoration and redevelopment of George Gilbert
Scott's Gothic façade as the grand St Pancras
Renaissance hotel.

If we don't wish to be seen, St Pancras station
– gateway to the Continent as well as the northern
heartland of England – is where we head. No need for
dark glasses, berets or the removal of wedding rings;
most people are on the move here, and either much
too excited or too irritated to pay attention to anyone
else. Our favourite spot for a clandestine drink is the
Champagne Bar on the railway concourse mezzanine,
facing the Eurostar arrivals and departures. It is
attached to the St Pancras Grand restaurant, but

we always find the service in the latter disappointing because the trade is by and large transitory. The Champagne Bar staff, on the other hand, are perky to a man, because their punters are usually en route to Paris and in celebratory mood, so tip well.

When we want more privacy, lower lighting and comfier chairs, we drift along the station mezzanine to the side entrance of the Booking Office: the St Pancras Renaissance hotel's bar. We recall this hallway as the old ticket office, and always marvel at the oak linen-fold-panelling booths, Arts and Crafts tiling and high Victorian ceilings. The hotel has kept the listed features and built a smart, dark bar around them, with partitioned tables and discreet corners. Whether or not your intentions are honourable, you can't beat one of the Victorian punch concoctions that have been reimagined for a modern palate. We like the Dickens Memorial Punch (rum, cognac and demerara sugar), which is served by the cup (£9) or the bowl (£100). The Season Ticket (cider, sherry, orange curaçao and lemon) is also a nice icebreaker.

St Pancras Renaissance Hotel, Euston Road NW1
Tel. 020 7841 3566
Tube: King's Cross St Pancras
www.bookingofficerestaurant.com

YE OLDE MITRE £

We'd walked Hatton Garden, London's diamond district, for years without noticing the Ely Court cut, which leads to the city's most clandestine public house. We'd also walked past the gated Ely Place countless times, not realizing that it too hides a passageway that leads to Ye Olde Mitre. The original pub was built in 1546, the twilight of Henry VIII's reign, for the servants of the bishop of Ely, whose palace stood on this site. The façade of oak and leaded windows that we see today was built in 1772, when the Crown sold the lands and demolished the bishop's palace.

Still, the oak-panelled bar and snug with ancient mismatched chairs and tankards hanging from the ceiling beams echo the Tudor original. History buffs will enjoy the sight of a cherry tree trunk trapped behind glass between the outer wall and the front bar, with a sign reading 'The cherry tree marks the boundary between the bishop's garden and the part leased by Sir Christopher Hatton.' Hatton was a favourite of Queen Elizabeth I, who gave him the bishop's lands and was known to have visited him several times, hence the tale that she danced a volta round Ye Olde Mitre's cherry tree. Perhaps she did. Like her mother, Anne Boleyn, Elizabeth I was a mistress of the arts of flirtation and dance.

"After your pint of London Pride, do walk through into Ely Place to view St Ethelreda's church, which was built in the thirteenth century and is the oldest Catholic church in England."

What we like about Ye Olde Mitre is the sanctuary it offers, and we are reliably informed that the draught ales, such as Harvest Pale, Rare Breed and Honey Dew, are decent coves. There's no pretence of being anything other than a solid, traditional pub that will serve you a plate of sausages or a pickled egg with your claret or ale. After your pint of London Pride, do walk through into Ely Place to view St Ethelreda's church, which was built in the thirteenth century and is the oldest Catholic church in England. The church and the vaults beneath – where Henry VIII and Catherine of Aragon feasted in

1531 – are all that's left of the bishop's palace.
The medieval ceiling of the church is one of the
finest in England.

1 Ely Court, Ely Place EC1
Tel. 020 7405 4751
Tube: Chancery Lane
www.yeoldemitreholborn.co.uk

Where to drink ...
in historic interiors

THE FRENCH HOUSE ££

The few regulars who haven't dropped off the perch by
now will agree that the French hasn't looked the same
since the smoking ban. To be honest, we never knew
what it looked like anyway, because the smoke was
always so thick that you couldn't see the hands dipping
into your wallet, your pork scratchings or your Levi's.
Trading since 1910, the French earned its nickname
in 1940 when the exiled General de Gaulle and his
Free French Forces appointed the Soho hostelry as
an alternative headquarters to Carlton House Terrace
during the Second World War. It was said that de
Gaulle wrote his 'France has lost a battle. But France
will not lose the war' radio address here. (Presumably
nobody responded with 'It's the drink talking.') The
pub was actually called the York Minster, and it wasn't
officially rechristened the French House until 1984.

The French's noble war record was eclipsed in the
second half of the twentieth century when a generation
of drunken, promiscuous, marauding artists, actors
and writers adopted the pub that famously won't serve

pints (the bar area is minuscule) and specializes in vino, spirits and Ricard. Francis Bacon and George Dyer, Lucian Freud, Oliver Reed, Peter O'Toole, Jeffrey Bernard and Richard Burton were all alumni of the French, as are pop, art and fashion flotsam Lisa Stansfield, Suggs, Pam Hogg and Damien Hirst. The ground-floor bar is still packed and poky, with sepia photographs all over the walls and a series of waist-high hatches open to the street so that those inside can fraternize with their smoking chums outside. We're sure more Ricard is consumed here than anywhere else in Britain.

The dining room upstairs has gone through many incarnations, including a brief moment in the sun as Polpetto. It was run by a rather harassed group of ladies on our last visit, and although the food was pleasant the atmosphere was austere and unwelcoming. We couldn't wait to get back downstairs, where – at £25 a pop – it would have constituted criminal negligence not to write off the afternoon to tuck into another bottle of Mâcon-Villages 2012. The French serves more than thirty champagnes and wines by the glass, although we suspect this is a ploy to make regulars like you and me feign responsibility then admit defeat after the sixth glass and order by the gallon. All together now: 'You talkin' to me?'

49 Dean Street W1
Tel. 020 7437 2477
Tube: Leicester Square
www.frenchhousesoho.com

THE TEN BELLS £

Since we're not of a superstitious bent, there aren't many historic buildings in London that bring out the

Madame Arcati in us. But one Victorian East End pub genuinely chills to the marrow. Stand under the faded signage for the Ten Bells public house, in the shadow of Hawksmoor's Christ Church, Spitalfields, on a black night, and tell us you don't feel it too. It was on this corner of Commercial and Fournier streets in 1888 that the prostitute Mary Kelly plied her trade and was last seen before her murder at the hands of Jack the Ripper. Her friend and fellow victim 'Black Annie' Chapman had taken a last drink at the Ten Bells before being cast out into the night; her mutilated body was discovered just before 6 am in a yard behind neighbouring Hanbury Street.

"Only a plaque naming the Ripper's victims acknowledges the Ten Bells' macabre history, but the pub certainly doesn't need ghoulish memorabilia to have presence."

Only a plaque naming the Ripper's victims acknowledges the Ten Bells' macabre history, but the pub certainly doesn't need ghoulish memorabilia to have presence. It has a quiet, melancholy dignity that we find satisfying as well as unsettling. The spartan bare floorboards, wooden furniture and witness-box bar flanked by a looking-glass panel are much as they would have been in the 1880s. It is poignant to think that the glorious High Victorian tiled walls and gaily coloured mural *Spitalfields in ye Olden Times* would have provided Mary Kelly and Annie Chapman with the only colour and comfort in their otherwise grim lives.

On a lighter note, the restaurant Upstairs at the Ten Bells caused a sensation in 2011/12 when the Young Turks collective (Isaac McHale, Daniel Willis and Johnny Smith) ran the austere second-floor dining room as a pop-up. The pop-up is now permanent and perfectly decent, but we prefer to direct you towards McHale's Clove Club in Shoreditch Town Hall (see **Restaurants**). As for London pubs of historic provenance, we are spoilt for choice, although many are much later pastiches of earlier periods. For the genuine articles, may we suggest the riverside Tudor inn the Prospect of Whitby in Wapping; London's last galleried coaching inn, the George in Borough High Street; or the City's one surviving Victorian gin palace, the Viaduct opposite the Old Bailey.

84 Commercial Street E1
Tel. 07530 492986
Tube: Liverpool Street
www.tenbells.com

YE OLDE CHESHIRE CHEESE £

Harold Clunn writes in his excellent *The Face of London* (1970): 'A peculiarity of Fleet Street is the long unbroken stretch of buildings extending from Shoe Lane to Fetter Lane without any side streets, but containing a veritable warren of courts and alleys, guaranteed to confuse even a regular frequenter.' Down one such pickpocket's alley, Wine Office Court, lurks Ye Olde Cheshire Cheese. Above ground, the oak-panelled warren of snugs, chop rooms, private dining rooms and bedchambers dates from 1667, when the pub was rebuilt after the Great Fire of London. The Cheshire Cheese is perennially dark because it is permanently overshadowed, making a necessity of open fires and candlelight that lend the murky corners a picaresque quality. Sawdust is still scattered on the bowed floorboards as it was in the days when

William Thackeray and Dr Johnson frequented the pub. Although Dickens was what we'd call a regular, Johnson, who lived in nearby Gough Court, is the pub's literary father. His chair lives in the Chop Room below a reproduction portrait.

Those who venture down the narrow, rickety stairs will be rewarded by two cellar storeys with whitewashed vaulted ceilings that are thought to be the foundations of a thirteenth-century Carmelite monastery once on this site. We braved the cellar bar with its refectory tables for a most acceptable pie and a pint. Ye Olde Cheshire Cheese is still popular with the solicitors of the Temple across the road, but all the pubs in Fleet Street are much diminished since the exodus of the newspaper offices that lined the street well into the 1980s. Evelyn Waugh painted an amusing picture of pre-war Fleet Street in *Scoop* (1938), and one can well imagine 'Boot of *The Beast*' getting lost in search of Ye Olde Cheshire Cheese. Then, Fleet Street's taverns were where London's press and power brokers intrigued, and Ye Olde Cheshire Cheese apparently had phone lines installed for every major newspaper so the editor could contact an errant or inebriated hack.

> *"Sawdust is still scattered on the bowed floorboards as it was in the days when William Thackeray and Dr Johnson frequented the pub."*

The fact that William Caxton's apprentice Wynkyn de Worde set up the first printing press in London on Fleet Street, near Shoe Lane, in 1500 makes the loss of the newspaper trade all the more tragic. Stroll down Fleet Street after your drink and you'll see the sinuous chromium-and-clear-glass art

deco façade of the former Express Building. But inside
Ye Olde Cheshire Cheese you're in the era of Johnson,
Boswell and Goldsmith. It hasn't changed since
Old & New London (1878) described it thus: 'A little
lop-sided, wedged-up house that always reminds
you, structurally, of a high-shouldered man with his
hands in his pockets.' On a cold winter's night there's
nowhere as cosy as the high-backed settle booths in
the Chop Room for mulled wine and mutton stew.

145 Fleet Street EC4
Tel. 020 7353 6170
Tube: Temple

Where to drink ... for a touch of camp cabaret

CAFÉ DE PARIS £££

In the depths below Piccadilly, the Café de Paris was
once the queen of the night: a cabaret and supper
club that opened in 1924 but was designed in the belle
époque style of a Parisian dance hall. The two-tiered,
pillared horseshoe of supper tables surrounds the
oval dance floor, toplit by a magnificent chandelier.
A sinuous split staircase sweeps around the stage from
a Moulin Rouge-style gilded orchestra balcony. Film
buffs will recognize the Café from countless movies,
although none are so evocative of its glory days as the
silent *Piccadilly* (1929), starring the exotic Anna May
Wong as a tragic cabaret queen.

In the 1930s the Café was patronized by the
young royal set surrounding the Prince of Wales
(later King Edward VIII) and the Earl and Countess

of Mountbatten, who invariably ordered a dozen and a half oysters and steak Diane as a midnight snack. Cole Porter introduced some of his most famous compositions at the piano here and, despite a direct hit during the Blitz that killed eighty guests, the Café rose from the ashes to become the most famous cabaret stage in London in the 1950s. Grace Kelly, the Aga Khan, Princess Margaret and the Oliviers would gather to see masters in the art of song interspersed with affable conversation from such figures as Noël Coward, Marlene Dietrich and Hermione Gingold.

The Café has survived disco, the Blitz, the club-kid phenomenon, techno and trashy raves relatively unscathed. In 2002 it was restored by its current owner, Brian Stein, and that year it celebrated its eightieth birthday with Dita von Teese performing her infamous Martini-glass striptease. With the London Cabaret Society and Showtime Cabaret Club now in residence, it is business as usual at the Café. A word of caution, though: dinner and a show begins at £75 and the sword-swallowers, strippers, fire-eaters and magicians on the bill are more Benidorm Palace than Moulin Rouge. The curse of the hen party has struck the Café de Paris, so we prefer a glass of champagne and a toast to Marlene from a balcony seat to salute this plucky, lucky survivor.

3 Coventry Street W1
Tel. 020 7734 7700
Tube: Piccadilly Circus
www.cafedeparis.com

CELLAR DOOR ££

It's not the most savoury of subjects, but the lack of public lavatories in London is approaching a scandal.

Those that survive charge 50p and are guarded by turnstile. It's a salutary lesson that if one is suitably dressed, one can always dive into the nearest ritzy hotel should one be caught at a disadvantage. Still, it's an ill wind and all that. In the 1960s the gentlemen's loo at the crossroads of Aldwych and Strand was a popular assignation point for such theatrical types as *Entertaining Mr Sloane* playwright Joe Orton. It would please Orton's sense of the absurd that mischief is still made in the basement bunker that now plays host to the Cellar Door cabaret and cocktail club.

'Just big enough for cats to swing', according to its website, Cellar Door is a Weimar-era Berlin meets Warhol's Factory hot box that hits the spot should you dive like a kestrel down the lavatory stairs in desperate need of a Negroni and a mad half hour. The cocktail list is exhausting and progresses from a classic Old Fashioned, Manhattan or Brown Derby to wild, wonderful house specialities with imaginative names like Never Trust a Flamingo, Gingerbread Ladyboy and Vampire's Kiss. Even the American Bar at the Savoy would struggle with such an ambitious list, hence our recommendation that you visit the Cellar Door for a quickie or stick to the same poison if you're going to get down and dirty with the drag queens, show girls, illusionists and acrobats.

"Just big enough for cats to swing ..."

Cabaret is committed nightly until 1 am, and we defy anyone in London's nightworld to resist a club night called Saturday Night Diva. Cellar Door has Life's a Drag for your delectation on Mondays, the Kit Kat Kabaret on Thursdays and a tasty open-mike night called Trash Tuesday hosted by the lovely

Champagne Charlie. Open mike takes karaoke skills to another level and is not for the faint-hearted or weak of vocal cords: many of the Cellar Door's Trash Tuesday punters are show boys and girls who bring their own sheet music. We've never been to Sunday Cinema, but love the idea of cult classic home movies shown on a projector in a former public convenience underneath Aldwych. It's more *Barbarella* and *Myra Breckinridge* than *Citizen Kane* and *Battleship Potemkin*, but *honi soit qui mal y pense*.

Zero Aldwych WC2
Tel. 020 7240 8848
Tube: Covent Garden/Temple
www.cellardoor.biz

THE CRAZY COQS £££

The lavish late-night showgirl spectacular belongs to Paris and the intimate supper-club cabaret to New York. Apart from a little drag and a pinch of jazz, however, London's cabaret scene has struggled since 1960. It was pronounced dead in 2010, when Pizza on the Park closed, where George Melly, Cleo Laine, Steve Ross and Barbara Cook all performed. In recent years we've seen a flurry of feather boas and the glint of rhinestone pasties as burlesque insinuated itself into the bars of our grander hotels the Rosewood, Savoy and Dorchester. But what London was lacking was a velvet-curtained cabaret clubroom for singers and musicians, like Feinstein's, the Rainbow Room or Don't Tell Mama in Manhattan. Not any more.

When Corbin and King took over the former Regent Palace Hotel's subterranean ballroom to open Brasserie Zedel (see **Restaurants**), they put pleasure above profit and dedicated a divinely sexy circular

room at the foot of a sweeping staircase to cabaret.
Christened the Crazy Coqs, it has interiors that are a
reimagining of Oliver Percy Bernard's 1930s art deco
hotel bar Chez Cup. The coqs in question are a neon-
light doodle on the room's original clock. The room
is a mad jazz pattern of lacquered black, white and
silver stripes and thick red-velvet curtains. Banquettes
facing the low stage snake around the perimeter
towards the bar, and café tables are dotted around the
room, which comfortably seats sixty. The bar staff are
a little more jazz hands than Corbin and King's usual
poker-faced professionals, and are as much part of the
show as the pros.

The Crazy Coqs is already much loved by West
End and Broadway stars who shine in those intimate
'evening with' floor shows, such as Issy van Randwyck,
Lorna Luft, Brent Barrett and Gary Williams.
Although the belting divas – Liza, Bernadette, Patti,
Idina et al – would be fabulous
in Crazy Coqs, they are simply
too big for supper clubs these
days, unless you catch them
after a show being invited to
sing. The club already has a
stable of performers, including
John Standing, Barb Junger,
Joe Stilgoe and Miss Hope
Springs, who call the Crazy Coqs
home. On Thursdays, West End
chorus boys and girls flock to the late-night open-
mike evenings to test new material, and Crazy Coqs
occasionally improvises as a private cinema, showing
such Hollywood classics as *Casablanca*, *Some Like
It Hot* and *Singin' in the Rain*. Doubtless Corbin and
King could make a ton of money turning Crazy Coqs

*"... West End
chorus boys and
girls flock to the
late-night open-
mike evenings
to test new
material ..."*

into another bar, but they love a cabaret as much as
London and Liza.

Brasserie Zedel, 20 Sherwood Street W1
Tel. 020 7734 4888
Tube: Piccadilly Circus
www.brasseriezedel.com/crazy-coqs

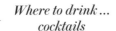

Where to drink …
cocktails

69 COLEBROOKE ROW £££

When the Savoy's barman Harry Craddock was
asked how best to drink a cocktail, he replied:
'Quickly while it's laughing at you.' Craddock
prefaced his *Savoy Cocktail Book* (1930) with the
legend 'Hereinafter learn all that is known about
cocktails.' Tony Conigliaro of 69 Colebrooke Row
appears to have taken up the challenge and moved
the cocktail beyond spirits, sugar, water and bitters
on ice. We first encountered his cocktail-laboratory
creations at the Zetter Townhouse, where we were
sent into raptures by a concoction of Beefeater gin,
gunpowder tea, dandelion and burdock, and Fernet
Branca. We'd only ordered it in homage to genius
comic writer James Hamilton-Paterson's *Cooking
with Fernet Branca*, but one taste sent us on an
alcoholic journey in the manner of Alice through
the looking-glass. We resolved to visit Conigliaro's
Islington headquarters, and went in search of the
lantern and red Martini awning. We also booked
a table, thinking that boded well for an evening of
elegant, grown-up entertainment.

People come to 69 Colebrooke Row for cocktail conversation, 'Juke Joint Gentleman' Mr Maurice Horhut tickling the ivories and, of course, the strange and extraordinary libations designed by Conigliaro. As devotees of Bob Fosse's film *Cabaret* (1972) we were thrilled to see Sally Bowles's favourite pick-me-up, the Prairie Oyster, on the menu. What appeared to be an egg yolk served on a porcelain oyster shell was in fact a delicate globule of vodka and tomato in gelatine spiced up with fiery horseradish. Divine decadence, darling! The Woodland Martini confirmed Conigliaro's status as the Heston Blumenthal of the cocktail universe: gin and amontillado flavoured and fragranced with 'woodland bitters' referencing maple, cedar and redwood. The gentlemen of our party preferred the Death in Venice, a classic Campari and Prosecco cocktail kissed by grapefruit bitters and an orange twist.

> *"The Woodland Martini confirmed Conigliaro's status as the Heston Blumenthal of the cocktail universe ..."*

We relish the theatricality of the Zetter Townhouse, but No. 69 is Tony Conigliaro's home turf, and the bar room, which accommodates no more than forty with comfort and acceptable sound levels, has a certain *Le Chat Noir* charm about it. We're not over keen on the Essex Road after dark, and did momentarily think we'd prefer to sample No. 69's high level of cocktail concocting in an equally high-voltage interior such as the Mandarin Bar in Knightsbridge's Mandarin Oriental. Then again, there's pleasure in cocktails mixed in a straight-up kind of joint that keeps the pretension and the prices to a minimum. House cocktails at Colebrooke Row are

£9.50. You wouldn't get a slice of lemon for less than that in SW1.

69 Colebrooke Row N1
Tel. 07540 528593
Tube: Angel
www.69colebrookerow.com

THE MERCHANT HOUSE ££

Like Guns N' Roses, 'the British Empire was established on a thirst for adventure and trade fuelled by gin and rum. The histories of these fine libations are intertwined through merchant life shaping a world of commerce and expedition.' Thus the Merchant House introduces its cargo of over 250 premium and rare-as-hens'-teeth bottles of gin, rum and other blithe spirits to complement the two titans of the Englishman's drinks cabinet. The Merchant House is hidden down a shamble of alleyways off Bow Lane, and the most expedient way to find it is to locate the spire of St Mary-le-Bow and ask. We got lost twice looking for the infernal place, but once we found it we were pleased we hadn't given up.

Having heard a little about the colonial, swashbuckling, East Indian seafaring theme of the Merchant House, we were expecting nothing less than *Pirates of the Caribbean*. What we discovered in the candlelit basement bar below the shopfront was not so much a bar as an altar to Bacchus, with tier upon tier of artfully lit multicoloured glass bottles, including an intriguing bootleg gin packaged in a brown paper bag. The cavernous suite of cellar rooms is furnished with tobacco-leather chesterfields, a battered upright piano, the odd stack of clothbound books about wars and expeditions, and occasional posies of fresh flowers in porcelain jugs. It's moody, but convivial rather than theatrical.

Any barman who plays Ella Fitzgerald's Cole Porter recordings is our kind of barman. We particularly liked our guy, who introduced us to it 'both ways'. Let us explain. 'Both ways' is a neat serving of the poison that bit you to accompany the cocktail in which it is mixed. One has to think of the Merchant House as a library of gin. The barman will work like a bespoke perfumer to mix a drink that has just the right balance of strength and substance. We wanted to be amused by a gin infused with ginger, rosemary and pepper. Our barman produced a great favourite – Berry Bros & Rudd's King's Ginger cordial, made for Edward VII – and proceeded to mix a cocktail that made us wonder whether to drink it or dab it behind our ears. The Merchant House is a serious to-order cocktail bar, and for its skill and bravery, we salute it.

13 Well Court, off Bow Lane EC4
Tel. 020 7332 0044
Tube: Mansion House
www.merchanthouselondon.com

WORSHIP STREET WHISTLING SHOP ££

Much has been made of the twenty-first-century 'Ginaissance' in London with young independent distillers Sipsmith, the London Distillery Company, Jensen's and the East London Liquor Company creating connoisseur infusions. Many have tried to re-create the nostalgic 'corsets, looking-glass and gaslight' glow of the city's old gin palaces, with mixed success. Those who appreciate authenticity should look no further than the Salisbury on the corner of St Martin's Lane, decorated in 1898 with gilded cherubs holding glowing etched-glass globes and acres of mirror. Film buffs will recognize the Salisbury from Dirk Bogarde's film *Victim* of 1961. But we digress. However pretty, the Salisbury is a traditional pub. For full immersion in the gin-drinking East End hipster scene, we always don our tweed caps and instruct our driver to take us to the Worship Street Whistling Shop.

Worship Street isn't a gin palace per se, but it is a handsome evocation of an underground Victorian tavern kitted out with glazed wood panelling, standard lamps, mismatched nineteenth-century furniture and intriguing nooks. We love the drama of the private Dram Shop, with a bath still as a centrepiece and wax-sealed bottles in the gin closet offering the libation once sold as 'drunk for a penny' and 'dead drunk for two pence'. At the height of London's gin epidemic (circa 1751, when William Hogarth drew the nightmarish *Gin Lane*), the noxious spirit rotted the mind and body and was flavoured with peppermint to mask the foul taste. Infusions today make gin an art form, and we do appreciate the Whistling Shop's own Cream Gin – clear, despite its name, but touched with velvety richness – but tend to order the house Gin Fizz mixed with Tanqueray No. Ten.

> *"… wax-sealed bottles in the gin closet offering the libation once sold as 'drunk for a penny' and 'dead drunk for two pence'."*

Like other neo-gin palaces in the East End, the Whistling Shop prides itself on making its own bitters, syrups and mixers, with a little more personality than Schweppes. This artisanal approach to cocktails,

which some dismissed as a fad, appears to be no such
thing. One doesn't mind paying more than £10 for
a cocktail if it is made with a very, very, very large
measure, an interesting combination of flavours and
a huge amount of skill. Londoners and our regular
guests know that alcohol is one of the city's biggest
swindles. The £20 G&T made with a measure of
mass-produced gin and Schweppes tonic is basically
the Dick Turpin of the cocktail world. You have been
robbed. We like to drink where we can see the barman
work and where we know the ingredients are bespoke.

63 Worship Street EC2
Tel. 020 7247 0015
Tube: Old Street
www.whistlingshop.com

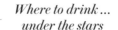

Where to drink ...
under the stars

KENSINGTON ROOF GARDENS £££

Clichéd it may be, but we can only liken the wonder
on first seeing the 1½-acre pleasure gardens on
top of the old Derry & Toms department store on
Kensington High Street to *The Wizard of Oz*. You truly
do leave the sepia world at street level and emerge in
glorious Technicolor. Pink flamingos (two of whom are
christened Splosh and Pecks) roam free in miniature
lakes stocked with fish. Mature trees planted by the
landscape architect Ralph Hancock in 1936 flourish
in nearly 5 feet of soil. A formal Spanish Garden with
flamingo-pink walls has an ornamental fountain and is
planted with palm, fig and olive trees, while crumbling

faux-Tudor red-brick walls and arches introduce
an English Woodland Garden. If Spain's Alhambra
Palace and Sudeley Castle had a child, Kensington
Roof Gardens would be the result.

The much-loved Roof Gardens are terribly
fortunate to have survived. Before Hancock was
commissioned, he masterminded an extraordinary
'Around the World in Eighty Days' enfilade of gardens
on top of the Rockefeller Center
in New York. Very little is left
of that grandiose scheme,
whereas the Roof Gardens have
been tended by tenants such
as Barbara Hulanicki's Biba
(the design team worked in the
old Tea Pavilion) and Regine's
nightclub. Richard Branson
acquired the Roof Gardens in 1981 and has protected
Hancock's legacy since, under the direction of head
gardener David Lewis. Lewis has restored various
lost elements, such as the box hedging, and enhanced
the collection of lavender, wisteria and roses in our
favourite part, the Tudor Garden.

> *"... the Roof
> Gardens have been
> tended by tenants
> such as Barbara
> Hulanicki's Biba ..."*

The pavilion at the heart of the gardens is a
private members' nightclub (open on Friday and
Saturday from 10 pm to 3 am) that's had rather a
revival now the princes William and Harry and the
Duchess of Cambridge have chosen Kensington Palace
as their official London residence. But God forbid we
suggest you insinuate yourself with a pack of honking
great Sloanes in order to enjoy the gardens. The
restaurant, Babylon, on the top tier of the pavilion
overlooks the English Woodland Garden and has
a fabulously smart al fresco cocktail terrace. We
recommend you book for dinner and walk the gardens,

champagne flute in hand, well before 10 pm, when the
Made in Chelsea set come out to play.

99 Kensington High Street W8
Tel. 020 7368 3993
Tube: Kensington High Street
www.roofgardens.virgin.com

RUMPUS ROOM £££

Our eyebrows arch when a new bar or nightclub seeks
to 'capture the essence' of the 1920s and the Bright
Young Things. The BYTs were a generation who'd
seen their elder brothers slain in the trenches and
who danced, drank and dashed at an insane pace
from Park Lane mansions to Brixton Black and Tan
clubs in order to forget. As Evelyn Waugh pointed out
in his dissection of the BYTs, *Vile Bodies* (1930), the
frantic, drunken antics of the jaded, lost youth who
lived to punish the parquet weren't half as much fun
as they looked. Besides, that 'flash in time' can't be
replicated any more than Tramp in the early 1970s or
the Atlantic in the early 1990s. So we were sceptical
about Mondrian London's decision to call the glass
cube on top of the old Sea Containers House the
Rumpus Room and reference the bright young things,
champagne cocktails and 'a time when a party was
more than a party'.

   We suspect that Mondrian will quietly drop
the marketing about flappers and dapper chaps in
monocles, because the vast glass Rumpus Room
is gloriously futuristic, more like a planetarium by
night. The views over the Thames towards St Paul's
and the City make one feel as if one is on the Bund
in Shanghai, though we sincerely hope the high-rises
aren't allowed to scrape any more sky in the near

future. There's a long outside terrace that we've yet to try without the benefit of mink, but it could be the most coveted real estate in London for cocktail drinkers come high summer. The banquette and red velvet vibe rather contradicts the design of the Rumpus Room, and we'd have been tempted to go to the other extreme by referencing Ludwig Mies van der Rohe and the Palm Springs Modern movement. In time maybe they will.

It is a concern for the Mondrian that not only has planning permission been given to develop the south side of the hotel, but also the site has been snapped up. When we visited the Rumpus Room and looked skyward, we could already see a vast concrete trunk thrusting up above Sea Containers House. It's quite a striking sight, as it happens, but not one we'd ever wished to see in the heart of London. Still, the construction of Mondrian London is spectacular, the Morgans Group has given us a much-needed new rooftop bar and the Rumpus Room was just settling its feathers when we popped in for a Red Rum Royale. So let's wish it well and look forward to seeing the Mondrian London when the hype has died down.

Mondrian Hotel, 20 Upper Ground SE1
Tel. 020 3747 1000
Tube: Waterloo
www.mondrianlondon.com

RADIO ROOFTOP BAR ££££

What is it about rooftop bars that make folk think they are modelling for a luxury yacht brochure? Perhaps London's peripatetic weather makes us stampede like determined wildebeest to the few decent terraces with spectacular views and, once ensconced, act like

Aristotle Onassis on board the *Christina*. We like the view from Vista on top of the Trafalgar Hotel, which places us eye to eyepatch with E. H. Bailey's sandstone statue of Nelson on top of his column. But the terrace is entirely open to the elements, and the cat is long out of the bag about this 'best-kept secret'. We turn instead, therefore, to the Foster & Partners-designed ME London hotel on the turn from the Strand to Aldwych.

ME London sits on hallowed ground. In 1903 the magnificent Richard Norman Shaw-designed new Gaiety Theatre was built on the site of the old Strand Music Hall. The Gaiety was demolished in 1958 and replaced by the impressive English Electric Company building. Foster's ME London hotel has a decidedly pale and uninteresting exterior that contributes precisely nothing to the area, but the observation deck on top is rewarding. On taking the express lift to the tenth floor of the hotel, you step on to a wraparound terrace surrounding a glass pavilion.

Radio has all the poise of a glacial Nordic blonde at a boat show. Low sofas with white-leather cushions and faux-chinchilla throws form intimate enclosures surrounding cocktail tables, and the 180-degree views from this modest height are, we think, perfection. Looking down from the Shard or the City skyscrapers makes London look like an ants' circus, but from Radio you feel like a commodore standing at the prow of a ship. When Radio first opened there was a purser with a clipboard bossing the passengers and telling them where to sit, and we also had the pleasure of a rather overenthusiastic DJ, who mistakenly thought he'd been booked to play Pacha in the Balearics. It has since calmed down. We do like to watch the sun set from here as the lanterns are lit and the city begins to sparkle like crystal. Radio is a particular delight in the winter, when the courtyard of Somerset House directly below is turned into an ice rink and lit like a funfair.

ME London, 336–337 Strand WC2
Tel. 020 7395 3440
Tube: Temple
www.melia.com

Where to drink ...
in evening dress

THE CONNAUGHT BAR £££££

If you'd like to show off your London Knowledge at the Connaught, turn right instead of left past reception and head towards the little-known candlelit Champagne Room, which seats twenty-five. The booth/bar in the corner gleams like the haunch of a Pullman railway carriage, and the list of champagne is first class. Eight prestige champagnes begin with Krug (£40 for a glass, £210 a bottle), and the forty rare vintages sold by the bottle include a £750 Vintage Pol Roger Sir Winston Churchill 1986 (Churchill famously drank his Pol for breakfast in a silver tankard, as they do at the Garrick Club).

Those who simply like to show off turn left for the staccato glamour of the Connaught Bar, which was decorated by David Collins in 2008. We say 'staccato' because the Connaught Bar has a sharp, angular quality inspired by Cubism that is as buffed and burnished as the exquisites who choose to drink here. The interiors and service – best described as White Star liner circa 1930 – shame anyone not

dressed to the nines to beat a hasty retreat back
out on to Mount Street. It is a thrill to be offered a
piquant little reviver by your waiter before ordering
the first cocktail, and the selection of *amuse-bouches*
devised by Connaught chef Hélène Darroze (duck
foie gras terrine, salmon tartare served with caviar
and horseradish dill cream) is a touch of pure class.
The maestro (or master mixologist) Agostino Perrone
has conducted the Connaught Bar since it opened,
and it is he who introduced the Martini Trolley (a
Ferrari, compared to Dukes Bar's vintage Bugatti),
upon which he stirs a lethal Tanqueray No. Ten gin
Martini, adding house infusions such as lavender,
cardamom and ginger should you so wish. Martini
drinkers, after all, have stronger opinions about the
perfect taste and temperature than Catholics do about
transubstantiation, so each to their own. But we're
of the opinion that any addition to a classic Martini
is a fleeting pleasure. We swooned on first tasting
cucumber in a G&T, but soon came to our senses and
reverted to lemon. At the Connaught you are in the
hands of the SAS of cocktail barmen, rather than mere
foot soldiers. Our favourite game is to name a base
(gin, vodka, whisky) plus a couple of high notes (lime,
mint) and leave the boys to improvise. They are never
out of tune.

The Connaught, Carlos Place W1
Tel. 020 7499 7070
Tube: Bond Street
www.the-connaught.co.uk

DUKES BAR ££££

Like the nimble tread of the feet of Fred Astaire,
Dukes Bar is quite simply the top. Cole Porter, who

wrote that lyric, had his shoes made across the road
at Lobb, although history doesn't record whether he
was a Dukes man. Ian Fleming was, however, and
drank the Martinis that he would place in the hand
of his hero James Bond. The Dukes Martini has since
become a London rite of passage for dapper chaps,
on a par with having a shirt made at 007's tailor,
Turnbull & Asser, and buying the spy's preferred
scent, Floris 89, on Jermyn Street.

It is facile to analyse what makes Dukes Bar
the best in London, if not in Europe. Its head
barman, Alessandro Palazzi,
is an alumnus of the Paris Ritz
Hemingway Bar, the Dorchester
and the Savoy. He is the godfather
– the Pappy – of London's
cocktail barmen. Having a
Martini mixed by Palazzi on the
low wooden trolley wheeled to
the table is poetry in motion.
A Dukes Martini, mixed with
Berry Bros No. 3 gin and Sacred
vermouth and served in a frozen
glass, is (to quote an esteemed
regular) like 'kissing the razor
blade'. One is not enough and
three are too many, so a segue into champagne or Her
Majesty's favourite, Dubonnet and gin, is advisable.

> "A Dukes Martini,
> mixed with Berry
> Bros No. 3 gin and
> Sacred vermouth
> and served in a
> frozen glass, is (to
> quote an esteemed
> regular) like
> 'kissing the razor
> blade'."

Although the walls of the three rooms that
comprise Dukes are adorned with fine oils and antique
prints of British dukes, the bar is not grandiose.
Standards are maintained, however, and the service
is immaculately old-school. There is no piped music,
and ebullient guests who raise their voices are quietly
and kindly asked to turn the volume down. Tables

can't be reserved and guests must be seated, so there is never a question of Dukes becoming boisterous or crowded. Our favourite seats are the two by the fireplace, since they allow a swift exit to the courtyard for a cigarette. It goes without saying that change at Dukes Bar is rarely welcome. The fringed curtains that were recently hung seem as inappropriate as a fart at a funeral, and the framed photograph of Sean Connery as Bond in the vestibule is a tad gratuitous. But as Joe E. Brown said at the end of *Some Like It Hot*, 'nobody's perfect.'

Dukes Hotel, 35 St James's Place SW1
Tel. 020 7491 4840
Tube: Green Park
www.dukeshotel.com

SCARFES BAR £££

London's hotel bars are some of the city's most sacred spaces. They satisfy particular moods. For a discreet Martini in patrician surroundings, one relies on Dukes Bar. If you're feeling amorous, the Savoy's sinfully glamorous Beaufort Bar is sufficiently lowlit for seduction. When life becomes film noir, there's Claridge's Fumoir to serve hard liquor in heavy Lalique crystal glasses, and the world-class Artesian bar at the Langham lifts the spirits with cocktails that could be mistaken for installation art. What, one wonders, can a new hotel bar do to compete with the premier league? If you're Rosewood London you keep your powder dry.

We first visited the bar at Rosewood London in 2013 in the company of its dashing managing director, Matthias Roeke. We enjoyed the mood of lazy, colonial languor enhanced by high ceilings, whip-smart waiters and the casually luxurious interior. Sipping a G&T and sharing bar snacks inspired by Indian street food, we felt like a disreputable aristocratic family who had absconded to Nairobi in its Happy Valley heyday. The light was as low as the velvet banquettes, allowing showpieces such as the long bar, library and fireplace to glow. We returned several times, but were drawn to the quieter, smarter Mirror Room beyond the hotel reception. In a stroke of genius, Rosewood's bar reinvented itself in April 2014 as Scarfes Bar, and it is a triumph. The only thing we don't like about it is the missing apostrophe in the name. The Scarfe in question is the political cartoonist Gerald Scarfe, the Cruikshank of contemporary London. His satirical cartoons have appeared in the *Sunday Times* for forty-four years, and now Rosewood's bar is his personal art gallery. The hotel commissioned Scarfe to paint a series of canvas panels that decorate the bar and delight the eye.

In a single *coup de théâtre*, Rosewood has given its bar personality – or rather multiple personalities – with gloriously irreverent cartoons of the Queen, the Beckhams, the Duchess of Cornwall, Prince George, Mick Jagger, Simon Cowell, Margaret Thatcher, David Cameron and Boris Johnson, to name a few. Scarfe promises to keep sketching newsworthy heroes and villains for his 'Current Affairs' and 'Artfully Current' corner canvases. Hats off to Rosewood for finding a way to connect the bar with London's past and its present. The hotel can't compete with the illustrious guestbooks of the Savoy or Claridge's, and the building itself has little history of note, but commissioning Scarfe nods to Bloomsbury's history as a home for diarists, satirists and, incidentally, the Cartoon Museum at 35 Little Russell Street, where

Scarfe's works are displayed. Although one wouldn't call Scarfes Bar a sacred space quite yet, an evening of Bunga Bunga cocktails in the company of the house chanteuse, Kitty LaRoar, is indecently good fun.

Rosewood London, 252 High Holborn WC1
Tel. 020 3747 8611
Tube: Holborn
www.scarfesbar.com

<hr />

Where to drink ...
if you want to dance

CLUB ROOM ££££

There is a dearth of grown-up London nightclubs, by which we mean natty little late-night supper clubs with whip-smart service, chilled champagne and a small dance floor. Perhaps this is because what used to be called the beau monde in the 1920s now all have occupations and don't relish a post-theatre white-tie supper and dance at the Embassy Club, Café de Paris or Quaglino's. It just strikes us that if there were more elegant places to dance after 11 pm, we would patronize them. Of course there are the classics, Annabel's (estalished 1963) on Berkeley Square and Tramp (1969) on Jermyn Street, but these private members' clubs are more *The Stud* and *The Bitch* than *Swing Time*.

We were dining at Bob Bob Ricard in late summer 2014 when glamour-puss owners Leonid Shutov and Richard Howarth casually asked if we'd like to see the new Club Room downstairs. The stairwell of Bob Bob is like the inside of an exquisite mirrored black-lacquer box, so it was all the more dramatic when the double doors flew open to reveal the perfect subterranean supper club. A sprung mahogany dance floor inlaid with backgammon-board marquetry is sunken centre stage, and surrounded by a glistening copper balconette and gold booths upholstered in scarlet leather, seating parties of eight around tables of claret marble. A bar ablaze with backlighting runs across one wall, a mirrored ceiling reflects the dance floor below and jazzy red ikat wallpaper adds exoticism to the opulence.

If Coco Chanel and Prince Felix Yusupov (the man who murdered Rasputin) had opened a nightclub together, this would be it. The 'Press for Champagne' buttons that originally made Bob Bob famous are in place at every Supper Club table, and Bob Bob's luxuriant Russo-English menu is served. We admire Shutov and Howarth because they understand the practicalities of pleasure. The acoustics in the Club Room are such that conversation can be heard over your strawberry soufflé and pink champagne while one or other of your party cuts a rug on the dance floor. The Club Room seats seventy (although I'm sure an extra lap can be found later in the evening) and is open until 1 am on Thursday, Friday and Saturday. We approve of these limited hours because, to quote Lady Bracknell, no one can live entirely for pleasure.

> *"If Coco Chanel and Prince Felix Yusupov ... had opened a nightclub together, this would be it."*

Bob Bob Ricard, 1 Upper James Street W1
Tel. 020 3145 1000
Tube: Piccadilly Circus
www.bobbobricard.com

LOULOU'S £££££

There is a precedent for illicit behaviour in Shepherd Market. The bawdy May Fair that gave the district its name was held on the site of 5 Hertford Street from 1686 until 1764. In the twentieth century Shepherd Market became synonymous with sex for heirs to the peerage, high-court judges and those who relish the sting of lashes administered by ladies in very high heels. Naughtiness and the promise of illicit thrills still hang like a mist around Shepherd Market after dark. Loulou's, the subterranean supper club below 5 Hertford Street, is one of those Halley's Comet nightclubs that come once a generation, where royalty, rock stars, models and tycoons feel entirely at liberty to meet and misbehave without fear of iPhones or idle gossip.

It was a stroke of genius on the part of Loulou's owner, Robin Birley, to employ the legendary Willie Landels and the fashion designer Rifat Özbek to design the interior, a labyrinth of lowlit, mirrored salons and private booths in what were once coal cellars. The look is Beatonesque in its opulence and the lighting is fiendishly clever, hence Loulou's appeal for those models of probity Kate Moss, Daphne Guinness and Mick Jagger. By comparison, the A-list nightclubs secreted in such new hotels as the London Edition and Chiltern Firehouse are by all accounts far too loud, frantic and merely fashionable. Loulou's truly does have a frisson of New York's Studio 54, where in the 1970s power, influence and artistry met glamour, talent and lust.

Unfortunately, Loulou's is open to members only and if, like us, you're not much of a joiner, you'll have to rely on moneybags friends or the kindness of strangers to gain entry. The club is named after Yves

Saint Laurent's muse Loulou de la Falaise, who was Birley's aunt. It is Birley's riposte to the sale of his late father, Mark Birley's, empire (including the infamous Annabel's in Berkeley Square) to Richard Caring. And how! The Duke and Duchess of Cambridge were early adopters of Loulou's, and the entire young royal set still swarms, as does the *jeunesse dorée* of London and the people who pay for them. The bill of fare is wickedly expensive, and it is rather exhausting being in the company of the genetically and financially blessed. But should you be guest rather than host, Loulou's is a must-see on the Grand Tour of London after dark.

2–5 Hertford Street W1
Tel. 020 7408 2100
Tube: Green Park/Hyde Park Corner
www.5hertfordstreet.co.uk

QUAGLINO'S £££

Quaggies, as it was known in the 1930s, hides on Bury Street in St James's, opposite Turnbull & Asser's bespoke shop. In its heyday Quaglino's was the fashionable, glittering subterranean art deco bar, dining room and dance floor, and comfortably welcomed 400 of London's wealthiest, prettiest and wittiest socialites. A sweeping chrome Astaire and Rogers staircase still leads from the balconied mezzanine bar to the dining room and makes one want to high kick like Zizi Jeanmaire at the Folies-Bergère. Opened in 1929 by the eponymous Italian Giovanni, the restaurant was café society's darling between the wars, with the celebrated American cabaret artist and lothario Leslie 'Hutch' Hutchinson playing hot jazz and serenading fast society countesses

Edwina Mountbatten and Idina Erroll. Quaggie's bar was a favourite of the Prince of Wales (the Duke of Windsor) and his joy-boy brother George, Duke of Kent, who shared apartments in St James's Palace, round the corner. It was at Quaglino's that the prince danced with his future wife, the scandalously twice-married Mrs Simpson. This was also the first London restaurant in which Her Majesty The Queen publicly dined, in 1956, and it hosted Judy Garland's fifth and final wedding reception months before her untimely death in 1969.

The great Terence Conran gave Quags a hip replacement in 1991, and the light-fingered among us still treasure the brightly coloured Q ashtrays filched as trophies of amusing evenings. In 2014 the decorator Russell Sage was commissioned to bring the faded lady back to life. His endeavours have been successful, with backlit tortoiseshell panels on the staircase and a fabulous matching *île flottante* bar dead centre in the dining room, surrounded by high leather bar stools. The whole joint is jumping with mad jazz-patterned carpets, upholstery and gleaming brass and steel. There's a private dining room up in the gallery, and a miniature cabaret stage with much promise. Disappointingly, Quaglino's to-die-for history isn't referred to anywhere, other than in the blurred black-and-white photographs thrown away on a corner wall.

Today one gets the impression that Quaglino's is an empty stage awaiting new stars. The 3 am licence and threat of DJ sets on weekend evenings strongly

> *"... the light-fingered among us still treasure the brightly coloured Q ashtrays filched as trophies of amusing evenings."*

suggests that it isn't chasing the post-theatre supper crowd who'd like a smart late-night bite and light conversation. That is a shame. London lacks such grown-up and glamorous venues, where conversation is king and dancing cheek to cheek doesn't mean twerking. So for the present we recommend taking a seat at the bar for cocktails and taking to the floor with a polished foxtrot when you're feeling refreshed enough to lead by example.

16 Bury Street SW1
Tel. 020 7930 6767
Tube: Green Park
www.quaglinos-restaurant.co.uk

Where to drink ...
alone

THE COACH & HORSES £

Soho is the first district in London to which we would direct anyone if they wished to drink alone and find amusing company. Beginning in the 1740s, successive waves of French, Italian, German and Russian immigrants carved up the narrow streets of tenements shared with artists, political dissidents and the ladies and gentlemen of pleasure who might or might not be offering love for sale. The culture of entertainment, exotic gastronomy, misbehaviour and brief encounters is so embedded in Soho's past that even now the much-sanitized square mile still has that grand frisson for people venturing out alone.

London's pubs are by and large truly democratic. You can sit and drink as long as the licence allows and will be welcomed by locals and strangers alike, as long as you don't commit the cardinal sin of being a bore. In Soho this code of honour among those who like to lift the elbow rather too much is practically a Masonic handshake. Like the French and the Colony Rooms, pubs like Soho's Coach & Horses were to the artists, writers and actors of the 1960s and '70s what the Georgian coffee houses had been to their counterparts two centuries before. The Colony's infamous landlady, Muriel Belcher, would greet her members with a friendly 'Hello c***', and the Coach & Horses landlord Norman 'London's rudest landlord' Balon would dismiss them with 'You're too boring to be in my pub.'

Not much changed in 2006 when Balon retired and Alastair Choat inherited the Coach & Horses. The satirical magazine *Private Eye* still holds fortnightly lunches there, and although high wooden bench seating has been installed outside, the down-at-heel Victorian interiors haven't been tarted up at all. This is a sensible move. In 1989 Coach & Horses regular Peter O'Toole starred as Coach & Horses regular (and *Spectator* Low Life columnist) Jeffrey Bernard in Keith Waterhouse's play *Jeffrey Bernard is Unwell*. The title was the disclaimer used every time the alcoholic Bernard missed his deadline, and the set was a carbon copy of the pub. The Coach & Horses thus brings many a literary and artistic type to Soho in homage to O'Toole, Bernard, Francis Bacon and Balon, who named his autobiography *You're Barred You Bastards*.

29 Greek Street W1
Tel. 020 7437 5920
Tube: Leicester Square
www.thecoachandhorsessoho.co.uk

MARK'S BAR £££

We don't presume to ask why you might find yourself in London looking for places to drink alone. But we don't envisage that your aspiration is to imitate Hopper's *Nighthawks*, or Degas's *Absinthe Drinkers* for that matter. New York has a healthy cocktail culture, making it perfectly normal for a guy (or gal) to walk into a bar and order an Old Fashioned. Perhaps in London this is seen as more acceptable in a pub than in a cocktail bar, but why precisely we can't imagine. Mark's Bar, below the eponymous Mr Hix's Soho restaurant, is acknowledged as one of the maestros of the modern cocktail, directed as it is by Nick Strangeway, so don't expect to head downstairs and find yourself a lonely bar stool.

The deep chesterfield sofas surrounded by the handiwork of Mr Hirst and Miss Emin are rammed from noon to 1 am with hipsters from either side of that Soho-Mayfair divide that is Regent Street. One plays the odds when drinking alone, and, this being a Hix restaurant, the odds are that the person or persons sitting on the next bar stool will be of the moving shaking variety rather than a bore with nothing to say. If you don't want to strike up a conversation, you could easily become engrossed in Mark's cocktail menu, which is divided by epoch and served up with historical notes that are erudite and entertaining. Of the 'Early British Libations', we were fascinated by the prototype Dirty Mojito discovered by Francis Drake on his voyages

> *"... the odds are that the person or persons sitting on the next bar stool will be of the moving shaking variety rather than a bore with nothing to say."*

to Chile and Peru. It's super to see a reference to the Hanky Panky, the invention of the Savoy's pioneering head 'barman' at the turn of the twentieth century, Ada Coleman, and fascinating to read about the first case of cocktail censorship, when in 1934 the St Regis Hotel in New York insisted the barman Fernand Petiot rename his Red Snapper the Bloody Mary.

Nick Strangeway was responsible for one of the most lethal inventions in the early 1990s, when he worked behind the bar at Damien Hirst's short-lived but achingly fashionable Pharmacy. He still serves the Espresso Martini at Mark's Bar – Belvedere vodka, an espresso shot and Kahlúa – that has a similar effect to sticking your fingers into a plug socket while doing a tequila shot. Mark's Bar wins the prize for best new cocktails in London with Strangeway's Ship Shape & Bristol Fashioned and the Stiff Upper Lip. Much as we might envy those progressing upstairs for a classic Hix lunch or dinner, we're equally contented to work our way down the list of bar snacks on the blackboard in Mark's Bar, lingering over Scotch quail's eggs with chorizo. Another round?

Hix, 66–70 Brewer Street W1
Tel. 020 7292 3518
Tube: Piccadilly Circus
www.marksbar.co.uk

POLO BAR £££

Built in 1955, the Westbury hotel is one of the unsung heroes of London's West End. The location is arguably the sweetest spot for a five-star hotel in W1, should designer shopping be your reason for living. The two-Michelin-star Alyn Williams restaurant is a hidden treasure, and one that we didn't shine a spotlight on for entirely selfish reasons. Dame Angela Lansbury was lunching there the last time we visited. But it is the Polo Bar that makes the Westbury essential for natives of Mayfair. Meetings and assignations are held there from breakfast to nightcap, and the barmen and women are a crack team that you'd trust with the code to your panic room.

Even the Polo Bar's separate entrance on Conduit Street glitters with Swarovski crystal and possibility. The mood is Manhattan in the 1950s, with dim lighting, a low ceiling and a soft carpet giving the room a sense of discreet luxury. A slightly raised mezzanine, brass railings, wood-veneer pillars and blue-velvet club chairs all conspire to make the interiors feel rich and the guests feel important. Perhaps we're being overdramatic, but we like to think that parcels of diamonds, memory sticks containing top-secret information and pilfered antiquities change hands clandestinely at the Polo Bar, although the likelihood is that nothing more sinister than business cards are slid across the tables.

> *"The mood is Manhattan in the 1950s, with dim lighting, a low ceiling and a soft carpet giving the room a sense of discreet luxury."*

We're rather fed up of hotels that tell the guests what they should be eating or drinking at any given time of the day or night. Sittings are the enemy of hospitality. If one wants a Bloody Mary at noon, sushi with breakfast or a salt-beef salad at 5 pm, a five-star hotel should deliver. This is where the Polo Bar is such a professional operation. The wine and spirits list anticipates every request and the bar menu knows what it is talking about. A spoonful of beluga, a light bite of smoked salmon served in a cone with crème fraiche, a robust Polo burger or salt-beef sandwich will appear miraculously from 11 am to 11 pm, and the bar itself is licensed until 1 am. Our favourite rule – no under-21s after 6 pm – guarantees that the Polo Bar maintains its dignity at all times.

Westbury Hotel, 37 Conduit Street W1
Tel. 020 7629 7755
Tube: Green Park
www.westburymayfair.com

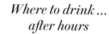

Where to drink …
after hours

FUMOIR ££££

Claridge's has a talent for making entrances. When Thierry Despont restored the hotel's public rooms in 1996, he set a mysterious Lalique glass panel above the doorway to the right of the foyer that hides the dark, smouldering 36-seat Fumoir bar. William Klein's portrait from 1956 of Lisa Fonssagrives blowing smoke through a dramatic black veil soars high above the marble horseshoe bar, and a tall proscenium arch behind the bar illuminates tiers of premium cognac, rum, port and tequila. The small but perfectly formed Fumoir has echoes of New York's Stork Club in its 1930s prime.

A seat in the Fumoir is highly prized because of the bar's inbuilt filter system. You don't see an ill-dressed person in Claridge's. Not ever. Full stop. So you're guaranteed to be drinking a Martini in the company of a well-groomed group. There is a no-reservations policy, although hotel guests clearly take precedence. Those who want to show off their peacock plumes and party frocks tend to gravitate towards the much more spacious Claridge's Bar; the more intriguing people who have reason for seeking a lowlit 1930s cocktail-lounge mood will discreetly slip into the Fumoir Bar. Many a deal has been brokered, romance begun and heart broken here.

We always look forward to being served a drink in the Fumoir's heavy Lalique crystal glasses, and thoroughly appreciate the barmen with encyclopaedic memories who know what we'd like before we name our poison. One evening a male American editor, evidently suffering from fashion-week fatigue and in need of a pick-me-up, handed his mobile to the barman while Christina Ong dictated the ingredients. We wished for the talent of an Al Hirschfeld or Annie Tempests to draw the cartoon of the Fumoir's reaction when an *Arena Homme+* editor had the arrogance or ignorance to ask for English Breakfast tea after 6 pm. Claridge's staff are far too polite to protest, but if your order isn't 40 per cent proof then you have no business depriving a serious drinker of his or her perch in the Fumoir Bar.

"... the more intriguing people who have reason for seeking a lowlit 1930s cocktail-lounge mood will discreetly slip into the Fumoir Bar."

Claridge's, 49 Brook Street W1
Tel. 020 7629 8860
Tube: Bond Street
www.claridges.co.uk

NIGHTJAR £££

If you are active in the late evening and early morning, we couldn't recommend richer pickings than Hoxton and Shoreditch, which have taken to the Manhattan Prohibition-era speakeasy trend like a melancholy Victorian housewife to laudanum. It's a scene around Silicone Roundabout on Old Street, with the Mayor of Scaredy Cat Town, Callooh Callay and Happiness Forgets all vying for the wallets of east London's answer to generation Zuckerberg and West End cocktail fiends slumming it in what is still a rather shady part of town. Hoxton suits a speakeasy, and you won't be disappointed when you step off the City Road and down the stairs into Lee Broom's infernal interiors at Nightjar.

Resembling Weimar Germany in the 1920s more than Manhattan's 21 Club, Nightjar is lit eerily and atmospherically by vintage Holophane pendants, two backlit art deco mirrors, the bar and the stage. The tin-tiled ceiling panels gleam in sinister fashion. Nightjar excels because, like New York speakeasies, it takes the music as seriously as the cocktails. Bands and soloists such as Dom Pipkin, Laurence Corns, the Basin Street Brawlers and the Lapazoos blow hot jazz and cool blues nightly. The music of Fats Waller, Cab Calloway, Billie Holiday and Bessie Smith works its magic as assuredly as the drinks menu.

> *"Nightjar excels because, like New York speakeasies, it takes the music as seriously as the cocktails."*

We particularly love bars like Nightjar and those of its ilk for reintroducing the no-standing policy that was second nature in a more civilized age. One has to book a table or take potluck on the door, and once the tables are filled the doors remain closed. Nightjar's cocktail list is divided into Pre-Prohibition (1880–1918), Prohibition (1918–32), Post War and Signature. We have to admit a penchant for the classic Pre-Prohibition cocktails, such as a Champagne Julep or Waldorf Gloom Lighter, rather than the authentic Prohibition numbers, which were often intentionally cut with overpowering mixers to mask the taste of harsh bootleg booze. Much as we applaud ingenuity, we do like our cocktails in lead-crystal glasses unencumbered by flowers, fruit, berries, dry ice, coconuts, sparklers or flames. Still, it's worth putting up with the odd artistic flourish in return for a civilized place to drink well-considered cocktails served in the old-school style until 2 am.

> *"We have to admit a penchant for the classic Pre-Prohibition cocktails, such as a Champagne Julep ..."*

129 City Road EC1
Tel. 020 7253 4101
Tube: Old Street
www.barnightjar.com

PHOENIX ARTIST CLUB £

Like the Dark Web, there are certain late-night addresses in London that are totally off the radar for all but those who intend to make mischief. Orientate yourself with the Charing Cross Road façade of the Phoenix Theatre, where Noël Coward's *Private Lives* was first performed, duck down Phoenix Street and you'll find the Phoenix Artist Club directly on your left. This members' club of thespians, critics, chorus boys and Soho socialites is open nightly until 2.30 am, and only strangers who arrive before 8 pm are allowed the chance to stay all evening. The rooms beneath the theatre were once rehearsal spaces and then a restaurant, hence the faded opulence of booths with threadbare curtains, a parquet floor laid down in the year Bonnie met Clyde, a long copper-topped bar and walls thick with black-and-white head shots of actors past and present.

The Phoenix was managed for nigh on twenty years by the late, great musical queen Maurice Huggett, who would (we kid you not) sip champagne from a china tea cup and mother the members through their triumphs and disasters. Although we have been down the Phoenix when more familiar faces, such as Rupert Everett and Guy Henry, have been at large, we can't confirm or deny that Grace Jones, Jude Law, John Hurt and Lady Gaga have also found the ruby slippers leading them down the stairs to the Phoenix. The Phoenix has a very high tolerance for alcohol (or should that be for inebriates?) as long as everyone plays nicely. The 'Gotta Sing' musical theatre open-mike nights every Thursday are terrific fun, but really the spectacle at the Phoenix Artist Club is invariably the regulars and their fortunate guests.

Apparently the Phoenix is nicknamed 'Shuts', because it never does, but we've never heard it referred to as such. There are signs that it might be growing a

> *"The Phoenix was managed for nigh on twenty years by the late, great musical queen Maurice Huggett who would (we kid you not) sip champagne from a china teacup ..."*

little respectable and po-faced since Huggett's death in 2011. In reference to its zero-tolerance drugs policy, the club's website sententiously states that 'staff include a former police officer, two former military personnel and a senior magistrate.' You're tempted to add: 'That's an act in itself.' But the Phoenix Artist Club does have that talent – which it shares with Madonna – of never appearing to age or know when to stop. So, much as we love the Groucho Club, it's always to the Phoenix that we'll go if we're in need of a laugh, a lick of Prosecco and a late night. As Elaine Stritch famously said to the barman, 'Just give me a bottle of vodka and a floor plan' ...

"... the Phoenix Artist Club does have that talent – which it shares with Madonna – of never appearing to age or know when to stop."

Phoenix Theatre, 1 Phoenix Street WC2
Tel. 020 7836 1077
Tube: Tottenham Court Road
www.phoenixartistclub.com

Fortnum & Mason

IV

Shops

Furniture & Interiors

For antique furniture

MALLETT

&JS

'Mallett, with Partridge, shares the pinnacle of the
fame (and fortune) of London's antique world,'
says the original *Discriminating Guide* of New Bond
Street's palatial near neighbours. Partridge, which
persisted in selling only eighteenth-century furniture
and paintings in the grand country-house style, went
into administration in 2009. Mallett, established in
1865, left New Bond Street in 2012 after a 104-year
residence, but relocated to the even grander Ely
House on Dover Street. In a classic case of survival
of the fittest, Mallett adjusted its interests to reflect
the tastes of a younger collector. The former bishop's
palace and gentlemen's club, built in 1772, displays
a vast stock of museum-quality eighteenth-century
furniture and objects in rooms of similar stately scale
to those for which the pieces were made. But you'll
also find nineteenth-, twentieth- and twenty-first-
century pieces displayed insouciantly next to the
Georgian glories.

Mallett understands that few clients today want an exclusively eighteenth-century interior in the English or French aristocratic style. Instead, they – or their decorators – think nothing of buying an extraordinary Walter Knoll K 428 cantilever chair, a Qing dynasty enamel basin and a George II tortoiseshell tea caddy in one visit. Mallett will always stock showpieces that museums and serious collectors covet, such as a suite of magnificent James 'Athenian' Stuart salon chairs made for Spencer House at the command of the 1st Earl. Far from mourning its old premises, Mallett must be delighted with Ely House. Now expertly restored and exquisitely decorated, it far surpasses the interiors of Bourdon House or New Bond Street.

"Mallett will always stock showpieces that museums and serious collectors covet ..."

Mallett's Meta project – a stroke of marketing genius – involves commissioning twenty-first-century designers such as Barber & Osgerby, Wales & Wales and Tord Boontje to work with craftsmen skilled in the handwork of the eighteenth century to create unique pieces for Mallett's London and New York showrooms. These future heirlooms are made from natural materials such as marble, leather, bronze and glass, designed to withstand the tests of time and taste. But the eighteenth century is Mallett's area of expertise, and we're always delighted to take a turn around Ely House to appreciate such masterpieces as a glorious brace of Thomas Chippendale George III gilt wood armchairs, a Louis XVI needlework cushion or a pair of Tsar Alexander II malachite tables. Mallett remains at the pinnacle of fame if not fortune of London's antiques world.

Ely House, 37 Dover Street W1
Tel. 020 7499 7411
Tube: Green Park
www.mallettantiques.com

For vintage furniture

RETROUVIUS

Adam Hills and Maria Speake were light years ahead of fashion when they established Retrouvius, a ramshackle former factory in north London that specializes in architectural salvage on a grand scale. Retrouvius finds beauty and nobility in good materials and well-made institutional objects reconditioned and reused in hip domestic interiors. They will take aged leather panels, used as shelving in the British Library when it was still housed in the British Museum, and fit them as bathroom cabinets. For the same project (an interior in Primrose Hill), Retrouvius took mahogany cabinets from the National Museum of Scotland to create a kitchen island and dishwasher door. On a more ambitious scale, Retrouvius bought acres of green slate cladding from a Blackfriars tower block and miles of teak floorboards from a London laboratory.

Although it is a bit of a hike to Kensal Green, it is terrific fun scurrying up and down the staircases at Retrouvius discovering families of frilly Vaseline glass wall lights, stacks of metal-framed bentwood chairs, walls of foxed glass mirrors and forests of sturdy Georgian timber doors. Retrouvius appeals to that very particular middle-aged trendy demographic who colonized the city's disused factories, warehouses and penthouses in the 1990s. Such architecture suits reclaimed institutional twentieth-century furniture made before plastic replaced noble, durable materials. We particularly like furniture designed by Retrouvius made from reclaimed wood, and vintage textiles such as 1950s Turkish flat-weave rugs and deliciously twee Welsh handwoven blankets. No, you're not going to find the Ardabil Carpet or a lost Le Corbusier here, but you will find handsome young design consultants who will charm you into buying half a dozen Scandi Modern brass wall lights as soon as look at you.

1016 Harrow Road NW10
Tel. 020 8960 6060
Tube: Kensal Green
www.retrouvius.com

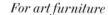

For art furniture

DAVID GILL GALLERIES

When David Gill opened his twentieth-century design gallery on the Fulham Road in 1987, the decorator David Mlinaric apparently heralded his arrival with 'Where have you been?!' The Fulham Road was (and still is) noted for its grand antique furniture dealers: Apter-Fredericks, Richard Courtney and Godson & Coles. The flamboyant Mr Gill was an early champion of Marc Newson, Tom Dixon and Ron Arad, as well as such London particulars as

Oriel Harwood and the transvestite potter Grayson Perry. In 2012 Gill opened a gallery in St James's, on a corner of Duke Street, near his first employer, the auction house Christie's. The gallery could compete with Hauser & Wirth or White Cube for ratio of space to exhibits, reminding us that the works on show are for a rarefied taste. Heal's or the Conran Shop will sell you the beautiful and useful; David Gill showcases the haute couture of contemporary furniture design.

The designers in the gallery's stable are some of the most celebrated in the world: Zaha Hadid, Mattia Bonetti, Fredrikson Stallard, Barnaby Barford and the Campana brothers, to name those given solo shows. Hadid's Liquid Glacial table, with what looks like a vortex of rippling water pouring into the table legs from a still pool of glass serving as the top, is a memorable modern masterpiece, as is Barford's mad customized Regency chandelier with a 'Jungle VIP' monkey swinging from it. We are most covetous of Stallard's Crush table – a glass box containing a sculpted piece of crushed gold aluminium – which echoes the artist Yves Klein's Perspex tables (1961) containing cobalt-blue pigment (also in the Gill collection). These statement pieces are not necessarily practical, but that's not the point. Is it furniture? Is it art? It is both.

> *"The designers in the gallery's stable are some of the most celebrated in the world."*

2–4 King Street SW1
Tel. 020 3195 6600
Tube: Green Park
www.davidgillgalleries.com

For contemporary furniture

SCP

The founder of SCP, Sheridan Coakley, has been in the business of modern furniture design and retail since 1985. He introduced Jasper Morrison and Matthew Hilton to Milan's Salone del Mobile in 1986, hence SCP's status as one of London's most important consultants. The firm has placed contemporary furniture in the Royal Opera House, the Barbican Centre and Goldsmiths' Hall. The East End showroom has always distinguished itself as having a sense of humour and delight in design, rather than appearing po-faced and too cool for school. On a recent visit we were amused by Reiko Kaneko's flying-saucer bone-china pendant lights, Wencke Barfoed's tall magazine rack, Lee Broom's cut-glass crystal-bulb pendant lights and Lucy Kurrein's Elmer sofa. We admire SCP's commitment to craft: it works with factories and artisans in the UK and sells textiles woven in Wales, ceramics made in Stoke-on-Trent and upholstery crafted in Norfolk.

SCP has always had the talent for choosing pieces that sit happily together in the showroom and inspire the client. As an East End institution, it is also a tastemaker, so we were intrigued to see brown furniture such as rosewood dining tables making an appearance, as well as garish 1970s German vases and madly patterned Hilos y Colores embroidered cushions. Twentieth-century classics are also well represented, such as the Charles Eames Dowel armchair and the Thonet bentwood café chairs No. 14 and No. 18. In addition to the furniture and a particularly good collection of lighting, SCP never fails to please with a vast collection of smaller glass, ceramic and metal household objects in the Philippe Starck school of pleasing silliness.

135–139 Curtain Road EC2
Tel. 020 7739 1869
Tube: Old Street
www.scp.co.uk

For silver, glass and china

THE LONDON SILVER VAULTS

&JS

In use as strongrooms for household silver, jewellery and documents since 1876, the London Silver Vaults are today a series of subterranean showrooms where the largest concentration of sterling silver and Sheffield Plate in the world is on sale from such firms as William Walter, Linden & Co. and I. Franks, the last of which has traded here for four generations. The vaults were Blitzed but never breached, and the anonymous 1950s building on top belies the magic beneath. One is transported to past centuries, when mirrored sterling-silver table centrepieces and quartets of tall Georgian candelabra were prized household possessions. Silver might have fallen out of fashion because it is high-maintenance and because there isn't an awful lot of use for spoon warmers, wax jacks, butter boats, asparagus tongs and brandy warmers. But it's an ill wind and all that; if, like us, you find a silver-set dining table life-enhancing, it's a buyer's market.

English silver has led the world since the twelfth century and is still sent to the Assay Offices in London, Birmingham, Sheffield and Edinburgh to be hallmarked. The hallmarking system, which precisely dates sterling silver, has been invaluable for collectors, who can buy eighteenth-century silver by master craftsmen Paul de Lamerie, Paul Storr and Hester Bateman knowing the provenance is correct. There isn't the need for an expert eye to verify or deny the authenticity, as there is with a Rembrandt. But the Silver Vaults are not solely for dealers and collectors in the market for an 1850 Mortimer & Hunt sterling-silver candelabra just shy of £75,000. The majority of visitors are seeking a traditional wedding or christening present, such as a Queen Anne porringer, a Georgian sterling-silver egg cruet set or a dainty box of Edwardian silver teaspoons.

Chancery House, 53–64 Chancery Lane WC2
Tel. 020 7242 3844
Tube: Chancery Lane
www.silvervaultslondon.com

THOMAS GOODE

&JS

Rather appropriately, Thomas Goode began trading in 1827 during the reign of King George IV, who commissioned from it the elaborate silver-gilt Grand Service that is still used for State Banquets at Buckingham Palace. Goode boasts that it makes and sells 'the world's finest tableware' from Ernest George's fine Queen Anne-style red-brick town house on South Audley Street. We happen to agree. The founder's son William Goode was the intrepid member of the family who travelled the world visiting such famous royal factories as Sèvres, Dresden, Meissen, Royal Copenhagen and Nymphenburg and acquiring services to sell. It was also he who cultivated 'twilight of the king-emperors' clients such as Tsar Nicholas II, Queen Victoria, Grand Duchess Vladimir and the kings of Romania, Norway and the Hellenes. William also commissioned the two 7-foot-tall Minton majolica elephants that were displayed at the Paris Exhibition in 1889 and now stand in the windows of 17–22 South Audley Street, with the Royal Warrants of Her Majesty The Queen and HRH The Prince of Wales near by.

Thomas Goode has been clever to keep in step with fashion, and now offers endless variations of the all-white table setting with the plainest modern Georg Jensen cutlery and Baccarat crystal glasses. But the firm has never been comfortable with minimalism, and we have to admit a bias for elaborate dinner services like the eighteenth-century pattern Green Garland made for the aforementioned Grand Duchess, the Lord of the Isles pattern co-designed by Prince Charles, and the Thomas Goode white-and-gold bone-china Versailles pattern. Thomas Goode has its own studio in Stoke-on-Trent, where it produces bespoke bone-china patterns developed with the aid of the in-house archive and museum. Since the Liberal peer Rumi Verjee bought this national treasure in 1995, Thomas Goode has enjoyed success with Peter Ting's Harlequin coffee service and Paul Smith's Stripes tea service, both of which are contemporary collector's pieces.

19 South Audley Street W1
Tel. 020 7499 2823
Tube: Green Park
www.thomasgoode.com

WILLIAM YEOWARD

Ordinarily, when shopping for crystal, we'd dash
to Harrods, the only London department store to
devote an entire room to Waterford and Wedgwood's
traditional patterns (on the second floor). Should we
want a more modern piece of glass, all the international
brands – Villeroy & Boch, Alessi, Riedel – are
represented, with everything in between. Peter Jones
on Sloane Square is also a terribly safe pair of hands
for glassware. But we urge you to take the No. 19 bus
(for there is no nearer Tube stop than Sloane Square)
to the further reaches of the King's Road to visit
William Yeoward's showroom. Established in 1995,
William Yeoward Crystal now holds Prince Charles's
Royal Warrant and is famed for making crystal by
hand, using cutting and etching techniques from the
seventeenth and eighteenth centuries.

A former decorator who worked for the late
Baroness Thatcher, Mr Yeoward is a creative
maelstrom, and his showroom is a sumptuous series
of room sets displaying his bespoke furniture,
upholstery, lighting, rugs,
textiles, ceramics and the
crystal for which he is perhaps
best known. To give you an
idea of the scale of Yeoward's
collection, his classics
include over thirty designs
for champagne glasses and
coupes. We particularly like
the Cordelia champagne flute, hand-engraved with
an intricate bunch of grapes. Every eventuality has
been allowed for: glass ice buckets and wine coolers,
caviar and seafood servers, candlesticks and hurricane
lamps and wildly over-the-top centrepieces in the

> *"...wildly over-the-
> top centrepieces
> in the shape of
> pineapples, urns
> and beehives."*

shape of pineapples, urns and beehives. In addition to the classics, Mr Yeoward has a smaller Country glass collection and an art deco American Bar set. From the latter we covet a set of tall Lillian Martini glasses, and from Country a mismatched set of sapphire, emerald and amethyst Fanny goblets (no sniggering at the back!).

270 King's Road SW3
Tel. 020 7349 7828
Tube: Sloane Square
www.williamyeowardcrystal.com

For textiles and carpets

FRANSES

&JS

Are we the only ones perplexed by those Persian carpet shops on and around Piccadilly, which haven't seen a customer since the Shah was deposed? Antique tapestry, carpets and textile art is an extremely rarefied trade these days, and you wouldn't trust that lot to sell you a welcome mat let alone an Aubasson. Now C. John, who holds the Queen's Royal Warrant, has left South Audley Street, there is only Franses remaining in the West End with world-class expertise on the subject. Founded in 1909 by Sidney Franses, the firm has developed a reputation as the Indiana Jones of antique carpets and textiles and has sold important pieces to New York's Metropolitan Museum, Boston's Museum of Fine Arts and the Victoria and Albert Museum in London. The Franses Tapestry Archive, kept on the same site, is the world's largest resource for the provenance of European tapestries, figurative textiles and carpets.

Franses still displays 'enormous tapestries of museum quality', as it did when the first *Discriminating Guide* visited the Knightsbridge showroom in 1977. One needs a chateau to display them, hence our interest in a glorious Louis XV Savonnerie carpet designed by Perrot circa 1745, a nineteenth-century needlework carpet owned by the Bismarck family, and a twentieth-century Arts and Crafts carpet designed by Charles Voysey circa 1900. For those who find Gobelin tapestries rather impractical purchases, we recommend looking at a superb eighteenth-century four-fold needlework screen from the chateau of the Duc de Brissac, curtains from 1876 printed in William Morris's Honeycomb pattern, and a rather lovely Queen Anne embroidery signed (in stitch) by thirteen-year-old Mary Davison.

80 Jermyn Street SW1
Tel. 020 7976 1234
Tube: Green Park
www.franses.com

LIBERTY ORIENTAL RUGS & CARPETS DEPARTMENT

&JS

According to Alison Adburgham's *Liberty's: A Biography of a Shop*, Arthur Liberty's first shop on Regent Street sold 'coloured silks from the East ... the sort of thing that William Morris, Alma-Tadema and Burne-Jones and Rossetti used to come in and turn over and rave about'. Liberty soon diversified into decorative Japanese ware and exotic oriental carpets.

Thus its justifiably famous Oriental Rugs & Carpets department is the oldest in the store today. A single intrepid buyer, Bruce Lepere, hunts down the 4,000 unique pieces on display in the fourth-floor showroom, on travels that take him to Afghanistan, India, Iran, Nepal and Morocco. Lepere will buy only handmade rugs and carpets, and is particularly fastidious about stocking antique carpets beyond the reach of less experienced trophy hunters.

It was reported in the first *Discriminating Guide* that 'some types of rug are cheaper at Liberty's than in Tehran.' This may or may not still be true, and we wouldn't care to test the theory. Suffice it to say that Liberty has arguably Europe's highest-quality list of oriental rugs and carpets priced between £100 and £200,000. We were most impressed that every carpet bought by Lepere is brought to London and washed, repaired and given a condition report should it be antique. We're equally impressed that Mr Lepere can say with absolute confidence of pieces recently bought in Iran that they are the 'antiques of the future'.

> *"It was reported in the first* Discriminating Guide *that 'some types of rug are cheaper at Liberty's than in Tehran.'"*

4th Floor, Liberty, Regent Street W1
Tel. 020 7573 9759
Tube: Oxford Circus
www.liberty.co.uk/oriental-rugs

TIMOROUS BEASTIES

When Glasgow School of Art graduates Alistair McAuley and Paul Simmons formed the print-design firm Timorous Beasties in 1990, the age of minimalism was just beginning. Wallpaper of any sort was desperately out of fashion and printed fabrics about as welcome as a cancan girl at a Vatican mass. However, slowly but surely Timorous Beasties has achieved what all great artisans wish: to master their craft and revive what many considered a dead language with original design. For example, Timorous Beasties took eighteenth-century *toile de jouy* and patterned it with what looked like a classical pastoral but was actually scenes from contemporary urban Glasgow. In the most recent works, 'Omni Splatt', 'Chic Blotch' and 'Grand Blotch Damask', rococo swirls and Victorian silhouette paper cuts are subverted with an attack of colour not dissimilar to a mash-up between Versailles brocade and the work of Jackson Pollock.

Timorous Beasties wallpaper and furnishing fabrics now furnish the Victoria and Albert Museum boardroom and Claridge's. McAuley and Simmons have collaborated with Fortnum & Mason, Liberty and Philip Treacy, to name a very few. Of the many patterns hand-screen-printed at the shop/studios in London and Glasgow, we particularly like the graphic Thistle, the Alastair Crowley-esque Devil Damask Lace and the terribly pretty Birdbranch. Allowing for multiple colourways, fabrics and paper treatments, the possibilities are endless. Just as Celia Birtwell used to say that everyone had to have a red room in 1960s London, we believe everyone with an ounce of style ought to have a Timorous Beasties room in 2015.

46 Amwell Street EC1
Tel. 020 7833 5010
Tube: Angel
www.timorousbeasties.com

For interior decorators

COLEFAX AND FOWLER

&JS

The earlier *Discriminating Guide* quotes *Vogue* as calling Colefax and Fowler 'the epitome of good taste'. The entry continues: 'The late Sybil Colefax and John Fowler set up shop in 1935 and have been responsible for some of the most beautiful rooms in England.' The story is slightly more complicated than that, however. With her fortune wiped out in the Wall Street Crash of 1929, Lady Colefax capitalized on her taste for interiors in the English country-house style by going into trade. She joined forces with Fowler who, after the war, took the lease on 39 Brook Street, where the firm remains. The society hostess Lady Colefax sold out to Nancy Tree, who, as Nancy Lancaster, would create the aesthetic for which Colefax and Fowler is still famous today. The English country-house style appreciates the inevitable ravages of time, disdains chic and values comfort over pose and effect.

> *"The English country-house style appreciates the inevitable ravages of time, disdains chic and values comfort over pose and effect."*

Many of Fowler's country-house chintz upholstery and wallpaper patterns are still sold in the classics range, such as the Bowood white rose repeat (copied from a fragment of wallpaper found in Bowood House, Wiltshire), Roses & Pansies, Chinese Toile, Plumbago Bouquet and Old Rose. There are quite literally thousands of delicate, faded chintzes, Regency stripes and micro-patterns in the Colefax and Fowler canon, but they are not the principal reason we're suggesting you visit 39 Brook Street. Since its inception, Colefax and Fowler has bought antiques, and there is always a nice collection for sale dotted about the house. The main showroom – the barrel-vaulted Yellow Room – is arguably one of the most important twentieth-century interiors in London. You will also see the courtyard garden behind, should you explore the whole house looking for the perfect eighteenth-century oval gilt wood mirror or Spanish leather trunk perfectly placed by Daniel Slowik, the manager of the antiques department. In December 2014 Colefax and Fowler hosted 'Beaton at Brook Street', an exhibition dedicated to interiors created by the society photographer Cecil Beaton.

39 Brook Street W1
Tel. 020 7493 2231
Tube: Bond Street
www.colefax.com

BEN PENTREATH

Architect, interior designer and amusing scribe for the *Financial Times*, Ben Pentreath is much in demand since the newspapers revealed that the Duke and Duchess of Cambridge had chosen him to redecorate Apartment 1A at Kensington Palace and Amner Hall on the Sandringham Estate. Actually, he was in demand before, having worked on the design of the Prince of Wales's new town Poundbury in Dorset in 2009, and has long been a champion of neoclassical architecture. In 2012 Pentreath wrote *English Decoration*, with a foreword by Nicky Haslam, in whose footsteps he dances. Pentreath's interior-design studio is led by Lucy Wilks (formerly of Colefax and Fowler), assisted by Luke Edward Hall. The Pentreath & Hall shop at 17 Rugby Street (www.pentreath-hall.com) stocks amusing, exotic small items for the home, such as Zulu baskets, ikat cushions, plaster paperweight Corinthian columns, jelly moulds, engraved tea glasses and ribbon-tied sets of multicoloured candles.

Pentreath's style of unselfconscious classicism can best be seen in photographs of his parsonage in Dorset, dating from 1820 and photographed in *English Decoration*. He applies David Hicks's cavalier attitude to colour and Terence Conran's love of time travel by mixing mahogany furniture, antique maps, willow-pattern china, Indian embroidered cushions and seagrass floor tiles and painting walls with colours a little less polite than those by Farrow & Ball. Pentreath's emphasis on comfort in even the grandest interior echoes the approach of Lady Colefax and John Fowler. It also resonates with the Duke and Duchess of Cambridge, who already have a history of doing as they do not as they ought, thus setting the tone and the fashion for the *Tatler* and *Country Life* set.

49 Lamb's Conduit Street WC1
Tel. 020 7430 2424
Tube: Holborn
www.benpentreath.com

ROBERT KIME

The antique dealer and collector of antique textiles Robert Kime knows how to put a room together, so much so that he has become Interior Decorator by

Royal Appointment to the Prince of Wales, for whom he redecorated Clarence House after the death of the Queen Mother in 2002. Kime's interiors can be characterized as 'aristocratic bohemian repatriated from Uzbekistan, who returns to inherit the family mansion armed only with a backpack filled with ancient native textiles and terribly good taste'. His two shops (on Kensington Church Street and Museum Street in Bloomsbury) tell his story beautifully, and serve first and foremost as showcases for his glorious appreciation of pattern: William Morris Daisy brocade carpets, Ottoman and Iznik embroidered panels, hand-sewn embroidered voiles from India, and yellow and buff woven silks in the eighteenth-century style.

Kime designed furniture – daybeds, nursing chairs, run-up stools and octagonal ottomans – and piles of cushions, curtains and lampshades are covered with his own printed textiles, which are instantly recognizable, Mughal Flower, Indus Linen, Field Poppy, Brother Rabbit Red and Twelve Colours being among the strongest statements. The ikats sold exclusively by Robert Kime include the sensational Harlequin, Peacock and Red Carnation patterns. We have often been grateful to Robert Kime for his collection of alabaster objects – tea-light domes, small vases and bowls – which have solved many a wedding-present dilemma and look a million dollars. Also, don't bother going anywhere else for reproduction Georgian lanterns,

We have often been grateful to Robert Kime for his collection of alabaster objects ... which have solved many a wedding-present dilemma and look a million dollars."

table-lamp stands and gallery lighting that are made in England, and antique-finished in brass, silver, gilt or gunmetal.

121 Kensington Church Street W8
Tel. 020 7229 0886
Tube: Notting Hill Gate
www.robertkime.com

Books

For signed first editions

HATCHARDS

&JS

Founded in 1797 and at 187 Piccadilly since 1817, Hatchards is the oldest bookseller in Britain and senior by forty-four years to the London Library in St James's Square, where many of the volumes it sells have been written and researched over the years. No other bookseller holds three Royal Warrants or the position in literary London of 'the author's bookshop'. Lord Byron, Oscar Wilde, Rudyard Kipling and Virginia Woolf were all customers (Woolf even mentioning Hatchards in her elegiac novel *Mrs Dalloway* of 1925), and literary lions Arthur Miller, Gore Vidal, Peter Ackroyd and Hilary Mantel have all signed their first editions and Hatchards' prized visitors' books, as have Alec Guinness, Bette Davis, the Duchess of Devonshire and Margaret Thatcher.

Hatchards celebrated its diamond jubilee in the year Emily Brontë published *Wuthering Heights* (1847) and its bicentenary when J. K. Rowling published her first Harry Potter novel (1997). It was the delightfully named Messrs Giddy and Joy who inaugurated Hatchards' annual Authors of the Year reception and high-profile book signings in the latter part of the twentieth century. The bookshop thus retains a stock of precious first editions by greats including W. H. Auden, T. S. Eliot, Christopher Isherwood, Nancy Mitford, P. G. Wodehouse, Jean Rhys and Muriel Spark, as well as a robust collection of works by and about Winston Churchill.

Now a part of the Waterstones group, bought by Russian benefactor Alexander Mamut and directed by James Daunt, Hatchards retains its aloofness and independent spirit largely thanks to a hugely knowledgeable staff, who can (brilliantly, as it happens) recommend Kathleen Winsor's *Forever Amber* for a more accurate portrayal of Barbara, Duchess of Castlemaine, than all the histories of Charles II's reign put together. Unlike the new Foyles, recently opened in the old Central Saint Martins building on Charing Cross Road, Hatchards is perfectly proportioned and easy to navigate, and always seems to have the book one wants or the suggestion of something better. The 'branch' in St Pancras station next to the miniature Fortnum & Mason is a scion grafted to the great oak that might or might not take.

> *"Hatchards ... always seems to have the book one wants or the suggestion of something better."*

187 Piccadilly W1
Tel. 020 7439 9921
Tube: Green Park
www.hatchards.co.uk

For antiquarian books

JARNDYCE

The demise of Charing Cross Road's second-hand book trade is much lamented by bibliophiles, and surely only the landlords can be happy with the unsightly ragbag of tat shops that have moved in. Jarndyce, named after Dickens's wards of court in his novel *Bleak House* (1853), is how one imagines a successful antiquarian bookshop should look. The house, built in the 1730s opposite what became the British Museum, was given a stucco façade in the 1850s and perfectly reflects the eighteenth- and nineteenth-century English literature and history that Jarndyce specializes in. Although Jarndyce was established in 1969, there has been a bookshop on this site for more than a century, and it feels lived-in. On our last visit we saw a late Victorian red leather-bound volume entitled *Where Famous Londoners Lived*, which listed the addresses of our great poets, statesmen, philosophers and authors. The heaven of a book being wrapped in anonymous brown paper and tied with string, as it would have been in Dickens's day.

Jarndyce produces eight catalogues a year of books on specialist subjects, such as Dickens, the Romantics, Women Writers, Etiquette and Education, and Bloods and Penny Dreadfuls. If you don't see what you're looking for, do ask, because the owners, Brian Lake and Janet Nassau, know their subjects, the auction market and the collectors who might be willing to buy or sell. The windows at Jarndyce are terribly popular with Bloomsbury locals because one displays 'Bizarre Books' with titles that never fail to raise a smile, such as *What to Say When You Talk to Yourself*, *The Leadership Secrets of Attila the Hun* and *How to Be Happy though Human*.

46 Great Russell Street WC1
Tel. 020 7631 4220
Tube: Tottenham Court Road
www.jarndyce.co.uk

For rare books and manuscripts

MAGGS BROS

&JS

Founded in 1853 by Uriah Maggs, this rare book and manuscript dealer has held successive Royal Warrants, from those of King George V to the present Queen. Maggs broke the auction record for a printed book when the firm paid £4.6 million for Caxton's edition of Chaucer's *Canterbury Tales* in 1998, negotiated the acquisition of the Gutenberg Bible of 1455 from the Soviet government in 1932 for the British Museum, and bought documents, books and intimate objects relating to Emperor Napoleon in 1916. Since 1937 Maggs has traded from 50 Berkeley Square, a picturesque historic late eighteenth-century town house that is said to be the most haunted property in London. Prime Minister George Canning died here, as, allegedly, did an *Upstairs Downstairs* cast of malcontents frightened to death.

Maggs may appear intimidating, dealing as it does with the world's ruling families, richest collectors and most august libraries, but the tone is set by the managing director and fourth-generation family member, 'Mr Ed' Maggs, who welcomes young collectors who may or may not become lifelong clients. There's an encyclopaedic stock sold for the low thousands, specifically manuscripts, letters and books signed by Charles II, Florence Nightingale, Princess Pauline Borghese, E. M. Forster, the Duke of Windsor and Stephen Tennant. Nelson, Wellington, Churchill and Queen Victoria are also well represented, but at a price. Each of Maggs' departments produces catalogues that represent the best in their field, be that early English illuminated manuscripts or naval and military subjects. A recent Charles Dickens catalogue displayed a remarkable collection of ten Cruikshank-illustrated first-edition monthly instalments of *Oliver Twist* from 1846, for £22,500. Maggs' startling Counterculture catalogues include photographs of Vivienne Westwood in Sex, her 1970s boutique on the King's Road.

50 Berkeley Square W1
Tel. 020 7493 7160
Tube: Green Park
www.maggs.com

———— *For new editions* ————

HEYWOOD HILL

&JS

Recommending Heywood Hill solely for new editions is rather like rating Fortnum & Mason only for its nougat. Heywood and his wife-to-be, Anne Gathorne-Hardy, opened Mayfair's favourite bookshop in 1936 so that 'the people we like can find the books they like', and that included antiquarian books as well as new editions such as James Joyce's *Ulysses*.

Hill's circle included Evelyn Waugh (who called the shop 'a centre of all that was left of fashionable and intellectual London'), Osbert Sitwell, James Lees-Milne, Cyril Connolly and Nancy Mitford, the last of whom famously worked at 10 Curzon Street during the war years. Heywood Hill has a titanic reputation in the literary world for such a small, albeit charming, shop, with its Georgian bow window and blue plaque to Mitford. That reputation is justified by the perfectly chosen selection of books old and new, covering precisely the subjects and authors that Heywood Hill's customers appreciate. If a book is not stocked, out of print or highly collectible, Heywood Hill will as a matter of course make the search become a quest.

Lifelong customer the late Duke of Devonshire (whose duchess, Deborah, was the youngest Mitford sister) was a major shareholder from 1991, and in 2013 the present Duke of Devonshire became sole owner, inviting Nicky Dunne to direct the family bookshop with Venetia Vyvyan. Those following in the footsteps of Lees-Milne or Mitford will not be disappointed by Heywood Hill. Scholars, socialites and the intelligentsia still consider the shop to be a place where minds meet. Heywood Hill's quarterly list of new books is invaluable now the quality of books generally has plummeted in inverse proportion to the quantity published annually. If there is such a thing as a perfect gift, surely it has to be Heywood Hill's choice of book delivered monthly for a year.

10 Curzon Street W1
Tel. 020 7629 0647
Tube: Green Park
www.heywoodhill.com

For antique maps and prints

ALTEA GALLERY

Although we've spent countless hours in Stanfords on Long Acre poring over modern maps and atlases, we've only paused to admire the windows of the Altea Gallery en route to St George's or Sotheby's opposite. Our only visit to Altea – in search of Richard Blome's map of St James's from 1685 – was rewarding. In addition to hundreds of antique maps dating from the fifteenth to the nineteenth century and a display of historic London cartography, the gallery director, Massimo De Martini, has amassed a precious collection of atlases, sea charts and globes. Cartography is a minefield for those not schooled in its subtleties. We were marvelling over the linen-laid William Newton *Map of London in the Early 16th Century*, thinking £1,500 was incredibly reasonable for an object of such great age, before being told tactfully that the map was produced in 1855.

> *"Cartography is a minefield for those not schooled in its subtleties."*

Altea was the first gallery of its calibre to catalogue its entire stock digitally and post prices online. While giving other dealers a point of reference in a notoriously secretive world, that does allow clients to do at least a little homework before coming to visit the gallery. You can spend anything from £100 to £100,000 at Altea, and what we appreciate is the generosity of the gentlemen in the shop should you share their passion for the subject. It isn't every day you can request to see Johannes Blaeu's *Theatrum*

Atlas of 1645 (yours for £45,000), with 120 hand-coloured maps enclosed in its gilded pages. Seeing such beauty makes one appreciate that Blaeu was to maps what Velázquez was to court painters in his day.

35 Saint George Street W1
Tel. 020 7491 0010
Tube: Oxford Circus
www.alteagallery.com

GROSVENOR PRINTS

In the eighteenth century London's print-shop windows were de facto tabloid front pages, to which the public flocked to see George Cruikshank or James Gillray's latest lampoon of the venal Prince Regent, drunk Charles James Fox or flirtatious Georgiana, Duchess of Devonshire. Today, antique print shops in central London are as rare as an honest politician. Those of us who value prints cleave to Grosvenor like survivors to the raft of the *Medusa*. The breadth of the stock can be gauged by the titles pencilled on each huge cardboard portfolio. British monarchs are divided by dynasty, and there are further folios for the world's kings and emperors. London is divided by borough and then into theatres, parks and palaces. Whereas other print shops might have a small section relating to dogs, Grosvenor has folios pertaining to working dogs, toys, terriers and hounds.

> *"Today, antique print shops in central London are as rare as an honest politician."*

What appears to be chaos is in fact extremely well ordered. Much of the stock is digitized, but for a collector there is no pleasure as great as a space being cleared on the ground floor of Grosvenor and one or two portfolios being left for one to peruse. The chase is the thrill; you might be looking for a print of Marlborough House and find it in a folio relating to Christopher Wren rather than, say, St James's or Queen Alexandra. If you're seeking a particular artist (Turner, perhaps?) or a famous engraver such as Houbraken, they will be catalogued in Grosvenor's online records, which list well over 100 'A's' in both artist and engraver. You'll appreciate, then, that Grosvenor Prints is an invaluable research resource as well as a joy to visit. Prints in superb condition are becoming increasingly rare, but they are also still relatively well priced. For its devotees, Grosvenor Prints is absolutely priceless.

19 Shelton Street WC2
Tel. 020 7836 1979
Tube: Leicester Square
www.grosvenorprints.com

HENRY SOTHERAN

Established in 1761 and trading in London since the Battle of Waterloo, Henry Sotheran is one of London's most venerable book and print shops, not to mention what we consider the most well-appointed. As a book dealer, Sotheran has an impeccable pedigree, having bought Laurence '*Tristram Shandy*' Sterne's library in 1768 and Dickens's after his death in 1870. Without the double ceiling height of Daunt in Marylebone, Sotheran still enjoys a sense of space, despite every wall being covered with glass-fronted bookshelves and the entire first floor being taken with desks and vitrines piled high with books pertaining to seventeenth- to twentieth-century literature, architecture, natural history, travel, architecture and children's literature. For bookmen who appreciate private press editions and bound sets, such as a twenty-six-volume collection of Dickens first editions bound in red leather by Bayntun, Sotheran's is Shangri-La.

For collectors of fine prints, the basement print room at Sotheran's is in a class of its own. In marked contrast to Grosvenor, Sotheran deals exclusively in the very top tier of decorative prints in absolutely tip-top condition. Each print is beautifully mounted and either displayed or stored in map chests, and each catalogue could be auctioned as is by Bonhams or Christie's. The jazzy 1930s travel posters for the French Riviera are as joyful as a production of *No, No, Nanette*, and the botanical prints (usually given their own window during the week of the Chelsea Flower Show) are glorious. In addition to the usual subjects (London views and 'Spy' cartoons), Sotheran is particularly strong on fashions from the 1870s to the 1950s. It is always a great pleasure to walk past the shop's windows every week and see gallery-quality posters to the left and books written by or bearing the ex-libris of such favourites as Patrick Leigh Fermor, Fleur Cowles, Hardy Amies and James Pope-Hennessy to the right.

> *"The jazzy 1930s travel posters for the French Riviera are as joyful as a production of No, No, Nanette ..."*

2–5 Sackville Street W1
Tel. 020 7439 6151
Tube: Piccadilly Circus
www.sotherans.co.uk

For bookbinding

THE WYVERN BINDERY

Moments from the Charterhouse and the ancient
Priory of St John is a fitting place for one of London's
few remaining bookbinderies, whose work would be
recognizable even now to the monks who inhabited
pre-Reformation Clerkenwell. The Wyvern Bindery
is not one of those pristine antiquarian bookshops
where one discusses the finer points of section-sewn
pages, hand-sewn headbands, decorative endpapers,
de-bossing and leather onlays from the comfort of
a polished club chair. This is a workshop chock-full
of young apprentices and piled high with samples of
leather, moleskins, marbled papers and gold leaf,
all waiting to produce bespoke bindings for one-off
commissions, editions and small runs.

There is quite literally nothing the owner, Mark
Winstanley, cannot do. His workshop turns its hand
to making bespoke boxes, slipcases, portfolios,
albums and periodical sets as
well as props for films, including
the Harry Potter franchise and
Sherlock Holmes. The last time
we witnessed Mr Winstanley at
work, he was two years into a
five-year project to restore and
rebind over 120 historic customer
ledgers belonging to Savile Row's
founding father, Henry Poole &
Co. He is arguably the only man in
London with the knowledge and
the number of trained apprentices to complete such a
task. In addition to binding books, Wyvern is expert

> *"This is a
> workshop chock-
> full of young
> apprentices ...
> all waiting to
> produce bespoke
> bindings ..."*

at repairing antique books, for which it is worth its weight in gold leaf.

56–58 Clerkenwell Road EC1
Tel. 020 7490 7899
Tube: Barbican
www.wyvernbindery.com

Clocks & Watches

ARTHUR BEALE

There are few more incongruous sights in London than the yacht chandler Arthur Beale on decidedly landlocked Shaftesbury Avenue. Founded in the sixteenth century by the ropemaker John Buckingham in the vicinity of the now lost Fleet River, which still runs beneath Holborn and down into the Thames, the firm now known as Arthur Beale sells shackles, bolts, hooks, rope, rigging, maritime flags, ship's bells, lifejackets and all things a decent ship's store should. Beale's was floundering of late, until new owners Alasdair Flint and Gerry Jeatt came aboard in 2014. The chaps are still finding ledgers of supplies sold to early Arctic and Everest exploration missions, and the old girl seems to be shored up for the present.

We must have sailed blithely past Arthur Beale for years without questioning how such an anomaly has survived for so long (400 years, according to the firm). We were stopped in our tracks by a wooden board in the window displaying a small family of maritime clocks and barometers that we know would appeal to smart landlubbers: brass and chrome wall-

mounted clocks with pronounced barrels, sold just
north of £100. The Breton navy-and-white-striped
long-sleeved tops and matching beanie hats that
are always on display in the window attract a steady
stream of fashionistas, who admire their authenticity.
Arthur Beale is also popular with interior decorators,
who can work wonders with an arum lily and a
monkey's fist.

194 Shaftsbury Avenue WC2
Tel. 020 7836 9034
Tube: Tottenham Court Road
www.arthurbeale.co.uk

PENDULUM OF MAYFAIR

One feels ever so slightly blasé saying that Pendulum
of Mayfair specializes in antique grandfather clocks
pre-dating 1810, as if this isn't an achievement in
itself. British long-case clockmaking was at its zenith
from the late seventeenth century to the turn of the
nineteenth, with masters such as Vulliamy, Lowndes,
Storr and Watts, and the director of Pendulum, Roy
Clements, has a decent representation of their work
in his London showroom. One always wishes to pause
when looking at these remarkable feats of art and
science to acknowledge that some of these timepieces
were marking the hour before the end of the Stuart
dynasty. If due care is given to these faithful fathers
of time and they survive as long again, they will be
keeping time 300 years hence, which is a sobering
thought in a society where an iPhone isn't expected
to last a year without being made obsolete by a
newer model.

Only a fraction of Pendulum's stock is on
show – the lion's share being kept in Suffolk, where

restoration and condition reports are undertaken
– although of course you will see some of the best
long-case, bracket, wall and carriage clocks in the
Mayfair showroom. Such is the vintage and quality
of Pendulum's stock that you won't find a decent
grandfather clock for less than the high thousands,
and it is more likely to be in the tens of thousands
if the name of an important maker is attached.
Although nothing can surpass the grandeur of a
walnut or mahogany long-case clock, we rather like
such classics as an Ambrose Coggeshall mahogany
wall clock of 1860, a rather fabulously fussy shagreen
and ormolu French clock (circa 1900) with porcelain
dial, and a collection of turn-of-the-twentieth-century
automatons in the shape of monkeys smoking, leaping
and playing the harp.

King House, 51 Maddox Street W1
Tel. 020 7629 6606
Tube: Oxford Circus
www.pendulumofmayfair.co.uk

THE VINTAGE WATCH COMPANY

Second-hand timepieces always remind us of those
wartime comedy spivs invariably played by George
Cole with a raincoat lining full of half-inched watches.
Resales of pieces made by the major marques Rolex,
Patek Philippe and Cartier now break auction records,
and the form for these commodities is studied as
keenly as the price of oil. The Vintage Watch Company
has found the perfect home in the Burlington Arcade
to concentrate exclusively on high-ticket historic Rolex
timepieces. There are over 750 watches in stock at any
given time, the earliest a silver officer's watch from
1916 with luminous hands and numerals, made only

eight years after Hans Wilsdorf named his London-based company Rolex. Although he subsequently moved to Geneva, in 1919, we like to think Wilsdorf's London years give the Vintage Watch Company a legitimate reason to trade in the Burlington Arcade.

The easiest way to choose a gift is by birthdate. This we tried, only to be rather horrified by an eighteen-carat white-gold Day-Date with matt black diamond dial and matching eighteen-carat white-gold president bracelet with a price tag of £26,900. We tend to find the earlier models more aesthetically pleasing, such as an Arabic numerical dial Rolex from 1931 with mechanical movement (£7,400), an eighteen-carat rose-gold Rolex from 1950 with large, round antique cream dial and mechanical movement (£12,400) and a chic 1920s ladies' Rolex Princess in steel and rose gold with rectangular mechanical movement and silk-cord strap. The Vintage Watch Company maintains workshops in the basement and will guarantee all its Rolex watches for two years. Although, since we were just waxing lyrical about late Stuart grandfather clocks lasting for three centuries, this might seem rather a stingy promise.

24 Burlington Arcade W1
Tel. 020 7499 2032
Tube: Green Park
www.vintagewatchcompany.com

Pens & Writing Paper

MOUNT STREET PRINTERS

A family stationer proud to specialize in die-stamping and engraving, Mount Street Printers opened in 1981 on what has become Mayfair's smartest street: smarter even than New Bond Street, where the firm's competitor Smythson resides. Much as we admire Smythson's history, the company has expanded worldwide and set its sights on the luxury handbag business, rather than engraving a dowager's coronet embellished with mother-of-pearl and gold leaf on Mayfair blue writing paper. So it is to the Cain family that we turn for correspondence cards, tissue-lined envelopes, invitations and calling cards.

"One falls a little in love with Mount Street Printers just because of the whimsical displays in the bow window."

One falls a little in love with Mount Street Printers just because of the whimsical displays in the bow window. On entering, it is pleasing to see that so much of the production and hand-finishing is completed on the premises. Should you have fantasies that Stephen Tennant ordered lavender writing paper here, be satisfied that you might be right. The same premises were taken by Queen Victoria's printer Henningham & Hollis in 1899. When MSP opened in 1981, one of the first customers was Ingrid Bergman.

At the last count, MSP employed more than twenty-five people, and the founders' son Alex was taking great pride in the number of apprentices continuing the trade. The design team lives on the top floor, but the rest of the house is essentially a series of workshops where die-stamping, foiling and gilt-edging are demonstrated. It is really rather brilliant to see work in progress and understand why the bespoke process is worth investing time and money to promote. You will find lovely ready-made cards and envelopes on the ground floor, a selection of which can be bought for the first time in the company's history from Fortnum & Mason. No fool Fortnum's to have recognized the need for a thoroughbred brand to help relaunch its stationery department.

4 Mount Street W1
Tel. 020 7409 0303
Tube: Bond Street
www.mountstreetprinters.com

PENFRIEND

A fight for the Burlington Arcade's soul was waged in 2014 that left rather too many shopfronts dark over Christmas while old tenants were ejected and fashionable brands, untroubled by the vast rent rises, were in no hurry to move in. Penfriend has clocked up more than twenty-five years in the Burlington Arcade, having been established in 1950 by a former Parker pen repairman, Ivan Mason. Pens, like gem-set jewellery, are a sublime product for the smaller shopfronts in the arcade: the higher the volume of high-ticket items crammed into the space the better. Of course the Achilles heel for pens and penmanship is the relatively low percentage of ladies and gentlemen who still write by hand, let alone always carry an instrument to do so. Of those, one has to wonder how many who possess a favourite pen would like a second that starts the collection.

The answer, as with so many elitist trades, is that the number of vendors shrinks, leaving the best to rise to the top. Although we've always loathed the name Penfriend – not having had a terribly good experience with Gallic penfriends in youth – we have come to treasure the shop at the Burlington Gardens end of the arcade. The royal family of maker's marques are all represented here, including Waterman, Montblanc, Visconti and Montegrappa. There is also a selection of antique pens, such as a handsome Conklin No. 18 black fountain pen made in 1918 and a Montblanc No. 144 from the 1940s. You will find pens crafted in all materials from precious woods and mother-of-pearl to eighteen-carat gold. Also on sale are those delicious coloured and scented inks that always remind one of Catherine de' Medici.

34 Burlington Arcade W1
Tel. 020 7499 6337
Tube: Green Park
www.penfriend.co.uk

Department Stores

FORTNUM & MASON

&JS

If Piccadilly were to be tailored a livery, it would be trimmed with Fortnum & Mason eau de Nil. Her Majesty's grocer from the age of Queen Anne (1707) to that of our present Queen is quintessentially West End, and as grand as a trumpet voluntary. Although pretenders such as Harvey Nichols temporarily stole its thunder in the 1990s, Fortnum & Mason has consistently delighted Piccadilly with magical window displays that promise tradition, celebration and spoiling treats. Setting aside the coffee counter and vitrines displaying handmade chocolates, Londoners tend to avoid the ground floor, even though it is glorious to watch gentlemen in tailcoats glide underneath the chandeliers in search of candied fruit or slabs of nougat as thick as the Elgin Marbles.

To celebrate its tercentenary in 2007, Fortnum's installed a carousel staircase down to the new fresh-food halls in the basement, with a 'doughnut' skylight reaching towards the upper floors. This was a risky but hugely successful move that has opened the doll's house that is Fortnum & Mason and encouraged us ever upwards. It succeeded only when the managing director, Ewan Venters, made sure there was a marvellous mix of historic and fashionable gorgeousness running the gamut from candles and stationery to perfume, nightwear, fine china, jewellery and millinery. We particularly like the games room and the top-floor Diamond Jubilee Tea Room, inaugurated by Her Majesty in 2012 on her first engagement with the Duchess of Cambridge and the Duchess of Cornwall.

> *"Fortnum's history basically covers the birth of the fashionable West End, but the firm wears its years lightly."*

Fortnum's history basically covers the birth of the fashionable West End, but the firm wears its years lightly. It could be said to have invented the picnic hamper, the Scotch egg and the vogue for serving comestibles in aspic, and it has the dubious honour of being the first retailer of Heinz baked beans. So many monarchs have ordered from what is essentially Buckingham Palace's corner shop that there seems little point in listing their peccadilloes. Fortnum & Mason is alive now as it hasn't been for decades: launching hot-air balloons and delivery vans and tending beehives on its roof. It is also expanding. St Pancras station and Heathrow Terminal 5 we can forgive; Dubai we cannot. Fortnum's famously dispatched beef tea to Florence Nightingale's Scutari hospital in the Crimean War in 1855. It did not open a concession.

181 Piccadilly W1
Tel. 020 7734 8040
Tube: Piccadilly Circus
www.fortnumandmason.com

HARRODS

&JS

By 1894 the small grocer's shop opened in Knightsbridge by Henry Harrod in 1849 could boast in a *Daily Telegraph* advertisement that 'Harrods serves the world.' By 1905 the domed red-brick palace of retail we know today, covering 5 acres and designed by Charles William Spencer, was completed, with more than a million square feet of selling space. Harrods' motto, *Omnia Omnibus Ubique* (all things for all people, everywhere), appears to hold true, even though the world-famous pet department – where Beatrice Lillie bought Noël Coward an alligator in 1951 and where Christian, the King's Road lion cub, was purchased in 1969 – closed in 2014. Harrods is, was and always will be all about shopping and spectacle, from installing the first escalators in 1883 (with an attendant at the top, armed with sal volatile and brandy) to former owner Mohamed Al-Fayed's Vegas-style Egyptian Halls and Escalator, retained by the shop's present owner, the Qatari royal family.

Although Harrods boasts over 300 departments, we have noticed many 'rationalizations' of late. The piano department closed in 2013, and we were dismayed not to be able to buy a bridge table in the games room, which is now in the basement. But, then again, one can't fault Harrods for the acres of Fine Watches and Fine Jewellery concessions on the ground floor, or the black-and-white Perfume Hall with its original Lalique panels. Harrods' Food Halls are one of London's most miraculous sights, particularly the tiles in the meat hall, painted with *Scenes from the Hunt* by W. J. Neatby in 1902, and the chandeliers that illuminate the cornucopia of fresh produce arranged daily like a Dutch old master still life. It is *Charlie and the Chocolate Factory* reimagined in a Romanov palace; an apposite reference, because the last tsar's daughters famously bought sailors' costumes at Harrods in 1913.

"Harrods is, was and always will be all about shopping and spectacle, from installing the first escalators in 1883 … to [the] Egyptian Halls …"

The Qatari acquisition of Harrods hasn't made a huge impact on the alignment of departments, although the bookshop has been reduced in size to accommodate the Cultural Essence of Qatar room. It is a mystery why the Qatari royal family has allowed the tasteless shrine to the late Diana, Princess of Wales, and Dodi Fayed to remain at the foot of the Egyptian staircase, along with a 10-foot bronze statue of Dodi, Diana and an albatross installed in 2005. We can't imagine that the Royal Warrants that Mr Al-Fayed allegedly burned – subsequently withdrawn – will return to the façade of Harrods as long as the shrine remains in place. A note on fashion: the *Discriminating Guide* is not going to list endless fashion flagship stores, either British or international, because we know the collections are available worldwide. Rather than hoof up and down Bond Street, Mount Street and Brook Street in search of designer womenswear, do save yourself the bother and find the cream of the crop on the first floor in Harrods' International Designer Rooms.

87–135 Brompton Road SW1
Tel. 020 7730 1234
Tube: Knightsbridge
www.harrods.com

Gifts

For flowers

McQUEENS

Although there is a bloodline of florists by Royal Appointment, from Constance Spry and Moyses Stevens to Kenneth Turner and Shane Connolly, one name not connected to royal weddings stands out as the most influential floral designer in twenty-first-century London: McQueen. Royalty was smiling down on its founder, Kally Ellis, who took over a failing Shoreditch florist in 1991, where the late Alexander McQueen's aunt had previously worked (hence the name).

"... the most influential floral designer in twenty-first-century London ..."

In 1994 *Vanity Fair* placed an emergency call to McQueens for last-minute help dressing the Serpentine Gallery for the magazine's annual party. It was the year Diana, Princess of Wales, appeared in her devastatingly curvaceous black 'revenge' cocktail dress, and so the party and the flowers were photographed to death. Today Ellis flies out to oversee personally the decoration of *Vanity Fair*'s parties after the Oscars and at the Cannes and Tribeca film festivals.

McQueens has distinguished itself through producing hand-tied sculptural arrangements of flowers in contemporary colour drifts using a minimum of different flowers and foliage. Its work for Claridges, the Berkeley and the Connaught is a constant delight, with a single flower – the blue delphinium, perhaps, or baby-pink peonies – deployed to fabulous effect in an arrangement of vases and bowls more akin to an installation than the old-fashioned single baroque tower of gaudy full-blown blooms. Pretty without being sugary sweet, and modern without looking harsh, McQueens' hand-tied bouquets are as subtly coloured as a Renoir. The Old Street location seems to discourage passing trade in favour of glamorous corporate clients, but McQueens does deliver in London.

70–72 Old Street EC1
Tel. 020 7251 5505
Tube: Old Street
www.mcqueens.co.uk

For chocolates

CHARBONNEL ET WALKER

&JS

As a prelude to seduction, Charbonnel et Walker Pink Marc de Champagne Truffles in a handmade heart-shaped, ribbon-tied box are hard to beat, unless of course one's inamorata is diabetic. Even the union of Mesdames Charbonnel and Walker has the whiff of regal misbehaviour about it. It seems that in 1875 the then Prince of Wales (later Edward VII) persuaded his favourite Parisian chocolatier, Madame Charbonnel of Maison Boissier, to come to London and set up shop with Mrs Walker. This she did, on Bond Street, and there Charbonnel et Walker remains to this day. Photographs of the ladies strongly suggest that neither would have been of interest to the prince, so we must assume that it was the quality of their truffles – and their effect on *maîtresse-en-titre* Lillie Langtry in the late 1870s – that prompted Wales's patronage.

How do we love Charbonnel et Walker? Let us count the ways. The pastel boxes foiled in gold and topped with the Queen's Royal Warrant make terribly pretty dinner-party gifts, whereas the mad, multicoloured boxes from the Princes Arcade chocolatier Prestat look as if they're from a joke shop rather than a historic maker of divine truffles, dark chocolate thins and candied ginger. We like the fact that at Charbonnel et Walker we're treading in the footsteps of truffle lovers Mrs Simpson, Princess Margaret, John Gielgud, Lauren Bacall, Noël Coward and Diana, Princess of Wales. But first and foremost we're absolutely wild about those pink champagne truffles, which are at their most seductive unwrapped alone rather than in company.

1 The Royal Arcade, 28 Old Bond Street W1
Tel. 020 7491 0939
Tube: Green Park
www.charbonnel.co.uk

For perfume
and scented gifts

D. R. HARRIS

Temporarily nudged off St James's Street, where it
was established in 1790, D. R. Harris was chemist to
the Regent and his St James's coffee-house circle.
The shop holds the Royal Warrant of Her Majesty The
Queen and the Prince of Wales, as well as the loyalty
and affection of the gentlemen's clubs that populate
this quarter of the fashionable West End. D. R. Harris
has a history of formulating classic gentlemen's
colognes, lavender waters and single-note English
flower perfumes that make the most marvellous gifts
should you know your host's tastes very well. We would
defy anyone with an ounce of discernment not to
appreciate a bottle of Harris's Bay Rum, Sandalwood
or Pink Aftershave. The firm doesn't use synthetics,
so colognes such as Mayfair, Marlborough, Windsor,
Arlington and Albany are fleeting pleasures. This we
much prefer to the strong designer eaux de parfum,
which stay for days like an unwelcome houseguest.

Much as we like the temporary sites – on Bury
Street down the road from Quaglino's, and the tiny
cabinet of a shop on Piccadilly – we were pleased to
hear that D. R. Harris is due to return to St James's
Street in 2015, with all the original mahogany
apothecary chests and cabinets reinstated. We are not
fans of mass production or flashy fashion brands, so
don't expect our hosts to be either. There's something
terribly modest and honest about the packaging for
a Marlborough scented candle, a ceramic pot of bath
salts or a box of three Lavender/Almond/Arlington

soaps from D. R. Harris. We always think the best gifts are those one's reluctant to give up, and there's barely a product in D. R. Harris that we wouldn't be delighted to receive.

52 Piccadilly W1
Tel. 020 7930 3915
Tube: Green Park
www.drharris.co.uk

FLORIS

&JS

Established in 1730, Floris is the oldest family-owned perfumer in the world. The royal crest above the door is that of King George IV, who gave the perfumer its first Royal Warrant, in 1820. The free-standing mahogany cases were made for the Great Exhibition of 1851, and one of the house best-sellers today, Bouquet de la Reine, was formulated in 1840 to celebrate the marriage of Queen Victoria and Prince Albert. Floris's appointment as Court Perfumer is a line unbroken from Queen Victoria to Queen Elizabeth II, for whom Bouquet de la Reine was reformulated in 2002 to celebrate her Golden Jubilee. The history of Floris is told in the charming museum and bespoke perfume room at the back of the shop, but the true story is told in the perfumes that date from the very beginning.

Private blends were produced for such illustrious customers as Russia's Grand Duke Orloff, who commissioned Special No. 127 in 1890, a favourite of that most unlikely of couples, Winston Churchill and Eva Perón. Ian Fleming preferred house blend No. 89 and mentioned the house in various James Bond novels. Records show that Marilyn Monroe, who visited London only once, in 1956, ordered Floris Rose

Geranium to be shipped to the Beverly Hills Hotel. Sadly, the ledgers don't record precisely what was ordered by the style icons Princess Marina, Vivien Leigh, Queen Marie of Romania and Lady Cunard. But, true to its past, Floris still makes such classics as Edwardian Bouquet, Night Scented Jasmine, Limes and White Rose. Of the new blends, we recommend Mahon Leather (made in honour of Juan Floris's birthplace, Menorca) and the rich, deep Leather Oud eau de parfum.

"Ian Fleming preferred house blend No. 89 and mentioned the house in various James Bond novels."

89 Jermyn Street SW1
Tel. 020 7930 2885
Tube: Piccadilly Circus
www.florislondon.com

--- *For cigars and snuff* ---

J. J. FOX & CO.

Fox's St James's heritage reaches back to 1787, when the firm acquired the tobacco vendor Robert Lewis. Lewis held the Royal Warrants of the Emperor Napoleon III, King Edward VII and his son King George V, as well as the loyalty of the Duke of Windsor, who donated his humidor from his Windsor folly Fort Belvedere to the Fox Museum, and Winston Churchill. Churchill's mother, Lady Randolph Churchill, for whom Lewis made gold-tipped filter

cigarettes, introduced her son to the shop in 1900.
He ordered fifty small Havana cigars and a box of
100 Balkan cigarettes, and remained a customer
until the day he died. Churchill's favourite battered
leather armchair stands in the basement museum,
as do documents pertaining to Oscar Wilde (whose
arrest left a cigar bill in arrears) and the oldest cigars
in existence, displayed in a glass casket as they were
at the Great Exhibition in 1851. For a cigar smoker, a
box or even a single Havana from J. J. Fox's St James's
Street shop is a gift from a shrine.

19 St James's Street SW1
Tel. 020 7930 3787
Tube: Green Park
www.jjfox.co.uk

For wines and spirits

BERRY BROS & RUDD

&JS

The earlier *Discriminating Guide* rather undersells
Berry Bros – royal wine merchant since the reign
of King George III – simply saying that the firm is
'best known in the trade today both for their superb
Port and excellent claret for drinking now, but the
offices themselves are worthy of a visit even if you're
not thirsty. The house, with its façade of five arched
windows, was built in 1730 and is unchanged.' This is
the most breathtakingly beautiful shop in London.
The floorboards of the principal reception room are
bowed with the tread of the Prince Regent, George
'Beau' Brummell, Lord Byron and Charles James Fox,

all of whom were weighed on the Great Scales, which still stand on the shop floor today. Not a bottle of wine is visible in this room, although friends of Berry Bros know that an inconspicuous staircase leads to two levels of cavernous cellar beneath.

Today the cellars house two of the firm's private dining rooms: the Napoleon Cellar (named after Emperor Napoleon III, who plotted his path back to power in the 1840s from Berry's cellars) and the Pickering Cellar, displaying historic bottles from the era when the vessel was more costly than the contents, including a bottle from 1661 celebrating the Restoration of Charles II. According to the firm's chairman, Simon Berry, the fabled secret passageway leading from Berry's cellars to those of St James's Palace has not been discovered, although a Tudor well was uncovered recently. Berry Bros may look unchanged, but that's because the brand director, Geordie Willis, has modernized the historic headquarters with great stealth and immense subtlety. One can actually see wine sold in the wings on either side of the entrance to No. 3, and Berry's scored an international hit with No. 3 London Dry Gin, which could do for the firm what Cutty Sark whisky did in the 1920s. Is there another wine merchant in London? Not that we're aware of.

"The floorboards ... are bowed with the tread of the Prince Regent, George 'Beau' Brummell [and] Lord Byron ..."

3 St James's Street SW1
Tel. 0800 280 2440
Tube: Green Park
www.bbr.com

Jewellery

For fine jewellery

MOUSSAIEFF

Matriarch Alisa Moussaieff is London's uncrowned
queen of diamonds. The family into which she married
has traded in diamonds and pearls for centuries, and
the House of Moussaieff has been based in London
since 1963. In 2007 Moussaieff opened a ritzy New
Bond Street flagship opposite Graff, although Mrs M.
still designs from a bunker headquarters in the Park
Lane Hilton hotel, where her billionaire clients still
prefer to meet. In recent years Graff and Moussaieff
have competed head to head at auction for the rarest,
largest and purest coloured diamonds, although it
was Mr Moussaieff (now retired) who began buying
coloured stones in the 1960s, and only Mrs M. knows
the extent of the family's stock. Impossibly rare stones
and flamboyant design meet in the jewels Mrs M.
sets and sells to ruling Gulf State families, among
others. As she says, 'we throw diamonds on the table
and together we choose the stones and the design.'
She will spend years collecting a parcel of perfectly
matched pink diamonds to create a line bracelet, and
even longer watching a rarity such as the Moussaieff
Red Diamond – at 5.11 carats, the largest of only five
red diamonds certified by the Gemological Institute of
America – adding millions to the price she paid.

Even an amateur looking at the window displays
of Moussaieff Bond Street will recognize the audacity
of her designs, using miracles of nature that alone

deserve a case in the Smithsonian Institution. Only Mrs M. could unite natural fancy intense pink and natural fancy vivid blue marquise-cut diamonds in a single ring, or show a suite of untreated Burma sapphires the size of dominos set as a demi-parure with D-E-F-quality diamonds. On our forays to the Moussaieff bunker at the Hilton, we've seen D-flawless diamond watches set with slivers of Golconda diamonds as the face, chameleon diamonds that change from yellow to green when exposed to light, and diamond-encrusted cuffs designed around star sapphires as big as golf balls.

"Even an amateur looking at the window displays of Moussaieff Bond Street will recognize the audacity of her designs ..."

The entry level for Moussaieff might be Middle Eastern sheikh's third wife, but we do urge you to visit New Bond Street and admire the most adventurous design of exceptional diamond jewellery in London or even the world.

172 New Bond Street W1
Tel. 020 7290 1536
Tube: Green Park
www.moussaieff.co.uk

SHAUN LEANE

In an echo of Judy Garland's 'Born in a Trunk' number from *A Star Is Born*, Shaun Leane cut his teeth doing bench work in Hatton Garden, restoring antique jewels by Cartier, Van Cleef & Arpels, Boucheron and so forth. Thus he says with deep humility: 'I admire the past masters who created fine jewellery that was distinctive of its time.' Leane, who founded the House

of Shaun Leane in 1999, went through a baptism of
fire working with his friend Alexander McQueen on
show-stopping pieces for every catwalk presentation
McQueen designed from 'The Hunger' collection in
1996 until his untimely death in 2010.

Leane's appreciation of past masters and his
wild decade making extreme pieces, such as the
ribbed metallic body sculpture for McQueen's muse
Björk, have nurtured an extraordinary talent for
jewellery design. Working with his creative director,
Ben Rowe, Leane has developed a cult following for
his sometimes dangerously beautiful designs, such
as the much-imitated 'Hook My Heart', 'Tusk' and
'Entwined' collections. He will explore a shape or
concept endlessly, interpreting a signature motif
such as his tusk in a simple sterling-silver pendant
then pushing the design onwards and upwards to
an exceptional conclusion, such as the extravagant
eighteen-carat yellow-gold tusk earrings set with a line
of perfectly matched emeralds.

Without huge fanfare, the House of Shaun Leane
has been producing one-off pieces of artist jewellery
that have had museums, collectors and auction
houses taking notice, including the eighteen-carat
white-gold-and-enamel White Light brooch, made
for the Forevermark 'Precious Collection' and set
with thirteen Steinmetz D-flawless pear-shaped white
diamonds, and Daphne Guinness's eighteen-carat
white-gold chain-mail Contra Mundum glove, pavé set
with 5,000 diamonds. One of Leane's most successful
(and award-winning) collections of late, 'Cherry
Blossom', began in vermeil but is now being made
in eighteen-carat rose gold embellished with pearls,
diamonds and white enamel. In 2014 Leane, an East
End boy, left Hatton Garden to take up residence in

a new town house in Mayfair, next door to Bonhams auction house. The three-storey house comprises showrooms, offices and top-floor workshops and can be visited by appointment should you wish to commission a unique piece from the House of Shaun Leane.

18 Woodstock Street W1
Tel. 020 7405 4773
Tube: Bond Street
www.shaunleane.com

SOLANGE AZAGURY-PARTRIDGE

In a quip worthy of Anita Loos, Solange Azagury-Partridge has already earned immortality in the quotation books by declaring: 'There comes a day in every woman's life when she wakes up wanting diamonds.' This Azagury-Partridge did in 1987, when she designed her own rough-diamond engagement ring. Today the jeweller holds court in the capital's most scrumptious town-house atelier, off Mount Street, keeps satellite stores in New York and Paris and has pieces in the permanent collections of the V&A and the Musée des Arts Décoratifs in Paris. Apart from a tenure as creative director of Boucheron at the invitation of Tom Ford, she has remained an independent force in contemporary jewellery design, and her body of work to date confirms that she is a modern master.

The decor of 5 Carlos Place says an awful lot about Azagury-Partridge's aesthetic: classical rooms are decorated with an anarchic colour palette of acid yellows, emerald greens and ruby reds. Star-shaped display cabinets and vitrines topped with scarlet ostrich plumes stand on psychedelic Op Art carpets.

The grand staircase is decorated with offcuts of clashing stars, rainbows and target-practice stripes. Imagine Cecil Beaton and Bridget Riley having a drug-fuelled one-night stand in an Edwardian town house and you've got the idea. There is mischief in some of Azagury-Partridge's designs; the ball-and-chain cufflink from the 'Alpha' collection, yellow-gold Fuck Off filigree ring and iconic enamel open-mouthed Hot Lips rings owe more to Linda Lovelace than to Salvador Dalí.

But it is the breathtaking creativity and exuberant sense of colour that will make Azagury-Partridge's pieces future heirlooms. Her Stoned bib necklace gathers a rainbow of coloured stones in a Byzantine collar that would look as striking worn with jeans as with a floor-length Jenny Packham dress. She paints with multicoloured cabochon stones in her latest Chromaphiliac drop earrings, and brings playfulness to a ring with her diamond fringe designs. We adore the sexiness of pieces such as the miniature pavé-set diamond disco-ball pendant, and the playfulness of the enamel Smartie Mother ring. Blackened gold that reveals the gleam of eighteen-carat yellow gold with touch and time is a speciality of Solange Azagury-Partridge, and makes a jewel unique to the wearer.

5 Carlos Place W1
Tel. 020 7792 0197
Tube: Bond Street
www.solange.co.uk

THEO FENNELL

As well as being one of the most amusing men in London, Theo Fennell is a relentless creative force in jewellery design. As he says, 'jewellery and silverware [at which he also excels] should be engaging and often romantic as well as beautiful. Above all it should give a thrill of pleasure each time it is looked at or worn.' Theo is the only jeweller in possession of a 44.87-carat blue topaz who would think 'what's missing here is a knuckleduster ring setting surrounding the stone with fish, seahorses and coral as if they are swimming in the stone.' Like Fulco di Verdura and Jean Schlumberger, Fennell has a surrealist's eye that can make

"... Fennell has a surrealist's eye that can make jewels ... delightful as well as intricate and ingenious."

jewels – such as his Masterworks rings inspired by *The Lion, the Witch and the Wardrobe, The Wizard of Oz* and *The Secret Garden* – delightful as well as intricate and ingenious. We know of no other jeweller who would on a whim make a series of eighteen-carat yellow-gold portrait rings of heroes and villains such as Abraham Lincoln, Winston Churchill, Chairman Mao and Eva Perón.

Fennell's early work (he founded his business in 1982) was characterized by baroque bejewelled crosses, keys and skulls beloved by Elton John and the late Gianni Versace. The baroque is still well in evidence, with poison rings set with stones the size of sheep's eyes and one-offs such as the Elizabeth I *memento mori* brooch with the queen's head a skull. But we're as fond, if not fonder, of smaller flashes of genius, such as Fennell's rock-crystal light-bulb cufflink backed with eighteen-carat yellow gold that glows in the right light, and his eighteen-carat yellow-gold lily-pad links with a white-gold frog in the centre of each. Fennell is one of the very few living jewellers who has a presence on the secondary market (JAR being another), and although he'd demur about buying to invest, we would prefer to put our trust in Fennell than in the Nikkei 225. The entry level is relatively low; a yellow-gold and mammoth-horn stick pin is £850, for example, and all the more appealing when Fennell tells the tale of an animal-rights protester who came into the shop and told Fennell he should be ashamed of using the horn of an 'endangered' species. Mammoths were extinct when, precisely? Some 4,500 years ago?

169 Fulham Road SW3
Tel. 020 7591 5000
Tube: South Kensington
www.theofennell.com

For antique jewels

BENTLEY & SKINNER

London's king of diamonds, Laurence Graff, did Bentley & Skinner a huge favour when he decided to expand into the former's New Bond Street premises. Nowhere in the world is there a higher concentration of magnificent diamond jewellery flagship stores than in Bond Street's 'diamond dash'. By moving to Piccadilly, across the road from Her Majesty's grocer, Fortnum & Mason, Bentley & Skinner acquired double the shopfront for its picture windows filled with tiers of antique diamond tiaras, natural pearl chokers, diamond collet necklaces and bejewelled insect brooches worthy of the V&A's jewellery galleries. The firm's managing director, Mark Evans, was equally sharp in allocating a window to his craftsmen's benches, thus displaying the house's talent in restoring and resetting important family jewels. To Bentley & Skinner's credit, the firm will not reset a jewel made by Chaumet in the 1890s because the second Mrs de Winter doesn't have the taste to appreciate it. In that respect, Bentley & Skinner is guardian as well as vendor of jewels set in the previous two centuries.

A liveried concierge greets clients to the twin houses, established in 1880 (Skinner) and 1934 (Bentley), a world of soft carpets, white gloves and antique vitrines filled with treasured masterpieces by Lalique, Garrard, Fabergé, Cartier and Bolin. The tiaras alone – such as an Edwardian diamond and natural-pearl fender (£95,000) – would have a debutante's white-gloved fingers twitching with anticipation. More thrilling is the knowledge that the jewels can be hired, as the producers of *Downton Abbey* did when Lady Mary had to be wed wearing the family tiara. Every piece sold by Bentley & Skinner is of the highest quality, whether signed or not, and it is reassuring to know that the Queen and the Prince of Wales are clients. One can spend the most rewarding afternoon shopping for treasures such as a perfect Fabergé pierced diamond bow brooch (£110,000), a Victorian sapphire, pearl and diamond insect brooch (£8,750), Cartier's 1950s gold-and-diamond dice cufflinks (£17,500) or a pretty art deco carved lapis-lazuli-and-diamond stick pin (£4,700).

55 Piccadilly W1
Tel. 020 7629 0651
Tube: Green Park
www.bentley-skinner.co.uk

LUCAS RARITIES

We have only touched on the West End antique dealers' rooms, discreetly hidden above shopfronts where serious collectors like to hunt for old masters, antique jewellery, antiquarian books and stamps in peace and with discretion. This we thought politic, rather than appearing to be a *Discriminating Guide* to a world of closed doors protected by security buzzers. However, we wouldn't wish to deprive you of the charming company of Sam Loxton, the director of Lucas Rarities, and his glamorous assistant Francesca Martin-Gutierrez. Loxton is an Indiana Jones of rare and precious jewels, with a particular expertise in and affinity with the great artist jewellery marques of the twentieth century, such as René Boivin, Suzanne Belperron, Paul Flato, Fulco di Verdura and the great Andrew Grima.

The Lucas Rarities rooms, above what used to be the showrooms of the bespoke tailor Wells of Mayfair, reward the intrepid with such collector's pieces as Flato's radically chic eighteen-carat yellow-gold, diamond, ruby and sapphire V-brooch, a rare Cartier ruby-and-diamond belle époque festoon necklace or Verdura's aquamarine-and-diamond starburst brooch. Loxton is particularly strong on gentlemen's dress jewellery, such as an early David Webb twisted-gold hoop cufflink, a Chaumet white-gold-and-moonstone dress set, and pretty black-tie lapel pins like Wiese's bar brooch in sapphire and eighteen-carat yellow gold. Loxton will always demur about

"... serious collectors like to hunt for old masters, antique jewellery, antiquarian books and stamps in peace and with discretion."

investment purchases, but, quite frankly, we'd rather follow his instincts than those of Warren Buffett.

47 Maddox Street W1
Tel. 020 7100 8881
Tube: Oxford Circus
www.lucasrarities.com

OBSIDIAN: HARRY FANE

As the single ladies of St James's (and not a few men) say, 'everyone's wild about Harry.' In 1978 Mr Fane and his partner in crime, the dashing Mark Shand, began dealing in *objets d'art*. The glamorous young bucks were as comfortable escaping headhunters in the Amazonian jungle as they were evading Andy Warhol and Halston on the dance floor of Studio 54 in New York City, so were unsurprisingly something of a hit with their jet-set clients. In the late 1970s and early 1980s, jewel houses had little interest in their past, and Fane and Shand found a passion for collecting antique Cartier. Timing is everything, and the dynamic duo were years ahead of the collector's market.

When an American friend of Fane's bought the archive of Count Fulco di Verdura – the society jeweller who found fame in collaboration with Gabrielle 'Coco' Chanel – Harry Fane decided to represent Verdura from the rooms he took above Duke Street in St James's. The Maltese Cross semi-precious jewelled cuffs that Fulco made for Chanel are his most famous design, but we are rather taken with the 1950s cocktail rings, the eighteen-carat yellow-gold and rock-crystal cage ring, and substantial yellow-gold link bracelets. Should you be invited upstairs to the studio, you will see Mr Fane's desk: a wonder of the St James's

world that is basically a life story told in antiquities
and *objets*. Fortunately, Mr Fane is at that stage in life
when he can sell what he likes made by whom he likes,
such as a small collection imported from Jaipur's
Gem Palace and William Welstead's delicate, modern
jewels, including briolette-diamond bead earrings
or sliced diamond wafers invisibly set on languid,
thin chains.

1 Duke Street SW1
Tel. 020 7930 8606
Tube: Green Park
www.harryfane.com

WARTSKI

Bangor isn't the most auspicious birthplace for
London's most revered dealer in antique jewellery, but
that's where Morris Wartski (great-great-grandfather
of the present-day chairman, Nicholas Snowman) set
up shop in 1865. In the 1920s Wartski had the foresight
to negotiate with the Soviet government, which was
selling off such tsarist treasures as a trove of Imperial
jewels and *objets* including the fabled eggs by the house
of Fabergé. Wartski's managing director, Geoffrey
Munn, is the Yoda of Fabergé studies, as was proved
once again in 2013 when the lost Third Imperial
Easter Egg was rediscovered, exhibited at Wartski
and sold for 'many millions'. There's a marvellous
eccentricity about Wartski selling the highest
examples of the jeweller's art from behind a Brutalist
1970s painted-bronze shopfront on Grafton Street.
There's no attempt to make the shop floor luxurious
or contemporary, and the portrait of Queen Alexandra
stares down disapprovingly at anyone vulgar enough
to suggest that refurbishment is necessary.

Wartski's windows aren't ablaze with diamonds. A Napoleonic acrostic bracelet, Paul Robin gem-set owl brooch (1880) or nephrite-and-silver-gilt picture frame that only a connoisseur would identify as Fabergé are all the clues you get that this treasure house owns an aquamarine given to Alexandra, the last empress, as a wedding present, a Fabergé jewelled box containing a note signed 'Nicky and Alix', very important tiaras (another speciality of Mr Munn) and a remarkable collection of Castellani and Giuliano jewels. That regal magpie Queen Mary was a client of Wartski, as are the Queen and Prince Charles. It was to 'Wartski of Llandudno' (as the firm still trades) that the Duke and Duchess of Cambridge turned for their wedding bands, traditionally crafted from Welsh gold.

14 Grafton Street W1
Tel. 020 7493 1141
Tube: Green Park
www.wartski.com

Ladies' Clothing

For haute couture

NICHOLAS OAKWELL

If only the house of Hardy Amies hadn't cashed its chips as an haute couturier and crossed the floor to designer men's fashion, Nicholas Oakwell would be a natural choice to succeed the late Mr Amies at 15 Savile Row. Then again, he doesn't need the distraction of Amies's archives, because since his haute-couture debut collection in 2011 Oakwell has become the darling of British actresses and international socialites, who flock to his Brook Street shop and his atelier in Clerkenwell. Unlike many Parisian houses, which now show 'Instagram' couture that looks startling in a picture but has nothing to do with the practicalities of a couture client's life, Oakwell makes heavenly dresses with stealthily practical glamour. His clients include Helen Mirren, Paloma Faith, Gillian Anderson and Natalie Dormer.

Not for Oakwell the mad Fan Bing Bing red-carpet crinoline dresses or evening gowns with unfortunate sheer panels, cut-outs and shapes that reveal too much flesh. Embellishment and interesting materials make his eveningwear outstanding: a speckle-feather pencil-skirt suit and a spiral-cut satin tassel dress from the 'Panthère' collection are prime examples of languid 1930s lines that are sexually charged while showing precisely nothing. Oakwell is something of a master of the feathered dress, as is demonstrated by his degradé woven-silk evening gown falling into a pool of blue ostrich feathers, from his 'Tsunami' collection, and gorgeous neck-to-knee ostrich party dresses from the 'Grima' collection, inspired by the great 1970s jeweller Andrew Grima. Oakwell can 'do' simplicity (such as the pleated cashmere knee-length dress from his 'Sylvia' collection), but he positively soars when given white organza and gold bugle beads with which to sculpt a goddess gown. In 2015 Oakwell promises a ready-to-wear collection with more emphasis on daywear and tailoring. He also moves into a seven-storey atelier in St James's, signifying that haute couture in London means business.

49 Brook Street W1
Tel. 020 7549 7950
Tube: Bond Street
www.nicholasoakwellcouture.com

STEWART PARVIN

Although he'll demur, because he's a thoroughly lovely
chap, Stewart Parvin is responsible at least in part
for what has become known as 'the new elegance'
of Her Majesty The Queen. Parvin, who holds the
Queen's Royal Warrant, is one of only three couturiers
entrusted with making the printed silk dresses and
brightly coloured monotone coats that constitute
Her Majesty's working wardrobe. He usually works in
tandem with the milliner Rachel Trevor-Morgan (see
entry), and the eye-popping colours favoured by the
Queen (worn so that she can be seen) are something
of a signature in Parvin's couture collections. He's an
absolute genius at making those neat little textured
wool or silk dresses with three-quarter sleeves,
flattering necklines and appropriate hems that have
been favoured by the rich and thin from Jacqueline
Kennedy to Anna Wintour. Like all good couturiers,
Parvin can flatter any figure. In 2012 he opened a
dedicated bridal atelier at 17 Beauchamp Place SW3,
the bridal dress being the Handel's *Messiah* of haute
couture, on which no expense is spared. Parvin's
wedding dresses are of the glacial, classical 1950s
princess type.

14 Motcomb Street SW1
Tel. 020 7838 9808
Tube: Knightsbridge
www.stewartparvin.com

WILLIAM VINTAGE

The vintage fashion phenomenon in London seemed to have exhausted itself, until William Banks-Blaney opened William Vintage in 2009. His Marylebone shop is a Mecca for the tastemakers, stylists and fashion-industry grandees who appreciate precisely what they are looking at. Banks-Blaney's knowledge of fashion history is second to none, and his eye for beauty and relevance is what sets him apart. Lord knows where he finds the couture pieces, but there they are in pristine condition and wearable sizes: a Jacques Fath black-velvet halter top and full satin skirt from 1953 (£2,575), a black Lanvin full-length evening dress from 1938 with beaded bow detail, and a superb Balenciaga haute-couture little black dress from 1940 (£2,250).

> *"… a Mecca for the tastemakers, stylists and fashion-industry grandees who appreciate precisely what they are looking at."*

As well as golden-age haute couture, Banks-Blaney can spot pieces from every period that will work in a contemporary wardrobe for cocktails, dinner, black tie or the boardroom, such as a knockout gold-sequinned strapless Bob Mackie showgirl dress from 1980 (£3,475), a neat, minimalist Halston Ultrasuede jacket from 1975 (£375) and a frilled silk Yves Saint Laurent taffeta shirt from 1977 (£525). Don't be put off by the four-figure price tags for the big game of the couture jungle. Banks-Blaney has a fashion editor's instinct for an unlabelled winner – garments he calls 'Great Unknowns' – so do consider the anonymous beaded chiffon 1920s and '30s flapper dresses and pieces that are exemplary of a period but not named. As Banks-Blaney will tell you, many are handmade by dressmakers.

2 Marylebone Street W1
Tel. 020 7487 4322
Tube: Bond Street
www.williamvintage.com

Fashionable boutiques

BROWNS

&JS

Joan and Sidney Burstein opened Browns on South Molton Street in 1970. By 1977 *James Sherwood's Discriminating Guide* was applauding 'the most comprehensive collection of carefully selected, beautifully designed and impeccably cut ready-to-wear clothes in London'. As Mrs B. would say of her ruthless defenestration of designer collections, 'I'm not dressing the world, just the woman who shops at Browns.' In order to appreciate her fashion genius, one has to remember that she introduced Sonia Rykiel, Calvin Klein (whom she met at Studio 54), Comme des Garçons, Missoni, Giorgio Armani, Donna Karan, Romeo Gigli, Jil Sander and Dries Van Noten to London. It was Mrs Burstein who gave all her windows to the most talented fashion graduates of the day, including John Galliano, Alexander McQueen and Hussein Chalayan.

So our respect for Browns, now directed by Mrs B.'s children, is unlimited. The fashion industry is of course global, and entirely driven by the many millions of pounds it makes the paymasters and shareholders today. But, thanks to Mrs B., Browns is still considered the Rosetta Stone of designer fashion: the boutique that can interpret trends and present a coherent point of view every six months. It is Browns' compliment that the boutique has not grown old gracefully and will still engage with the tastemakers such as Peter Pilotto, the Row, Roksanda Illincic, Jeremy Scott for Moschino, J. W. Anderson, Simone Rocha and Christopher Kane. Mrs B. has been a very vocal supporter of John Galliano, who was dismissed from Dior for an anti-Semitic rant caught on film, and has declared that she will stock her protégé's comeback collection for Maison Martin Margiela in 2015.

24–27 South Molton Street W1
Tel. 020 7514 0016
Tube: Bond Street
www.brownsfashion.com

PICKETT

Trevor Pickett was one of the Burlington Arcade's most popular, puckish characters who held court in his eponymous fancy-goods store – or from a bar stool in Cecconi's across the road. However, the march of the fashion brands taking over the coveted shopfronts in the Arcade saw the business Pickett established in 1988 close its doors in 2015, much to the chagrin of his well-heeled customers, including various members of the royal family. The Arcade lost a great character and a man passionate about luxury goods made in England. In true Trevor Pickett style, the doors closed in Burlington Arcade on a Friday and his new shop, at the top of Savile Row, opened the following Monday. The new Pickett is, if anything, grander than the last shop and stands at the gates of the historic

bachelor quarters Albany facing the Row. It was
Pickett who introduced the pashmina to London and
imported gaily coloured kilim slippers that are often
seen stalking the Fulham Road, not to mention the
corridors of Clarence House. Smart Londoners order
bespoke suitcases, carriers and holders from Pickett
rather than from Goyard. The ground floor of the shop
is a rainbow of ladies' leather gloves, leather wallets
concealing neon-bright lizard linings, silk/cashmere
scarves and neatly furled umbrellas. The luggage
lives downstairs in a basement as exotic as that of
the Moika Palace in St Petersburg. Pickett's green
carrier bags and hot-orange satin ribbons will, no
doubt, be carried down the Burlington Arcade and the
powers that be will perhaps live to regret losing such a
colourful tenant.

10–12 Burlington Gardens W1
Tel: 020 7493 8939
Tube: Piccadilly Circus
www.pickett.co.uk

For millinery

RACHEL TREVOR-MORGAN

Sometimes you really can't make it up. The atelier of
royal milliner Rachel Trevor-Morgan is in a crooked
seventeenth-century house backing on to Crown
Passage, in the shadow of St James's Palace and a
brisk trot away from Buckingham Palace. Trevor-
Morgan, who has made hats for Her Majesty since
2006 and was awarded the Royal Warrant in 2014,
actually works in rooms rented from the world's

oldest hatter, James Lock & Co. (see entry), and to say the first-floor parlour showroom has charm is the understatement of the century. The tiny room overlooking one of the last passages still to be lit by gas is filled with brightly coloured hats that perch like exotic birds on every conceivable surface.

As Trevor-Morgan knows from various royal ladies, a hat must frame, not hide, the face. Neither must it feel as though those exotic birds have landed unceremoniously on one's head. The Queen's hats are all of a type: a tipsy top-hat silhouette with upturned brim and minimal trim. The smaller hats in Trevor-Morgan's atelier are much more frivolous: a pert green fur-felt beret with a bow and pheasant-feather trim, a wool houndstooth pillbox with curled quills, and a striking fine straw 'flying saucer' in black-and-white target print. Trevor-Morgan has a talent with handmade silk flowers and petal trim, which she deploys underneath wider asymmetric brims or piles on to silk-satin Alice bands. All Trevor-Morgan's hats are made to order and hand-dyed (from £200 to £1,500), although she does sell showroom samples at the end of each season.

18 Crown Passage, King Street SW1
Tel. 020 7839 8927
Tube: Green Park
www.racheltrevormorgan.com

STEPHEN JONES

The divine Stephen Jones is a hero for followers of fashion. Within a year of graduating from St Martins in 1979, he had his first Covent Garden atelier, backed in part by the Blitz club impresario Steve Strange. As a New Romantic, he lived with Boy George and

Grayson Perry, and went on to make hats for Spandau
Ballet, Grace Jones, Madonna and Robbie Williams,
to name a very few. In 1987 Jones made the iconic
Vivienne Westwood Harris Tweed crown, and from
1993 he collaborated with John Galliano on every
own-label and Dior catwalk show until the latter's
dismissal in 2011. Jones's knowledge of fashion history
– shared with a favoured client, the late Anna Piaggi
– was demonstrated when the V&A asked him to
curate 'Hats: An Anthology', an exhibition that toured
the world. His work is captured on screen in Cate
Blanchett's *Elizabeth* (1998) and Audrey Tautou's *Coco
before Chanel* (2009).

Stephen's atelier in Great Queen Street is no
more than five minutes away from his first, on Endell
Street. His creations are displayed in his long, narrow
showroom on model heads with swan necks. The
milliner has many references to draw on from his
colourful and varied career as hatter to royals (Diana,
Princess of Wales), rock stars (the Rolling Stones,
Kylie Minogue and Marilyn Manson all in the same
year), fashion designers (Thierry Mugler, Jean Paul
Gaultier, Jasper Conran) and club kids. Although a
new collection is created each season, one does tend
to find favourite shapes (a tiny top hat, a marvellous
flowerbomb turban, an Edwardian Ascot picture
hat) recurring by popular demand. What only the
made-to-order clients see is Stephen's huge salon and
workspace concealed behind the narrow shopfront.
It is only by invitation that you see Wonderland.

36 Great Queen Street WC2
Tel. 020 7242 0770
Tube: Holborn
www.stephenjonesmillinery.com

For shoes

ANELLO & DAVIDE

A fashion editors' best-kept secret since it opened in 1922, and a cornerstone of West End theatrical costume designers, Anello & Davide is an absolute treasure of a by-appointment bespoke shoe shop. Those not in theatrical circles may recognize it as the maker of the Cuban-heeled ankle-length 'Beatle Boot' worn by the Fab Four in the early 1960s. The Queen has been wearing near-identical black patent-leather court shoes by Anello & Davide for half a century, although the heel has lowered to a more robust 2½ inches in recent years. The company's expertise in historic footwear from ancient Rome to the twentieth century makes it invaluable for costumes for the stage and screen. It also appeals to women who have the flair to wear an early nineteenth-century Empire pump or a 1920s twin bar shoe with a Louis heel. Such is the nature of bespoke and made-to-measure shoemaking that technically anything is possible. But, whereas fashionable shoemakers probably won't wish to stray too far from their signature style, Anello & Davide can meet any requirement, as it did last century for David Niven, Orson Welles, Gregory Peck and Marilyn Monroe.

> *"… an absolute treasure of a by-appointment bespoke shoe shop."*

15 St Albans Grove W8
Tel. 020 7938 2255
Tube: High Street Kensington
www.handmadeshoes.co.uk

JOHN LOBB

&JS

Managed by the fourth and fifth generation in the family business, and with a basement library of 12,000 lasts pertaining to 'live' customers, John Lobb is one of the titans of handcrafted gentlemen's requisites in St James's. Its eponymous founder opened his first London shop in 1866. The present shop is built on the site of Lord Byron's bachelor quarters before he moved to Albany. No. 9 is an absolute feast for the eyes, with workbenches to the left of the shop floor, a cabinet of antiquities (including Queen Victoria's last) and display cases of stock models in every conceivable colour and combination of leather, suede and exotic skin. Lobb makes only bespoke shoes, and will spend a minimum of six months producing the last for a first pair. The house maintains that its shoes measure up to factory-made shoes as 'a Rembrandt compared to a penny print'.

Every gentleman in the world who is in the market for bespoke shoes will be well aware of 9 St James's Street, hence our placement of the house in the ladies' pages of this book. Secreted in the basement are the lasts of the twentieth and twenty-first century's most stylish women: Katharine Hepburn, Vivien Leigh, Diana, Princess of Wales, and Madonna. The shoes

> *"The shoes are the antithesis of pretty, which is probably why such androgynously chic ladies as [Katharine] Hepburn were devotees."*

are the antithesis of pretty, which is probably why such androgynously chic ladies as Hepburn were devotees. Stock models are by and large low-block-heeled shoes with a masculine bent, such as the Ghillie Brogue and the Two Tone Brogue Two Strap. Open-toed court shoes with a decent heel are rather Lady Thatcher chic, and minimalists will appreciate the Three Button Golosh in leather and suede with a low heel. It's all terribly Vita and Violet *entre deux guerres*, and none the worse for that.

9 St James's Street SW1
Tel. 020 7930 3664
Tube: Green Park
www.johnlobbltd.co.uk

MANOLO BLAHNIK

Few shoe designers have embedded themselves so deeply in popular culture as Manolo Blahnik. The Florentine shoemaker of dreams Salvatore Ferragamo and the Frenchman Roger Vivier achieved cult status on screen, but that's nothing compared to Blahnik's starring role in *Sex and the City*, with a new pair seen on the trotters of Sarah Jessica Parker's character, Carrie Bradshaw, every week. It was American *Vogue*'s dragon empress editor Diana Vreeland who in 1970 instructed a young Manolo Blahnik to 'do shoes', and in fashion terms that was tantamount to a Papal Bull. Blahnik is entirely self-taught and makes every prototype by hand, and his sketches are so enchanting that they serve as advertising campaigns.

Blahnik was a protégé of the late, great Ossie Clark, for whom he designed the vertiginous 'cherry shoe', and went on to make shoes for US masters Calvin Klein, Isaac Mizrahi, Oscar de la Renta and Bill Blass. He also had a long creative partnership with John Galliano. Like Carrie Bradshaw, women become faintly hysterical about 'my Manolos', and collectors have been known merely to admire rather than actually wear a favourite pair. If Christian Louboutin's shoes are the Ferrari of stiletto heels and toe cleavage, then Manolo is a Rolls-Royce Silver Ghost. Devotees of Blahnik wouldn't buy his shoes anywhere other than at the Chelsea flagship tucked away on the rather modest Old Church Street.

49–51 Old Church Street SW3
Tel. 020 7352 8622
Tube: Sloane Square
www.manoloblahnik.com

Gentlemen's Clothing

For bespoke tailoring

ANDERSON & SHEPPARD

&JS

The original *Discriminating Guide* called Anderson & Sheppard 'an old-fashioned and traditional bespoke tailoring firm which still opens at 8.30 am so that their clients can have a fitting on their way to the City and whose clothes they describe as "elegant but not smart"'. A suit took two weeks to make and cost £230. No longer on Savile Row as it was in the 1970s, Anderson & Sheppard now resides on Old Burlington Street, equidistant between Bond Street and Savile Row. Suits are north of £3,000 and take nearer three months to make. A&S has always had a touch more glamour than the older, more traditional London tailors. The firm dressed the screen idols Rudolph Valentino, Fred Astaire, Cary Grant and Gary Cooper, as well as such exotic blooms as Serge Diaghilev, Cecil Beaton and Ivor Novello. Today it holds the Prince of Wales's Royal Warrant, and the Hollywood provenance makes it arguably the most famous British bespoke tailor in the US.

In 1931 the actor (and A&S customer) William Haines starred in the film *A Tailor Made Man*, for which a copy of Anderson & Sheppard was reconstructed on a soundstage by MGM. No. 32 Old Burlington Street has a similar film-set feeling, and might have been art-directed and staffed by Central Casting. Jack Cardiff couldn't have done a better job lighting each corner of the shop, from the warm library glow of the drawing room at the front to the dramatically lit cutting room visible beyond the changing rooms. A&S is a handsome shop that cuts handsome suits. A second shop, Anderson & Sheppard Haberdashery (17 Clifford Street W1, tel. 020 7287 7300), sells everything but the suit, and has to be a contender for the most beautiful new shop interior in London. There isn't a Donegal tie, paisley cashmere pocket square or Manolo Blahnik for A&S pink suede brogue that you won't covet.

32 Old Burlington Street W1
Tel. 020 7734 1420
Tube: Green Park
www.anderson-sheppard.co.uk

THOM SWEENEY

One always finds more adventurous drama off Broadway than on, and the same is true of the tailors who choose not to trade on Savile Row. Timothy Everest (see entry) famously said that opening on Savile Row would be like moving back in with his parents. Thom Whiddett and Luke Sweeney, both alumni of Tim Everest, must have had a crystal ball when they opened on a quiet corner of Weighhouse Street in upper Mayfair (the area closer to Park Lane than Regent Street). The district is now positively smouldering with hot international fashion brands keen to get close to Mount Street (the new Bond Street, don't you know ...). Thom and Luke are handsome chaps who look good in a suit, so they are their own best advertisement. They understand the traditions of Row tailoring but have considerably slimmed the silhouette and removed unnecessary detail, and encourage slightly braver choices of cloth from their bespoke clients.

The Weighhouse Street shop is a little bit clubby and cool, with scotch on the rocks the house drink and black-and-white portraits of the icons of snake-hipped suiting (Sinatra, Sammy D., Dino) on the walls. It doesn't try to be old school tie or St James's club, because that's not where the customer feels comfortable. Benedict Cumberbatch, David Gandy and Matt Smith have made no secret of being Thom Sweeney men, but we're more impressed by the seriously wealthy and influential guys who respect their technical skill but also want more style than they can get from the traditional Row tailors. A sharp ready-to-wear shop selling 'wardrobe ready' suiting opened at 33a Bruton Place in late 2014, suggesting that Thom Sweeney's ambitions may reach beyond London, let alone Savile Row.

1–2 Weighhouse Street W1
Tel. 020 7629 6220
Tube: Bond Street
www.thomsweeney.co.uk

TIMOTHY EVEREST

The only limitation that exists in bespoke tailoring is the taste of the customer. Timothy Everest's Georgian town-house atelier in the East End has consistently produced some of the most directional design work in recent British fashion history. That's because he, like the iconoclastic Savile Row revolutionary Tommy Nutter, with whom he apprenticed, attracts major creative talents with strong ideas of their own. Everest is in many respects the godfather of the Neo-Edwardian trend born in London's East End for tweed-clad bearded chaps on bicycles. It was in the early 1990s that Everest spotted designer-brand fatigue and decided to go back to handmade investment pieces 'cut like a dream with something extra, something unexpected, going on'.

Like Nutter, Everest (MBE) has an instinctive appreciation of cloth. He'd think nothing of cutting a three-piece suit in various sizes of dogtooth check so the chap looks like a walking Bridget Riley. Suits are lined with silk print maps, Melton under-collars are cut with hot orange felt, and every detail is considered to clash and complement in a 'good bad taste' fashion. Everest's town house is populated by bright young things from attic to cellar, and the creative energy is just marvellous. We remember that when the financial crisis of 2008 hit the more flamboyant traders would decamp to Everest's atelier just to spend a carefree hour considering herringbone and horn buttons. Regular collaborations with such cool brands as Rapha, Eley Kishimoto, Brooks and Fox Bros keep Timothy Everest on his creative toes and inform his adventures in bespoke tailoring. We recommend

Elder Street, but he does have a Mayfair address too, at 35 Bruton Place W1 (tel. 020 7629 6236).

32 Elder Street E1
Tel. 020 7377 5770
Tube: Liverpool Street
www.timothyeverest.co.uk

--------- *For gentlemen's outfitters* ---------

CORDINGS

Now that businesses established in 1971 are calling themselves 'heritage brands', it is easy to close one's ears when bombarded with dates and the names of dead customers. But let's put the country outfitter Cordings in perspective. When it opened on the present Piccadilly site in 1877, Queen Victoria had just been proclaimed Empress of India. When John Charles Cording founded the firm, in 1839, it was the year of the First Opium War. In the twentieth century King George V was a customer, as was the Duke of Windsor as Prince of Wales and King Edward VIII. Now bear in mind that London could have lost Cordings, had the dapper chap Eric Clapton not financed a management buyout in 2003. For huntin', shootin', fishin' country coves, Cordings is the only relevant gentlemen's outfitter, and the firm still specializes in paddock jackets, house-check field coats, plus twos and plus fours, Hunter wellies, shooting socks and garters, Tattersall check shirts, and moleskin and needle-cord jeans.

It is many years since the old dress codes – such as the ban on 'brown for town' shoes or tweeds in the

City and St James's – crumbled. We'd go so far as to say that London men's fashion is being led by the garments Cordings has sold for more than a century. The firm isn't unaware of this now, being a major sponsor for the tweedy game birds and boys who cycle in the annual Tweed Run. On our last visit to Cordings, we noticed quite a few fashionistas who wouldn't know one end of a gun barrel from the other going into raptures over rust-coloured moleskin trousers, Tattersall checks in bright yellow and brick red, amethyst shooting socks with clashing tasselled garters, and the gorgeous field-inspired tie and pocket-square prints. The sterling-silver cufflinks are to die for: pheasants, shotguns, leaping hares and waddling ducks.

19 Piccadilly W1
Tel. 020 7734 0830
Tube: Piccadilly Circus
www.cordings.co.uk

DASHING TWEEDS

The will-o'-the-wisp of the urban tweed movement, Guy Hills, is a sight to behold in Mayfair, cycling hither and thither in psychedelic tweeds woven by his partner, Kirsty McDougall, shot through with glow-in-the-dark Lumatwill™. What began as a cult cloth-design house, as advertised by Hills's vast bespoke wardrobe, has developed into a credible biannual ready-to-wear collection sold from a Sackville Street *boîte* with interiors by his brother's design consultancy, Retrouvius (see entry). The ethos of Dashing Tweeds is contemporary, streamlined separates made in high-tech performance fabrics but with the appearance of traditional tailoring. Take its cycle blazer (£950): it has a strong shoulder line and a neat fit to the waist,

but it is incredibly lightweight and the double vents
are sewn with reflective flaps. In addition to tweeds
there are lovely summer-weight City shorts suits made
in seersucker or cotton jacquard. Dashing Tweeds still
sells cloth by the yard (we like London architecture-
inspired patterns Lloyds Building, Centre Point and
Gherkin), and offers a made-to-measure service should
one wish to go off-menu.

26 Sackville Street W1
Tel. 020 7439 8633
Tube: Piccadilly Circus
www.dashingtweeds.co.uk

EDE & RAVENSCROFT

Ede & Ravenscroft's Chancery Lane headquarters is
the only shop in London (if not the world) where one
of those rare unicorns, men seeking full white tie and
tailcoat, can be kitted out from black silk plush top
hat to black patent-leather toecaps. Furthermore, that
can be done ready-made, to-measure and bespoke.
Although it is thought to be older, the firm chose 1689
– the coronation of William III and Mary II – as its
date of foundation. It has tailored coronation robes for
every monarch since, as well as being the acknowledged
master of ceremonial tailoring, be that robes for
parliamentary, chivalric, clerical or judicial grandees.
Gents ordering their buff Royal Ascot waistcoats on the
picturesque ground floor of the shop won't be aware
that below stairs the ceremonial department might be
tailoring gold-embroidered robes and hand-making
wigs for the Chancellor of the Exchequer.

Considering Ede's is one of a very elite group to
hold three Royal Warrants and is acknowledged to
be the oldest tailor in London, it doesn't do an awful

lot of shouting about it. Its order books are filled
with the vital statistics of kings, dukes, high-court
judges and archbishops, but Ede's is discretion itself.
We have relied on the firm's employees for well over
a decade to suggest acceptable shirt, tie, waistcoat
and pocket square combinations – mismatched but
complementary – for Royal Ascot, and they have never
got it wrong. Because the firm tends to dress very
successful, flamboyant men from the legal profession
who, let's face it, have more in common with actors
than with academics, the seasonal palette for shirts
and ties is always that little bit bolder. We like the
progress the firm's design director, Michael McGrath,
is making in exploring less formal separates, and will
be eternally grateful to Ede's for continuing to sell
tunic shirts with stud collars: now an endangered
species outside the legal profession.

93 Chancery Lane WC2
Tel. 020 7405 3906
Tube: Chancery Lane
www.edeandravenscroft.com

 *For evening dress*

ALEXANDER McQUEEN

We are stringent about not describing London
designer flagship stores that are cloned everywhere
from Mumbai to Chengdu. The 'same shop, different
time zone' approach to luxury retail is stifling
the pleasure of shopping, just as that online boa
constrictor Net-A-Porter is strangling it. So it is with
great joy that we saw the House of McQueen keeping

its promise to its late founder, Alexander (Lee) McQueen, by quietly developing a bespoke service in the basement of its London menswear flagship at 9 Savile Row. The ready-to-wear collection designed by the company's creative director, Sarah Burton, is shown on the ground floor, as are various stock models from the archive.

Inevitably there is 'something of the night' about the House of McQueen, not least stemming from the late designer's obsession with the macabre and Victorian tailoring, and his suicide in 2010. McQueen's bespoke department, headed by the Savile Row-trained Richie Charlton, is the closest one will get to a marriage of couture and bespoke in London. McQueen has access to embroiderers, lacemakers, feather-dyers and jacquard weavers who can meet any requirement. Clients use the collection and archive upstairs as a creative starting point for a bespoke commission. On our last visit, Charlton was perfecting a bespoke dinner jacket and white-tie tailcoat incorporating a subdued version of McQueen's pagoda shoulder; these were quite frankly two of the most exquisitely sculpted garments we had seen on Savile Row for a long time. We predict that McQueen bespoke garments made today will be pored over in wonder by fashion historians in years to come.

9 Savile Row W1
Tel. 020 7355 0088
Tube: Piccadilly Circus
www.alexandermcqueen.com

EDWARD SEXTON

The elder statesmen in London's tailoring trade will admit that Edward Sexton is the most naturally gifted cutter of his generation. Working from his first-floor atelier in Beauchamp Place, Mr Sexton can practically measure up by sight, and he is one of the few bespoke tailors who can pull off a straight finish minus the two or three fittings that are usually taken to sculpt the suit slowly. An Edward Sexton suit is distinctive: the shoulder line stands a little prouder than most, and the coat is cut with a sinuous waist and a skirt with length and flair. One of the many actors whom Mr Sexton has dressed on screen and off confessed that the cut of Edward Sexton's trousers gave him an erection. Mr Sexton is equally adept at tailoring for ladies, and has dressed Twiggy, Bianca Jagger and Annie Lennox. The only tailor deserving the epithet 'legendary', he cuts pure bespoke for favoured clients and consults on ready-to-wear for Chester Barrie.

Edward Sexton is a master of the art of 'romancing the suit', his phrase for dressing it up with a flamboyant tie, a rich silk pocket square or a cornflower in the lapel. He and Tommy Nutter were leaders of London's peacock revolution when they first invaded Savile Row in 1969. The Rolling Stones, the Beatles, the Duke of Bedford and Hardy Amies appreciated that Sexton and Nutter brought sex appeal to Row tailoring for the first time in the history of the street. Nutter's styling and Sexton's talented hands created a new bespoke block and a more flamboyant attitude to men's evening dress: velvet double-breasted smoking jackets with grosgrain trim, ivory three-piece trouser suits (worn by Mick and Bianca) and horizontal-pinstripe suits cut with houndstooth patch pockets and facings. Mr Sexton's

> *"Edward Sexton is a master of the art of 'romancing the suit' ..."*

Tommy Nutter suits are now on display in the Victoria and Albert Museum and the Met in New York.

26 Beauchamp Place SW3
Tel. 020 7838 0007
Tube: Knightsbridge
www.edwardsexton.co.uk

SIR TOM BAKER

Soho tailors traditionally have more licence for risk-taking and creativity than those in Mayfair, whose rents need feeding with endless grey chalk-stripe and navy City suits. Sir Tom Baker trained on Savile Row (including five years at Hardy Amies) before establishing himself as a classically trained, avant-garde bespoke tailor in 1996. Although it is important to note that he can cut City suits that wouldn't cause brows to furrow at Coutts bank or the Athenaeum club, he does excel when a client agrees that the very point of fine tailoring is 'to feel lusted after and look strong'. His cocktail suits are especially desirable, in particular the silhouette we have christened the 'Northern line'. The Northern line came about when Sir Tom had only enough chartreuse-green-and-black ribbed silk cloth to cut a one-button evening coat and waistcoat. These he made with a classic slim evening trouser in black wool. We have repeated the 'Northern line' order several times with black and silver bouclé wool and royal blue duchesse satin.

The Sir Tom Baker bespoke block rocks. His cutting and his choice of cloth – brocades, leather, lamé – make his evening dress distinctive. There's a slight flare to his cuffs, a longer length to his coats and a rather clever chevron point to the back of the collar. Sequin cloth is the very devil to tailor, and Sir Tom makes the best black or sapphire-blue sequin dinner jackets in London. The black bow window of his D'Arblay Street shop (the site of a gruesome multiple murder in the nineteenth century) is a Soho landmark. Those who step inside will see a rail of ready-to-wear that (unsurprisingly) has caught the eye of many rock musicians who invariably order bespoke. Sir Tom is brilliantly bright and very amusing company, and keeps a good cellar of robust Argentinian Malbec.

4 D'Arblay Street W1
Tel. 020 7437 3366
Tube: Tottenham Court Road
www.tombakerlondon.com

For shirts and ties

EMMA WILLIS

Emma Willis MBE is the First Lady of Jermyn Street. She arrived in St James's in 1999, having had the foresight to bring her talent as a bespoke shirtmaker to the offices of City gents and, subsequently, to the Palace of Westminster at the invitation of Lord Astor. Today you can't walk five paces in the Royal Enclosure at Royal Ascot without seeing an aristocrat or socialite wearing Willis's charming combinations of shirt and tie in powder blue, baby pink, lilac and white. The shop is pretty with colour drifts of ties surrounding a huge vase of meadow flowers. Walls are stacked with striped, checked, textured and plain shirts in sea island cotton, silk and linen. All the colours complement one another, making men shopping for themselves eternally grateful. Downstairs is a clubroom where Emma measures bespoke clients. It is here that you can see her silk and cotton dressing gowns (a baby-blue-and-white silk gown with piped edges is a beauty), and her boxer shorts made from a mad patchwork of shirting cloths. Emma Willis is a made-in-England enterprise; more specifically, all her garments are made in her listed Georgian factory in Gloucester. Emma's charity, Style for Soldiers, makes bespoke shirts for servicemen and women injured in conflict, and is supported by the Prince of Wales and the Duchess of Cornwall.

66 Jermyn Street SW1
Tel. 020 7930 9980
Tube: Green Park
www.emmawillis.com

HARVIE & HUDSON

&JS

Although St James's was traditionally the home of gentlemen's requisites – everything but the suit – the shirtmakers who have lined this street since the early twentieth century have all expanded their repertoire. Harvie & Hudson (established 1949) is the only shirtmaking firm on Jermyn Street still owned and run by the family that founded it. At the time of writing, third-generation guv'nors Richard Harvie and Andrew Hudson have just refurbished Nos 96–97. The corner site was always a bit dark and befuddled, but we are pleased to report that the seven tall arched windows have been opened up so the light-filled shop floor is visible on all sides. The traditional gentlemen's-outfitter aesthetic hasn't been swept away, and one can appreciate the tall Edwardian haberdasher's cabinets now they are properly lit and framed. A smart made-to-measure room at the back has green-velvet-curtained changing rooms and cutting boards. We adore the story of H&H wishing to brighten up the shop window in the 1960s, and cutting stock shirts in flamboyant striped pyjama material that is now a house signature.

H&H is solidly reliable for country clobber that allows townies like us to pass unnoticed at the Burghley or Chatsworth horse trials: fantastic Tattersall check shirts (which would be quadruple the price at Ralph Lauren) that make bright-pink, lavender and cornflower-blue knitted ties stand out in a mile of style; guardsman-red waistcoats; miniature gun-cartridge cufflinks; rich forest-tone paisley silk cravats; and a rainbow of boxcloth braces with brass fittings. We thoroughly respect H&H for keeping an eye on prices and (tell no one) rely on the shop for our stocks of knee-length red socks.

96–97 Jermyn Street SW1
Tel. 020 7839 3578
Tube: Piccadilly Circus
www.harvieandhudson.com

HILDITCH & KEY

Hilditch & Key versus Turnbull & Asser might sound like a famous Wimbledon doubles final, but it is in fact one of the great professional rivalries in London's West End. The firms are roughly of an age (Turnbull founded in 1885 and Hilditch in 1899) and face each other on Jermyn Street, across Bury Street. As any St James's dandy will tell you, however, there the similarity ends. Comparing Hilditch to Turnbull just because they both make shirts is like debating the merits of Klimt and Rothko because they both chose to work in paint on canvas. In late 2014 Hilditch & Key reopened after an extreme makeover of what was a very tired shop. The new fit is cleaner and brighter, with dedicated spaces for the vast ready-to-wear shirt collection and accessories, a cutting table in the Jermyn Street window and a cloth-lined bespoke room beyond.

It is a truism that with something as ostensibly simple as a shirt and tie there are absolutely endless variants in colour, cloth, surface pattern and silhouette, and that's before one even considers the details. We applauded Hilditch for restraining the core shirt collection to a tight edit of blues and whites with a classic collar and double cuff, then limiting the choice of tie and pocket square to blues, claret and grey and variations on spots, stripes and textured plains. The house livery is navy blue, and this is played out in accessories such as attaché cases, hip flasks (a vital piece of kit long forgotten) and wallets. Forays into tailoring – slim trousers in navy flannel, a hot-orange V-neck, a quilted gilet – promise much. Bates, the venerable Jermyn Street hat business annexed by Hilditch & Key when it lost its premises, is at present at the Jermyn Street end of the Princes Arcade. We understand it will move again, but sincerely hope it survives and thrives.

73 Jermyn Street SW1
Tel. 020 7930 5336
Tube: Piccadilly Circus
www.hilditchandkey.co.uk

TURNBULL & ASSER

&JS

Lewis Carroll's Red Queen from *Through the Looking-Glass* always comes to mind when we cross the threshold of Turnbull & Asser: 'Why, sometimes I've believed as many as six impossible things before breakfast.' Such is the cult of heritage in fashion and luxury goods (established 1978 and all that) that there's an awful lot of cant about authenticity and appropriateness. Turnbull & Asser weighs in at 1885 and keeps a mighty archive of shirt patterns that proves great wealth gave licence to exuberant colours. The Edwardians could easily match the peacocks of the late 1960s/early 1970s for rainbow-bright gentlemen's requisites. In periods of T&A's recent past there has been a tendency to be too polite.

The shop into which T&A moved in 1903 is arguably the most glittering historic interior on Jermyn Street. The mahogany shop fittings with gold-leaf calligraphy form a stage set as prestigious as the Theatre Royal Drury Lane that legitimizes the products on display. The bespoke shop round the corner in Bury Street is where patterns for Winston Churchill, Charlie Chaplin, Cary Grant, Michael Caine, President Reagan and all the Bonds from Connery to Craig are on display, but T&A is about so much more today. The firm's head of design, Dean Gomilsek-Cole, has already proved himself with collections inspired by spies featuring silk jacquard playing-card dressing gowns and ties, pocket squares and smoking jackets printed with amusing repeats of dominoes, dice, newsprint, matches and light bulbs. It's all terribly luxurious, but with a wit, dash and bravery that will write history rather than shy away from it. In 1980 Prince Charles awarded T&A his first Royal Warrant; the princes William and Harry are also customers, as was their mother, the late Diana, Princess of Wales.

71–72 Jermyn Street SW1
Tel. 020 7808 3000
Tube: Green Park
www.turnbullandasser.co.uk

For gentlemen's requisites

BUDD SHIRTMAKERS

The Burlington Arcade, built in 1819 to a design
by Samuel Ware, tends to eclipse London's other
shopping arcades by dint of its extraordinary age and
length. Actually, John Nash's Royal Opera Arcade
in St James's is a year older, but it feels terribly
neglected and is in great need of regeneration.
The late Edwardian Piccadilly Arcade is the happy
medium. This conduit between Mayfair and St James's
contains only twenty shops, and Budd has been in
residence since the arcade was built, in 1910. Until
the Savile Row tailor Huntsman bought Budd, the
shop looked as if it were still supplying requisites for a
gentleman of the Edwardian era: sock garters, ribbed
knee stockings, nightshirts, braces, starched wing
collars and stiff bib-fronted evening shirts to be worn
with white tie. The shop has been spruced up without
sacrificing charm, and is now a cult destination among
the new generation of dandies who dress in the Neo-
Edwardian style. The manager, Andrew Rowley, is a
reassuring presence who has worked at Budd for more
than thirty years. He is the guardian at the gate for the
bespoke shirtmaking and pattern-cutting that happen
above his head.

There are still many bespoke shirtmakers to
choose from on and near Jermyn Street, but it is the
delightful accessories for which we rely on Budd. We
go for the ribbed yellow knee-length socks (which
the late Duke of Devonshire used to buy from Budd),
cream poplin pyjamas with blue piping, claret and
white polka-dot silk dressing gowns, cravats, bow

ties and pocket squares. The young peacocks come to Budd because gentlemen's requisites are an entry point to the world of Savile Row and Jermyn Street bespoke, to which they aspire. Any firm that has the confidence that its customer will buy pink boxcloth braces or a lavender sock is our kind of establishment.

3 Piccadilly Arcade SW1
Tel. 020 7493 0139
Tube: Piccadilly Circus
www.buddshirts.co.uk

JAMES LOCK & CO.

&JS

The history of Lock is the history of London. The name has been linked to St James's Street since 1676, and the firm has traded from No. 6 as a hatter since 1765. One of Nelson's last acts before taking ship for the Battle of Trafalgar in 1805 was to settle his bill at Lock's for a cocked hat with green eyepatch, which covered his right eye, blinded at the Battle of Calvi. The 1st Duke of Wellington was a customer, as were St James's architects John Nash and the Adam brothers, the actor David Garrick and George 'Beau' Brummell, whose Lock hats were delivered to his Turkish bath in Covent Garden. On his arrest in 1895, Oscar Wilde left an unpaid account at Lock. King Edward VII fell foul of the company as Prince of Wales; his grandson the Duke of Windsor, on the other hand, was devoted to Lock's for life and always settled his bills on time. Today Lock holds Royal Warrants from the Duke of Edinburgh and the Prince of Wales, and had the distinction of measuring the Queen's head with the company's conformature when the Imperial State Crown was remodelled for the Coronation in 1953.

Lock couldn't be less like a museum, however. The house wears its age lightly, and the walls of trilbies, panamas and homburgs in colours from classic black, navy, grey and chocolate to camel, green and plum are brightly lit. A room at the back of the shop is devoted to tweed flat caps, and there is always something to make one smile, such as the more specialist hats: the Coke (bowler) made by Lock in 1850; the fez; the smoking cap; the fur Davy Crockett hat; and the antique black silk top hats that Lock reconditions for Royal Ascot. Men from the princes William and Harry to David Beckham, Jude Law and Johnny Depp are seen shopping at Lock rather than sending equerries or stylists. We like the classics, but youngsters might prefer a Lock & Roll trilby with a lower crown and stingy brim.

6 St James's Street SW1
Tel. 020 7930 8874
Tube: Green Park
www.lockhatters.co.uk

JAMES SMITH & SONS

&JS

The oldest and largest vendor of umbrellas and walking sticks in Europe, James Smith & Sons was established in 1830, and has been on this not particularly salubrious site since 1857. Then again, if this handsome high Victorian emporium had been in a more desirable shopping quarter, such as Mayfair, perhaps it would not have survived relatively unaltered for 150 years. Efficient young chaps forbid photography, keeping the tourists who swarm outside the shop with cameras and selfie sticks at bay; in a world where even infants seem to know how to take

a selfie, this camera-shy attitude is very welcome.
Buying an umbrella is now considerably more of an
investment than it was in 1977, when the original
Discriminating Guide quoted Smith's umbrellas as
'from £4'.

You can still buy a very decent Fox-frame
umbrella with nylon hood for under £100. But if
you're looking at one-piece umbrellas with crooks
carved from maple, oak, walnut or ebony and you'd
like the sterling silver lapband monogrammed,
the price will climb towards £300. Smith has a
terrific selection of ladies' parasols with ivory or
white hoods, and the most adorable frilled ladies'
umbrellas with incredibly slim sticks that are
terribly popular with London's 'Goodwood Revival'
girls, who dress in a variation of 1920s to 1950s
vintage fashions united by authentic accessories.
You don't tend to see swagger sticks or City canes
being given an outing in the West End, unless they
are employed as walking sticks. Perhaps there will
be a revival of the ebony crook cane, but that has yet
to happen. It may be that safety rather than fashion
will bring back the City stick. Our favourite design
at Smith (apart from the Whangee cane umbrella)
is the replica of Henri de Toulouse-Lautrec's
hardwood-and-silver 'drinking stick', hollowed out
to contain two shot glasses and a flask. In common
with many items sold on the shop floor, it is crafted
in the basement workshop.

Hazelwood House,
53 New Oxford Street WC1
Tel. 020 7836 4731
Tube: Tottenham Court Road
www.james-smith.co.uk

GEO. F. TRUMPER

Opened on Curzon Street in 1875, Trumper was strategically placed in the heartland of residential Mayfair's aristocratic town houses. Those born to the purple have been patronizing Trumper ever since. No. 9 Curzon Street has been looking a little threadbare of late, largely because the clients didn't want the spell to be broken, but a sensitive, almost imperceptible facelift has improved the barbershop floor immensely. Trumper is primarily cherished for barbering, manicures and wet shaving, but we like to recommend the shopfront counter (underneath the portraits of five generations of monarch) for smart bathroom-cabinet requisites. Combs, shaving-brush handles, razor shanks and shoehorns can no longer be made in ivory or tortoiseshell, but Trumper has perfected simulacra of tortoiseshell combs and brushes for barnet, beard and moustache, and also offers a lovely collection of faux-ivory accessories. We are great fans of Trumper's pure badger-bristle shaving brushes, chrome dome razor stands and leather-trimmed hot-orange canvas wet packs. We defy you to leave the shop without an extra, such as Extract of Limes cologne or delicious Rose Shaving Cream.

"We are great fans of Trumper's pure badger-bristle shaving brushes, chrome dome razor stands and leather-trimmed hot-orange canvas wet packs."

9 Curzon Street W1
Tel. 020 7499 1850
Tube: Green Park
www.trumpers.com

For shoes

G. J. CLEVERLEY

British bespoke tailoring operates on similar principles to Jedi knights: power and pedigree are handed down from master to pupil. The eponymous George Cleverley died in 1991 at the age of ninety-three, having handmade shoes for Rudolph Valentino, Humphrey Bogart, Clark Gable, Winston Churchill, Laurence Olivier, John Gielgud and Ralph Richardson. Thus his pupils George Glasgow and John Carnera inherited a name that is to shoemaking what the Cartier Tank is to watches. Cleverley's showroom in the Royal Arcade (built in 1879) has upstairs workshops that are a wonder of the bespoke world, containing a library of lasts belonging to the men who make London tick.

Cleverley rules the world of British bespoke shoemaking from the Royal Arcade. The firm has a full diary of international appointments, which are largely undertaken by Mr Glasgow's son George Jr, who divides his time between London and Los Angeles. Cleverley shoes walk the line between dainty, pointy Italian lasts and the more traditional, pragmatic English style. Perhaps the most famous shoe was made for the firm's most respected customer: the black leather Churchill with imitation lacing and elasticated fan sides.

13 The Royal Arcade,
28 Old Bond Street W1
Tel. 020 7493 0443
Tube: Green Park
www.gjcleverley.co.uk

GAZIANO & GIRLING

Although their brand may sound like an invitation
to a marriage between two Italian crime dynasties,
Tony Gaziano and Dean Girling are messianic about
handmaking shoes in England. Their factory in
Kettering is the first to be set up under a bespoke shoe
trademark in more than 100 years. In a roundabout
way, they remind us of the Savile Row revolutionaries
Tommy Nutter and Edward Sexton (see entry), who
brought a bit of flair and fashion to a straight-laced
trade. Established in 2006, Gaziano & Girling sold
their flamboyant bespoke and bench-made shoes
from Chittleborough & Morgan's basement studio on
Savile Row, and now have a flagship on Savile Row
that appears to be outclassing their elders. They
describe their Deco line thus: 'The lasts are acute,
the designs original and the handwork extreme.' This
is all a bit *Top Gear* for us. However, the contours of
their Deco shoes are as sinuous as a Stradivarius, with
a cinched 'spade waist' and elongated, elegant toe.
Made to measure in such exotic materials as stingray
and alligator, they are lethally smart. The in-house
patina service, whereby a shoe can be recoloured with
judicious polishing, is as satisfying as being able to
spray your Bentley a different colour every month.

39 Savile Row W1
Tel. 020 7439 8717
Tube: Green Park
www.gazianogirling.com

TRICKER'S

Jermyn Street now boasts as many shoemakers as
shirtmakers. A helpful rule of thumb is that the
St James's Street end is preferable. This will change

with the redevelopment of the Regent Street end, but for now Tricker's is in pole position. The small shop, with its austere dark wood panelling, brown furniture and old-fashioned carpet, makes no attempt to look modern. So while other shoemakers attempting clean and minimalist simply look bland, Tricker's has bags of character and lets the shoes speak to the hoards of bearded boys in their twenties and thirties saving up the £370 for a prize pair of Bourton brogues. Tricker's has been making shoes in Northampton since 1829, when King George IV was still (just) on the throne. It has pretty much perfected the Bourton brogue – a derby shoe with bellows tongue, natural Barbour welt, leather uppers and linings, and commando rubber-stitched sole – which has become hugely fashionable in red, green, white and purple leather as well as the classic acorn, espresso, black and navy. Tricker's offers a bespoke service as well as made-to-measure, and produces all the classic City and country shoes, although for the present the brogue is the British bulldog leading the pack.

"... the brogue is the British bulldog leading the pack."

67 Jermyn Street SW1
Tel. 020 7930 6395
Tube: Green Park
www.trickers.com

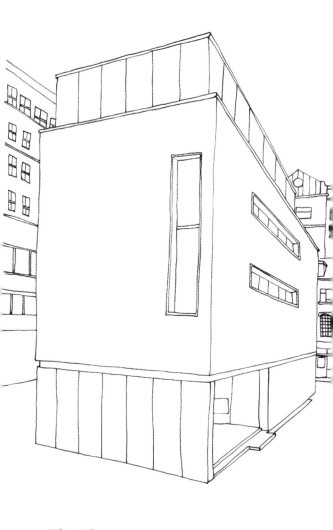

White Cube

Culture

THE BRITISH MUSEUM

The British Museum is London's most popular
tourist attraction and welcomed 6.8 million visitors
in 2013/14. We would go further and say the beloved
BM is the world's greatest and most comprehensive
repository of human cultural and artistic endeavour
between 2500 BC and AD 2000. The BM was born
in 1753 when Hans Soane bequeathed over 71,000
pieces from his collections to King George II for the
nation. At the time of writing the collection exceeds
eight million objects, of which only 1 per cent can be
displayed in Robert Smirke's quadrangular galleries
of 1857. The Great Court alone – reopened in 2000
topped by Norman Foster's ingenious undulating glass
ceiling surrounding the old Reading Room tower –
covers an area of 2 acres.

The museum's collection expanded with the
British Empire as antiquities from ancient Egypt,
Rome, Greece, China and beyond were brought like
trophies back from the colonies. The early nineteenth
century was a particularly rich period of discovery
and acquisition. The Rosetta Stone, a multilingual
tablet carved in 196 BC that has been used to decipher
hieroglyphs, was brought to the BM in 1802, and
sculptures from the Parthenon (the 'Elgin Marbles')

by the 7th Earl of Elgin in 1806. King George IV donated his father's library to the museum, and in 1898 Baron Ferdinand de Rothschild made the Waddeston Bequest of over 300 pieces of Renaissance jewellery, plate, enamel, carving, glass and majolica. Even with the Natural History objects removed to South Kensington in the 1880s, and all the books and manuscripts removed to the British Library in 1997, the British Museum collection seems undiminished.

The most popular galleries in the BM are those on the upper floors dedicated to the ancient Egyptian cult of death and the mummies; and the most controversial are the Duveen Galleries, which house the Elgin Marbles. We admit a bias towards the less well-attended galleries containing Etruscan gold and Grecian vases. Should we wish for peace and beauty we head to the Chinese Ceramics gallery, the wonderful Clocks & Watches rooms and the Prints & Drawings collections. A word on the former King's Library rooms: these long, tall galleries now form a wonderful cabinet of curiosities containing many of Soane's original bequests, pieces collected by Captain Cook and William Hamilton, and magical objects such as the dark materials of Queen Elizabeth I's sorcerer Dr John Dee.

The British Museum's special exhibitions are epic in scale and demonstrate the high esteem and respect in which the institution is held worldwide. Recent highlights include 'Life and Death in Pompeii', 'Beyond El Dorado' and 'Ming'. We find the paying exhibitions in the old Reading Room tower the most successful. The new Sainsbury Exhibitions Gallery is vast, vacuous and cold: the 'Viking' exhibit couldn't fill it, and even the Ming emperors' treasures were overwhelmed. The World Conservation and

Exhibitions Centre, built in 2014 alongside the
Edward VII wing, ensures the museum's future at
the heart of collecting and conservation, and the
policy of free admission holds true to Soane's belief in
the education and enjoyment of the public. Although
the cafés and the restaurant on top of Smirke's tower
are perfectly charming, a good way of avoiding all
those bodies the BM attracts is to nip to Pied Bull
Yard, where you'll find the Café le Cordon Bleu
(www.lcblondon.com), which has courtyard tables
for a clement day and serves home-made soups,
sandwiches and absolutely peerless patisseries made
every morning by the Cordon Bleu masterchefs.

Great Russell Street WC1
Tel. 020 7323 8299
Tube: Tottenham Court Road
www.britishmuseum.org

10 not to be missed at the British Museum

- Room 4: Statue of Amenhotep III (1370 BC)
- Room 4: Rosetta Stone (196 BC)
- Room 18: The Parthenon ('Elgin')
  Sculptures (438 BC)
- Room 22: Gold oak wreath with a bee and
  cicadas (350–300 BC)
- Room 26: Aztec turquoise mosaic mask
  (AD 1400–1521)
- Room 38: Mechanical Galleon clock,
  Augsburg (AD 1580–90)
- Room 40: Lewis Chessmen (AD 1150–75)
- Room 51: Mold gold cape (1900–1600 BC)
- Room 52: Oxus Treasure Persian gold model
  chariot (5th–4th century BC)
- Room 95: David Vases (AD 1351)

THE COURTAULD GALLERY

When Mr Sherwood published the first *Discriminating Guide*, the notorious Soviet spy Anthony Blunt had stepped down as director of the Courtauld only three years previously. Then, as now, the Courtauld was a world-class institute for scholars of fine art in Somerset House, with a series of public galleries for displaying works bequeathed by its founders, Samuel Courtauld, Viscount Lee of Fareham and Sir Robert Witt. When the Courtauld was established in 1933, the eponymous collector's taste in French Impressionist and Post-Impressionist art was not universally appreciated. In fact, when the Courtauld collection was offered to Oxford's Ashmolean Museum, the then curator is said to have replied that even if those things were left on the doorstep he wouldn't give them wall space. Just shows how wrong you can be.

Among Samuel Courtauld's collection was Manet's masterpiece *A Bar at the Folies-Bergère*, Renoir's *La Loge*, *Two Dancers on a Stage* by Degas, eight works by Cézanne and important works by Monet, Toulouse-Lautrec, Seurat, Gaugin, Van Gogh and Modigliani. The collection is now on permanent display in the North Wing of Somerset House, designed by William Chambers in 1780 for the Royal Academy, the Royal Society and the Society of Antiquaries. We must confess that when on an expedition to see the French modern masters we tend to overlook the ground-floor Medieval gallery, where Bernardo Daddi's *Crucifixion with Saints* is shown, and head straight for the vertiginous spiral staircase that leads to the first-floor galleries.

Once upstairs, we're so impatient for Van Gogh's 'Selfie with Bandaged Ear' that we don't give earlier work, such as Cranach the Elder's *Adam and Eve*, a second glance. Perhaps the answer is to pay a separate visit to appreciate the Courtauld family silver, the painted Florentine wedding chests and canvases by Pieter Bruegel the Elder, Rubens, Gainsborough and Goya. The Courtauld is positively intimate compared to the vast sprawl of the National Gallery or Tate Britain, and is very rarely blessed with crowds, so it is an absolute pleasure to spend a little time with Manet's barmaid, Gauguin's dusky maidens or Degas's dancers.

The second floor contains further treasures, including Roger Fry's collection of works by such Bloomsbury Group artists as Vanessa Bell and Duncan Grant, as well as works by Modigliani, Raoul Dufy, Oskar Kokoschka and Egon Schiele. In addition to the works on show, the Courtauld has a collection of over 7,000 drawings and watercolours and 20,000 prints. They form the core of the special exhibitions that study a subject or artist in great depth, and include important works borrowed from other international institutions. Particularly successful in the recent past were 'Becoming Picasso', 'Beyond Bloomsbury', 'Goya's Witches' and a study of Toulouse-Lautrec's muse Jane Avril, 'Beyond the Moulin Rouge', that was storytelling curation at its best.

> *"The Courtauld is positively intimate compared to the vast sprawl of the National Gallery or Tate Britain, and is very rarely blessed with crowds ..."*

Somerset House, Strand WC2
Tel. 020 7848 2526
Tube: Temple
www.courtauld.ac.uk/gallery

10 not to be missed at the Courtauld Gallery
First-Floor Galleries
- *Adam and Eve* by Lucas Cranach the Elder (1526)
- *A Bar at the Folies-Bergère* by Edouard Manet (1881–82)
- *Two Dancers on the Stage* by Edgar Degas (1874)
- *La Loge* by Pierre-Auguste Renoir (1874)
- *Self-Portrait with Bandaged Ear* by Vincent Van Gogh (1889)
- *Young Woman Powdering Herself* by Georges Seurat (1888–90)
- *Ta Rerioa* by Paul Gauguin (1897)
- *The Card Players* by Paul Cézanne (*c.* 1892–95)
- *Jane Avril in the Entrance to the Moulin Rouge* by Henri de Toulouse-Lautrec (*c.* 1892)

Second-Floor Galleries
- *Female Nude* by Amedeo Modigliani (1916)

KENWOOD HOUSE

Hampstead Heath is the closest London comes to a countryside idyll, hence its popularity with the Romantic poets. Kenwood House, framed by 112 acres of naturalistic Humphry Repton landscaping on the crest of the heath, is a neoclassical Adam villa of breathtaking beauty. It is a remote one, too – miles from the nearest Tube – and therefore an absolute joy to visit unencumbered by the herds of gum-chewing, iPod-playing wildebeest who stampede all over more central museums such as the National Gallery and the National Portrait Gallery. Remodelled for the 1st Earl of Mansfield between 1764 and 1779, Kenwood is Robert Adam's London masterpiece. Although its contents were sold off in 1922, the 1st Earl of Iveagh (a scion of the Guinness family) bought Kenwood and subsequently left the house and his formidable art collection in perpetuity to the nation.

And what a collection! The earl had exquisite taste and a terribly good eye for seventeenth- to nineteenth-century art, with a bias towards the great British portrait artists Thomas Gainsborough, George Romney and Joshua Reynolds. Of the sixty-three Iveagh Bequest paintings, the earl bought a Rembrandt self-portrait, a jewel of a Vermeer, a nice early Turner and a monumental Claude de Jongh. Before the £6 million restoration and reopening in 2013, Kenwood House played second fiddle to the art it contained. Today we get a much clearer impression of the Earl of Mansfield's eighteenth-century Adam interiors. The library, or Great Room, has been restored to the earliest colours (pale blue, pink and white), transforming the painted ceiling by Antonio Zucchi. The pale-blue entrance hall is equally enchanting. Imagine a great curator taking the best painting from each gallery in the National and removing it to a charming country house, and there you have Kenwood.

Although one or two pieces of furniture from the Earl of Mansfield's day have been bought back, there isn't an awful lot to give one the impression of eighteenth-century life at Kenwood. That said, the Music Room, which contains Gainsborough's marvellous portrait of Mary, Countess of Howe, is evocative of card parties and musical evenings. If we have one criticism of Kenwood, it is the same of all English Heritage-managed properties: that the emphasis on children's activities is out of proportion. What a waste to see the Orangery furnished only with beanbags and a blackboard. We were also disappointed on a recent visit that the upstairs rooms, which contained the Sussex Collection – a fascinating family of Jacobean portraits – were closed owing to a lack of attendants. But it would be outrageous not to end on a note of high praise for the restoration at Kenwood House, the intelligence of the rehang and the marvellous Brew House café with its tables dotted around the former fruit, flower and vegetable gardens.

Hampstead Lane NW3
Tel. 020 8348 1286
Tube: Hampstead
www.english-heritage.org.uk

10 not to be missed at Kenwood House

- *Mary, Countess of Howe* by Thomas Gainsborough (*c.* 1764)
- *Old London Bridge* by Claude de Jongh (1630)
- *Dressing the Kitten* by Joseph Wright of Derby (1768–97)
- *The Hon. Mrs Tollemache as 'Miranda'* by Joshua Reynolds (1773–74)
- *Hawking in the Olden Time* by Edwin Landseer (*c.* 1831)
- *Coast Scene with Fishermen Hauling a Boat Ashore* by J. M. W. Turner (*c.* 1803–4)
- *Portrait of the Artist* by Rembrandt van Rijn (1665)
- *The Angerstein Children* by Joshua Reynolds (*c.* 1782–83)
- *The Guitar Player* by Johannes Vermeer (*c.* 1672)
- *View of Dordrecht* by Aelbert Cuyp (*c.* 1652–53)

THE NATIONAL GALLERY

According to Mr Sherwood Sr, the National Gallery is 'one of the greatest delights in Europe', and it is still free of charge. Unlike the Prado, the Louvre and the Palazzo Pitti, the National Gallery does not benefit from centuries of art amassed by a deposed monarchy: Her Majesty's art collection remains in her palaces, thank you very much. The magnificent haul of thirteenth- to nineteenth-century European art housed on Trafalgar Square since 1838 is made up of bequests and acquisitions latterly funded by public appeal, such as Raphael's *Madonna of the Pinks*, which was saved for the nation in 2004.

Since the addition of the Sainsbury Wing in 1991, the National Gallery has a floor area the size of six football pitches. Needless to say, you'd need rollerblades and sharp elbows to view seven centuries of art history in a morning, and it can be overwhelming without a plan of campaign. The further you stray from the madly popular Impressionist and Post-Impressionist rooms (43–46), the higher your chances of communing with masterpieces in relative peace. But arrive early, bite the bullet, turn left from the foyer and see these remarkable rooms smothered with Manet, Monet, Renoir, Degas, Cézanne and Van Gogh.

"Needless to say, you'd need rollerblades and sharp elbows to view seven centuries of art history in a morning, and it can be overwhelming without a plan of campaign."

The nation's collection of British art was moved to the Tate after 1897. However, Room 34 (English Old Masters 1750–1850) suggests that the National kept the best, including Stubbs's *Whistlejacket* (*c.* 1762), Constable's *The Hay Wain* (1821), Turner's *The Fighting Temeraire* (1839), Wright of Derby's eerie *An Experiment on a Bird in the Air Pump* (1868) and

Gainsborough's *The Morning Walk* (*Mr and Mrs William Hallett*; 1785). Hogarth's *Marriage A-la-Mode* series in Room 35 is an endlessly fascinating study if you're seeking a window on louche London in the eighteenth century. Such is the depth of the national collection that entire rooms have been dedicated to single artists, and it is satisfying to focus on one room should one have half an hour to kill. The National Gallery has one of the world's finest collections of work by Rembrandt (Rooms 23–24), Rubens (29), Van Dyck (31), Canaletto (38) and Holbein the Younger (9).

Prince Charles called early designs for the Sainsbury Wing a 'monstrous carbuncle on the face of a much loved and elegant friend'. The Venturi, Scott Brown and Associates design that was chosen instead is entirely satisfying: monumental, minimalist and flooded with light. Were these largely religious early Renaissance works hung in some of the gloomier galleries at the back of the old building, they would be totally ignored; presented on the white walls of the Sainsbury, the rich pigments and gold work glister. Jewels in the collection include *The Wilton Diptych*, Uccello's *Battle of San Romano* (*c.* 1438–40) and Botticelli's *The Adoration of the Kings* (*c.* 1470–75).

Unlike the National Portrait Gallery, one cannot become a friend of the National Gallery for an annual fee, so there is no shortcut for priority entry to the annual blockbuster exhibitions, such as Leonardo da Vinci (2012), Vermeer (2013), Veronese (2014) and 'Rembrandt: The Late Works' (2015) – unless, of course, your company is a corporate sponsor. The best way to approach the National Gallery is to emulate Princess Margaret, who would view one painting per visit. This is a lovely way to acquaint oneself with the national collection. May we suggest Bronzino's

An Allegory with Venus and Cupid as an intriguing place to start?

Trafalgar Square WC2
Tel. 020 7747 2885
Tube: Charing Cross/Leicester Square
www.nationalgallery.org.uk

10 not to be missed at the National Gallery
Sainsbury Wing
- Room 53: *The Wilton Diptych* by artist unknown (1395–99)
- Room 56: *The Arnolfini Portrait* by Jan Van Eyck (1434)
- Room 57: *The Virgin of the Rocks* by Leonardo da Vinci (*c.* 1491–1508)
- Room 60: *The Madonna of the Pinks* by Raphael (*c.* 1506–7)

National Gallery
- Room 8: *An Allegory with Venus and Cupid* by Agnolo Bronzino (*c.* 1545)
- Room 21: *A Woman Bathing in a Stream* by Rembrandt van Rijn (1654)
- Room 24: *A Young Woman Standing at a Virginal* by Johannes Vermeer (*c.* 1670–72)
- Room 41: *Madame Moitessier* by Jean-Auguste-Dominique Ingres (1856)
- Room 43: *The Water-Lily Pond* by Claude Monet (1899)
- Room 44: *Bathers at Asnières* by Georges Seurat (1884)

NATIONAL PORTRAIT GALLERY
Established in 1856 and in its present St Martin's Place premises since 1896, the National Portrait Gallery is a joy for those with a love of figurative

painting, British history and famous faces of heroic and villainous repute. The original collection placed little value on artistic merit, and subjects had to be a decade deceased before being deemed eligible for inclusion. Today the Lerner galleries on the ground floor are cacophonous theatres of debate where London gathers to pass judgement on the new portraits of the celebrated faces of today, commissioned each year by the trustees from important, sometimes controversial artists and photographers. Just as Georgian London would meet outside the print shops of St James's Street to gawp at Cruikshank's caricatures of high society, we come to the NPG's engine room on the ground floor to debate whether Alastair Adams intended to make Tony Blair's portrait so mad-eyed, if James Lloyd meant Dame Maggie Smith to look so woefully dishevelled, and why Paul Emsley's painting of the Duchess of Cambridge (patron of the NPG) in 2013 aged her so terribly. Meanwhile the chattering classes coo over Sam Taylor-Johnson's film of a sleeping David Beckham and Nicky Philipps's handsome dual portrait of princes William and Harry.

> *"... the Lerner galleries on the ground floor are cacophonous theatres of debate ..."*

The galleries on the upper floors are curated chronologically and hung with the 11,000 pieces in the primary collection. The escalator in the foyer of the Ondaatje Wing – monumental and impressive, though at the expense of gallery space – takes one directly to the low-lit Tudor galleries, where the oldest works in the collection are displayed. The gallery's scholars, curators and restorers keep the permanent collection

alive with new acquisitions and loans, such as the
portrait of Katherine of Aragon (1520) reunited in
2014 with a contemporary portrait of Henry VIII, and
solve cases of mistaken identity, such as a full-length
Lady Jane Grey that proved to be Henry's last queen,
Catherine Parr. The restoration in 2013 of Anne
Boleyn, upon whom I gaze at least once a month,
revealed a rosier complexion for Henry's bewitching
second queen.

The galleries progress through England's history
by means of the faces of monarchs, philosophers,
statesmen, artists, authors and reformers. Society
portrait painters, such as Thomas Lawrence, John
Everett Millais and John Singer Sargent, are well
represented, as are the Bloomsbury Group in the
20th Century Gallery. Entry to the NPG is free,
including to the special exhibitions on the upper
floors, which have explored such diverse subjects as
the Duke of Wellington, Queen Caroline of Brunswick
and Vivien Leigh. One can also photograph almost
all of the permanent collection, without flash. The
NPG's Digital Gallery on the foyer mezzanine is
invaluable for students, researchers and historians, as
is the print-on-demand service, which gives access to
fascinating images not on show, such as the Bassano
Archive of late nineteenth- and early twentieth-
century portrait photography.

The NPG's blockbuster paying exhibitions usually
focus on a particular subject (Audrey Hepburn,
Elizabeth I) or artist (Sargent, Beaton, Bailey), and
go beyond artworks. The Virginia Woolf exhibit in
2014, for example, displayed her suicide note to her
husband, Leonard. The NPG's basement bookshop
is a hidden treasure for historical biography, fashion
monographs and fine-art photography, although the

cafeteria is cramped and oversubscribed by those who haven't discovered the rather smart rooftop Portrait Restaurant, with its glass viewing deck facing Trafalgar Square.

2 St Martin's Place WC2
Tel. 020 7306 0055
Tube: Leicester Square
www.npg.org.uk

10 not to be missed at the National Portrait Gallery
Lerner Galleries (ground floor)
- Room 35: *Germaine Greer* by Paula Rego (1995)

First Floor
- Room 24: *The Brontë Sisters* by Patrick Branwell Brontë (*c.* 1834)
- Room 28: *Aubrey Vincent Beardsley* by Jacques-Émile Blanche (1895)
- Room 31: *Dame Edith Sitwell* (aluminium bust) by Maurice Lambert (*c.* 1926–27)
- Room 32: *Queen Elizabeth II* by Pietro Annigoni (1969)

Second Floor
- Room 1: *King Henry VIII; King Henry VII* ('Whitehall cartoon') by Hans Holbein the Younger (*c.* 1536–37)
- Room 2: *Queen Elizabeth I* ('Ditchley portrait') by Marcus Gheeraerts the Younger (*c.* 1592)
- Room 4: *William Shakespeare* associated with John Taylor (*c.* 1600–10)
- Room 18: *George Gordon Byron, 6th Baron Byron* by Thomas Phillips (*c.* 1835)
- Room 20: *Arthur Wellesley, 1st Duke of Wellington* by Thomas Lawrence (*c.* 1820)

SIR JOHN SOANE'S MUSEUM

If you seek a monument to the neoclassical architect
John Soane, do not look to the Bank of England, Royal
Naval College or Dulwich Picture Gallery. In 1792
Soane acquired the first of three adjacent town houses
on the north side of Lincoln's Inn Fields that he would
successively demolish and refashion into a cabinet of
curiosities for his numerous collections and laboratory
for his architectural studies. Soane, who was professor
of architecture at the Royal Academy, began collecting
antiquities having embarked on his Grand Tour in
1778. The centrepiece of the Soane Museum is the Ante
Room and catacombs beneath, built on the site of the
mews behind No. 13. Natural light falls from a skylight
above the galleried Ante Room, creating the most
extraordinary chiaroscuro effect upon treasured stained
glass, stone, terracotta, plaster and wax objects hung
from cellar to ceiling.

Soane paid £2,000 for the semi-translucent
alabaster Sarcophagus of Seti I (1370 BC) in 1824.
It now rests in the catacombs beneath the museum,
and is seen to greatest advantage during the candlelit
tours held on the first Tuesday of every month at
6 pm. The Ante Room is a gift that keeps on giving the
more often one visits, although a guide is necessary
to separate the plaster casts and reproductions from
the genuine antiquities. A wooden mummy case looks
undistinguished until we're told that it belonged to the
Duke of Richmond and was the first to arrive in London.
Similarly, the cast of the *Apollo Belvedere* becomes
interesting when we're told it was made in 1917 for Lord
Burlington and previously lived at Chiswick House. The
Naseby Jewel (1630) – a cavalier hatpin embellished
with rubies – was so called because the doomed King
Charles I dropped it at the Battle of Naseby.

The sculpture collection is spectacular, but the entire house is a repository for Soane's treasures, and one that he would open to the public even in his lifetime. Perhaps the best metaphor for his approach to collecting is the ingenious picture gallery with a Russian doll system of cupboard doors that open to reveal layer upon layer of framed canvases. One has to befriend a guard or guide in order to open the doors and reveal such glories as Hogarth's *A Rake's Progress*, a series of eight canvases that take Tom Rakewell from Mayfair to Bedlam. Relatively little of Soane's collection of paintings and drawings is on display, and similarly the library contains a fraction of his 6,000 volumes. Neither is there room to display his 30,000 architectural drawings, including Christopher Wren's sketches for Hampton Court Palace and 57 volumes of works by the great Robert and James Adam.

From 2016 we will be able to see Soane's collection of architectural models, including his own for the Bank of England and nineteenth-century cork models of the Pantheon in Rome. Soane's living quarters are fascinating, because the ground floor echoes his collection (his breakfast room is domed and Byzantine) while the first and second floors are of the early nineteenth-century fashion. The yellow drawing room on the first floor, with views from the glazed loggia, is a beauty, and we look forward to seeing Soane's second-floor bedroom and bathroom when the restoration project to 'open up' all three of the houses is completed in 2016.

13 Lincoln's Inn Fields WC2
Tel. 020 7405 2107
Tube: Holborn
www.soane.org

10 not to be missed at Sir John Soane's Museum

- The Naseby Jewel (1630)
- The Cawdor Vase (4th century BC)
- The Ephesian *Diana* (2nd century BC)
- Terracotta bust of Charles II by Arnold Quellin (1684)
- Sarcophagus of Seti I (1370 BC)
- Wooden patera from the Painted Chamber of the Palace of Westminster (13th century)
- *Apollo Belvedere* plaster cast (1719)
- *A Rake's Progress* by William Hogarth (1733)
- Cork model of the temple of Zeus by Domenico Padiglione (*c.* 1820)
- Sir Gregory Page of Wricklemarsh's Cantonese chair (1721)

TATE BRITAIN

One can't help but feel that Tate Britain was much diminished by the opening of Tate Modern in 2000. To cut a long story short, Sidney R. J. Smith's neoclassical national gallery of British art was inaugurated in 1897 and became known by the name of its founder, Henry Tate. Twentieth-century bequests and acquisitions added important pieces of international art to the core collection. The Tate Gallery as was made perfect sense: to the left an enfilade of galleries mapping the stately progress of British art from 1500 to 1900, and to the right a glittering constellation of energetic, provocative twentieth-century paintings and sculptures by Picasso, Miró, Braque, Dalí, Johns, Warhol and Hockney.

The decision made by the director of the Tate, Nicholas Serota, to remove and rehouse the non-British twentieth-century collection to the former Bankside power station was a sound one. But for

Tate Britain it was as if a crack team of international art thieves had made off with the most valuable and recognizable canvases: Warhol's *Marilyn Diptych*, Lichtenstein's *Whaam!*, Mondrian's *Composition with Yellow, Blue and Red*, Léger's *Still Life with a Beer Mug* and a room full of Rothko, to name a few. In 2013 Tate Britain emerged from a multimillion-pound facelift and rehang after a two-year closure. Was it a success? Well, yes and no.

The galleries are now hung as a chronological walk through the history of art from 1545 to the present. Why it begins in the furthest possible gallery from the entrance and then flows counter-clockwise in a U-shape is anybody's guess, although I suspect the position of the gift shops was a consideration. Rooms are curated by date rather than school or theme, which either produces a fascinating dialogue between divergent contemporary artists or is really rather jarring, depending on your sensibilities.

About 1,000 of the 70,000 pieces in the collection are on display. The left enfilade, taking us from 1545 to 1915, is successful, although such crowd-pleasers as Henry Wallis's *Chatterton* are notable by their absence, Tate Britain being rather disdainful of Victorian sentimentalism. Crossing to the right wing, the Tate Modern plunder begins to show. Apart from a couple of cracking Francis Bacons, two galleries of Henry Moore sculpture and the much-loved Hockney *A Bigger Splash* (1967) and *Mr and Mrs Clark and Percy*, the timeline begins to unravel. The layman begins to lose the will to live as room follows room of obtuse, ugly installations and brutal abstract canvases in a chamber of Turner Prize-esque horrors.

The Clore Gallery annex, which houses the Turner collection, looks like a 1980s comprehensive made from Lego bricks. If you are of the 'seen one, seen them all' school, the bright and beautiful Turner galleries within are an education in the artist's progression towards abstraction. But the works of William Blake are hidden in a second-floor gallery so dark you need a miner's helmet to see the work properly. Other than the direct Thames Clipper from Tates Modern to Britain, it is an effort to get to Millbank (the site of Victorian London's grimmest women's prison), and the museum must work hard to earn our time. Fortunately, the Rex Whistler Restaurant, opened in 1927 and decorated with the artist's *Expedition in Pursuit of Rare Meats* murals (recently restored), is famed as 'the most amusing room in Europe'.

Millbank SW1
Tel. 020 7887 8888
Tube: Pimlico
www.tate.org.uk

10 not to be missed at Tate Britain
500 Years of British Art Galleries
- 1760: *Colonel Acland and Lord Sydney: The Archers* by Joshua Reynolds (1769)
- 1780: *Emma Hart as Circe* by George Romney (*c.* 1782)
- 1810: *Flatford Mill* by John Constable (1816–17)
- 1840: *The Lady of Shalott* by John William Waterhouse (1888)
- *Ophelia* by John Everett Millais (1851–52)
- 1890: *Mrs Carl Meyer and her Children* by John Singer Sargent (1896)
- 1910: *The Resurrection, Cookham* by Stanley Spencer (1924–27)

- 1940: *Three Studies for Figures at the Base of a Crucifixion* by Francis Bacon (1944)
- 1950: *The Pond* by L. S. Lowry (1950)
- 1960: *Mr and Mrs Clark and Percy* by David Hockney (1970–71)

TATE MODERN

To begin with a disclaimer, Tate Modern – opened in May 2000 in George Gilbert Scott's former Bankside power station – is a raging success. It is London's fifth most popular tourist attraction, and had almost five million visitors in 2014. Solo shows such as 'Matisse: The Cut-Outs', 'Lichtenstein: A Retrospective' and Gilbert & George are masterfully produced, and commissions for new work to be displayed in the Turbine Hall have given London some of its most memorable installations, by Anish Kapoor, Carsten Höller, Olafur Eliasson and Ai Weiwei. Such is the success of Tate Modern that the architect Herzog & de Meuron has been called in again to develop the disused tanks as gallery spaces and build the tower annex behind the iconic original brick structure.

However, when there isn't an exhibit such as Eliasson's burning sun projection or Weiwei's field of sunflower seeds in the Turbine Hall, the gallery does seem half empty, however overwhelming the space itself. The permanent collection is displayed on levels 2 and 4, and from the beginning has been curated by theme rather than date of inception or school. On our last visit, three of the four galleries were open: Energy & Process, Poetry & Dreams and Structure & Clarity. The fourth was taken by the once-in-a-lifetime Matisse exhibit. Here, more than in any other gallery in London, we did get the feeling that people were wandering aimlessly around because they should, rather than because they wanted to.

Those of an age gather around the works of Picasso, Gris, Dalí and Kandinsky like survivors on the raft of the *Medusa* relieved to find something familiar in hall upon hall of obscure works about which the curators have decided we ought to be told. On our last visit we didn't see such (admittedly obvious but much-loved) pieces as Warhol's *Marilyn Diptych* (1962), Alberto Giacometti's *Walking Woman* (1932/33–36) or Rothko's Seagram murals (1958–59), although in the case of the last it could be our error for losing the will to live. There is a huge emphasis on controversial installation art in Structure & Clarity (of course) that may make one think but rarely makes one smile. The aforementioned tanks (opened in 2012) are dedicated to more installation and performance art ... words that have us fleeing for the exit.

Tate Modern's chief executive, Nicholas Serota, has a huge responsibility leading this charitable organization for the nation. He holds the purse-strings for the acquisition of new works for all the Tate galleries nationwide, as well as the power to dispose of items in the collection that he deems no longer 'on message'. It is a dangerous game to decommission the national art collection, and we hope that fashion and political correctness do not play as large a part in disposal as they clearly do in acquisition. Still, as Oscar Wilde should have said, 'only an auctioneer can admire equally all schools of art.'

Bankside SE1
Tel. 020 7887 8888
Tube: Southwark
www.tate.org.uk

10 not to be missed at Tate Modern
Level 2: Poetry & Dreams
- *The Three Dancers* by Pablo Picasso (1925)
- *Mobile* by Alexander Calder (*c.* 1932)
- *Portrait of a Young Woman* by Meredith Frampton (1935)
- *Metamorphosis of Narcissus* by Salvador Dalí (1937)

Level 4: Energy & Process
- *Lingotto* by Mario Merz (1968)
- *Trip Hammer* by Richard Serra (1988)

Level 4: Structure & Clarity
- *Still Life with a Beer Mug* by Fernand Léger (1921–22)
- *Six Mile Bottom* by Frank Stella (1960)
- *Swinging* by Wassily Kandinsky (1925)
- *Bottle and Fishes* by Georges Braque (*c.* 1910–12)

VICTORIA AND ALBERT MUSEUM

The V&A presents a history of the civilized world narrated by 5,000 years of the decorative arts in more than 145 galleries. Scholars can spend their lives studying a single object, be that the Ardabil Carpet, Shah Jahan's white jade cup, Tipu's Tiger or the Duchess of Manchester's Cartier tiara. The world's largest collection of the decorative arts began with a kernel of works purchased for the nation from Prince Albert's Great Exhibition of 1851, and grew largely thanks to bequests and the avoidance of Britain's pernicious inheritance tax. Thus treasures have poured into the gallery's collections of ceramics, glass, jewellery, costume, sculpture, books and prints, photography, textiles, metalwork, furniture, drawings and paintings.

The museum's former director Roy Strong recommends: 'Walk through, disciplining yourself not to look at things in detail, just to get the feel of the nature and scale of the museum ... under no circumstances try to "do" the Victoria and Albert all in one go.' The advice is as true today as when it was given to Mr Sherwood Sr in 1977, although much has since changed in the museum. Most recently, Cast Court – where scale models of Trajan's Column and Michelangelo's *David* are displayed – was restored in 2014. The jewellery gallery is particularly fine, with pieces dating from ancient Egypt and all times since, although the sheer scale is somewhat overwhelming. We could, and do, spend hours in the ceramic and glass galleries. Stained glass alone runs the gamut from the twelfth century to the present by way of the Pre-Raphaelites.

> *"The jewellery gallery is particularly fine, with pieces dating from ancient Egypt and all times since ..."*

Costume, jewellery and textiles are rather stealing the limelight at the V&A of late, thanks to such sell-out closed (read paying) exhibitions as 'Hollywood Costume', 'Pearls', 'Alexander McQueen: Savage Beauty' and 'Shoes: Pleasure and Pain'. We rather enjoy the octagonal Fashion Gallery, with its mezzanine under the dome, where the permanent collection is displayed chronologically incorporating appropriate objects from the wider museum collections. Although we regretted the loss of the Theatre Museum in Covent Garden (now the restaurant Balthazar; see entry), that collection has greatly enhanced the V&A and brought performance in from the cold, and the collections of Kylie Minogue and David Bowie have attracted a new generation to the museum.

The most successful curation in the V&A is the formidable British Galleries, which walk us from the Tudor period to the Victorian era, bringing together objects – embroidery, silver, furniture, paintings and costume – that crystallize each period of English aristocratic taste. Highlights in the collection include Henry VIII's writing desk (*c.* 1525), the Great Bed of Ware (1590–1600) mentioned in Shakespeare's *Twelfth Night*, James II's embroidered wedding suit (1673), Chippendale chairs (1750–80) and glorious tiles by the Pre-Raphaelite William De Morgan. Perhaps most spectacular of all are the interiors salvaged from London's lost palaces, such as the rococo Norfolk House Music Room (1756), rescued from St James's Square in the 1930s. The V&A never gathers dust, and is an extremely precious museum for London because it offers unprecedented access to its collection for students, researchers and the public over and above the breathtaking displays on the 12-acre site in South Kensington. For those who mourn the loss of the British Museum's Reading Room, do seek and find the V&A's National Art Library.

Cromwell Road SW7
Tel. 020 7942 2000
Tube: South Kensington
www.vam.ac.uk

10 not to be missed at the Victoria and Albert Museum

- Portland Vase by Josiah Wedgwood (*c.* 1790)
- The Heneage Jewel by Nicholas Hilliard (*c.* 1595)
- The Great Bed of Ware by Hans Vredeman de Vries (1590–1600)
- *The Day Dream* by Dante Gabriel Rossetti (1880)

- Wine cup of Shah Jahan (1657)
- The Ardabil Carpet (1539–40)
- Leonardo da Vinci notebooks (1490)
- The Gloucester Candlestick (1107–13)
- The Manchester tiara by Cartier (1903)
- Wedding suit by artist unknown (1673)

THE WALLACE COLLECTION

Like Mary Poppins, the Wallace Collection is practically perfect. Although only moments from Oxford Street, Hertford House stands on the north side of Manchester Square as impervious and imperious as a dowager, keeping modern London at bay behind its walled carriage forecourt. As H. V. Morton wrote in *In Search of London* (1950), 'there is nothing else in London like the Wallace Collection: it is a little Louvre Museum. There is probably in the world no more surprising display of the acquisitive abilities of a few wealthy and cultivated aristocrats.' The sumptuous, refined collection was acquired for the house by four generations of Hertford marquesses and an illegitimate son, Sir Richard Wallace.

"Like Mary Poppins, the Wallace Collection is practically perfect."

The 4th bachelor marquess and Sir Richard were voracious collectors of the French rococo art and furniture for which the Wallace is famed, hence the treasure trove of Boulle furniture, Boucher paintings and Sèvres porcelain that is unrivalled in the UK if not the world. Sir Richard's widow, Lady Wallace, left the lot to the nation in 1897, and Hertford House opened as a museum in 1900. The brilliant Lady Wallace also insisted on a codicil that

nothing could be added to or taken away from
the collection.

The plain red-brick exterior of Hertford House does
not prepare one for the sumptuous gilded staterooms,
lined with rich silk brocades and hung with glorious
old masters and decorated with cabinets, salon chairs,
bronzes, clocks and chandeliers. A first visit to the
Wallace Collection is a delicious experience if one simply
immerses oneself in all these riches without trying to
examine every diamond-set rock-crystal snuffbox and
Sèvres coffee cup. Stop occasionally to greet familiar
faces, such as Boucher's *Madame de Pompadour* (1759)
in the Oval Room or Reynolds's *Strawberry Girl* in the
Boudoir. Return to spend a rewarding hour finding the
vases made for Madame du Barry in the Dining Room
cabinets, or conduct a lengthy Judgement of Paris
between the three portraits of the actress/courtesan
Perdita Robinson by Gainsborough, Romney and
Reynolds hanging in the West Room.

The Oval Drawing Room and Study are incredibly
special because they contain the largest collection of
Marie Antoinette's furniture outside France. If you can
tear your eyes away from Fragonard's *The Swing*, look
above the fireplace in the Oval Room for two gilt bronze
wall lights (*c.* 1780) from the queen's Games Room at
Fontainebleau. Look below Fragonard's *The Souvenir*
(*c.* 1776–*c.* 1778) (another great favourite) in the Study
and you'll find Marie Antoinette's oak secretaire, sold
with the contents of the Petit Trianon after the French
Revolution. One could spend days gazing dreamily
at Boucher's delicious nudes, Nattier's rouged court
beauties and Watteau's flirtatious *fêtes champêtres*.

Lady Wallace's codicil has not bound successive
directors' hands because it mentioned nothing about
improvements to Hertford House. The restoration of

the Grand Gallery in 2014, with the addition of a skylight, has made the room much less gloomy. For the Centenary Project in 2000, the architect Rick Mather glazed the central courtyard, creating a restaurant and sculpture garden, and realigned the basement to create 30 per cent more public space, including temporary exhibition halls and a lecture theatre. On a sunny day, the conservatory restaurant (run by Peyton and Byrne) is a delight for breakfast and lunch. On Saturday and Sunday night it is a super, secret location for a civilized dinner.

Hertford House, Manchester Square W1
Tel. 020 7563 9500
Tube: Bond Street
www.wallacecollection.org

10 not to be missed at the Wallace Collection
Ground Floor
  Front State Room
  • *Margaret, Countess of Blessington*
   by Thomas Lawrence (1822)
First Floor
  Great Gallery
  • *The Laughing Cavalier* by Frans
   Hals (1624)
  East Galleries I
  • *Self-Portrait in a Black Cap* by
   Rembrandt van Rijn (1637)
  East Drawing Room
  • *The Adoration of the Magi*
   by Peter Paul Rubens (*c.* 1624)
  Oval Drawing Room
  • *The Swing* by Jean-Honoré
   Fragonard (1767)

Study
- Marie Antoinette's oak secretaire by Jean-Henri Riesener (1780)

Study Cabinet
- Carved rock-crystal, gold and diamond snuffbox (*c.* 1730–40)

Boudoir
- *The Strawberry Girl* by Joshua Reynolds (1772–73)

Grand Staircase
- *The Rising of the Sun* (1753) and *The Setting of the Sun* (1752) by François Boucher

West Room
- *Mrs Mary Robinson (Perdita)* by Thomas Gainsborough (1781)

Art Galleries

For contemporary art

HAUSER & WIRTH

It is dismaying to see what is left of old London demolished by avaricious developers to make way for yet another monumentally bland glass cube with no regard for buildings that are their elders and betters. Equally perplexing are the rent rises that threaten those streets historically linked to one trade, such as Savile Row (bespoke tailoring), Cork Street (fine art) and Jermyn Street (shirtmaking). So it was sad on many levels when English Heritage's Savile Row office, Fortress House – a peculiar but charming structure built in 1950 – was demolished in 2009 to make way for an office block designed by Eric Parry Architects.

However, the Row's tailors should be giving Hauser & Wirth three cheers for relocating its West End showrooms from St James's to 23 Savile Row. The tomb-like ground-floor galleries wrap around both corners of the Savile Row façade, and floor-to-ceiling windows give passers-by a peek at the future of contemporary art. H&W's reputation in the international art market is such that it serves as a magnet for discerning wealth; in short, precisely the demographic of financially blessed men that Savile Row likes to dress.

H&W represents such artistic giants as Louise Bourgeois, Mark Wallinger, Paul McCarthy, Ron Mueck, Martin Creed and Richard Jackson, all of whom work on a scale that is appropriate to these vast spaces. It is such fun to walk past H&W and find oneself stopped in one's tracks, lost for words and occasionally convulsed with laughter at a giant Bourgeois spider, a Mueck monster turkey strung up from the gallery ceiling or Jackson's plastic models of life-size little boys with their pants pulled down defecating multicoloured paint on to the gallery wall. For sheer street theatre alone, Hauser & Wirth deserves neighbourly support.

23 Savile Row W1
Tel. 020 7287 2300
Tube: Oxford Circus
www.hauserwirth.com

WHITE CUBE

There are probably as many contemporary art galleries in Mayfair as there are Caffè Neros, but only one has consistently broken through into popular culture and captured the attention of the masses, whether for good or for ill. Jay Jopling founded White Cube on Duke Street, St James's, in 1993. It was at this diminutive gallery, designed by Claudio Silvestrin, that Jopling introduced the Young British Artists Tracey Emin, Jake and Dinos Chapman, Damien Hirst and Mark Quinn. By 1997, the work of YBAs from the collection of Charles Saatchi – bought largely from White Cube – was exhibited in the Royal Academy's 'Sensation' exhibition. Conceptual, controversial and calculated to infuriate the bourgeoisie, Jopling's exhibitions made the art scene deeply fashionable and the artists multimillionaire members of a New Establishment.

The Duke Street gallery closed in 2002, and White Cube migrated to Hoxton Square (where else?) in the East End. Today it lives in a cavernous 1970s space in Bermondsey and in Mason's Yard behind Duke Street. Mason's Yard is an impressive building and the first free-standing structure to be built in St James's for more than thirty years. One of the first works to be shown there was Hirst's £50 million diamond-encrusted skull *For the Love of God* (2007), set by the historic Piccadilly jeweller Bentley & Skinner (see entry). The godfather of contemporary British art still represents the artists he helped to create, and exhibitions at Mason's Yard are still relatively hot tickets on the London social scene, particularly when everything stops in October for the Frieze Art Fair.

25–26 Mason's Yard SW1
Tel. 020 7930 5373
Tube: Green Park
www.whitecube.com

For old masters

PHILIP MOULD

Philip Mould OBE is your man in London for English old-master portraits and miniatures with royal and noble provenance. He and his former associate, Dr Bendor Grosvenor, are responsible for discovering lost (read misattributed) works by Van Dyck, Thomas Lawrence and Thomas Gainsborough owned by museums such as Tate Britain and the Bowes or languishing, soot-blackened and unloved, in the stately homes of England. As you'd imagine, their expertise in finding these 'orphans of art history' makes the Dover Street gallery a magnet for owners hoping their old masters are by Peter Lely, Godfrey Kneller, Johann Zoffany or Joshua Reynolds.

Mould's buccaneering career as the Indiana Jones of portraiture was recorded in his book *Sleuth: The Amazing Quest for Lost Art Treasures* (2011), and he and Dr Grosvenor co-star on the BBC's 'question of attribution' series *Fake or Fortune?* Their instinct that a portrait might be 'right' can elevate a 'school of' extra into a museum-quality star. There is little Mould doesn't know about Tudor portraits of Henry VIII, his wives and children; he has authenticated, dated and sold such important works as the Clopton Portrait of Queen Elizabeth I (1558), the first known likeness of the queen painted after her accession that year.

One of Mould's most audacious finds was the discovery that an eighteenth-century oil of a fat, ugly matron was in fact a portrait of the celebrated transvestite the Chevalier D'Eon, a spy for Louis XV and French ambassador to London. The National

Portrait Gallery subsequently acquired the chevalier for its permanent collection. Of course, the perfect storm for collectors is a subject of sufficient beauty and/or fame painted by one of the greats. We don't know how he does it, but Philip Mould keeps striking gold.

29 Dover Street W1
Tel. 020 7499 6818
Tube: Green Park
www.philipmould.com

RICHARD GREEN

In 1936, the year of Richard Green's birth, his father opened an art gallery on St James's Street. Now, nearly eighty years later, Mr Green is one of the most powerful dealers in seventeenth- to twentieth-century art in the world, with two Bond Street galleries displaying his stock of old masters and modern art with a book value in excess of £100 million. Mr Green's reputation as a bellwether for the international art market has been proven repeatedly. He has been collecting L. S. Lowry for more than thirty years, and put his marker on Victorian, sporting and modern British art years before the market caught up. The Bond Street *flâneur*, ourselves included, will always pause outside Richard Green's windows to be rewarded by a delicious Jan Davidsz. de Heem still life, a lyrical Boudin seascape or a pretty little Degas study of a dancer.

   In late 2011 the family opened magnificent new premises at 33 New Bond Street, next door to Sotheby's. Directed by Green's sons Jonathan and Matthew, No. 33 specializes in developing the market for twentieth- and twenty-first-century paintings and sculpture, although it draws the line at BritArt. Showing great respect for Bond Street's architectural history, Green commissioned the architect George Saumarez Smith to design a neoclassical façade with a Hellenistic frieze in Portland stone set above the *piano nobile* windows. The five-storey town house contains 6,366 square feet of gallery space displaying the French masters Morisot, Renoir, Sisley, Pissarro, Picasso and Helleu and the best of the twentieth-century British artists David Hockney, Dame Barbara Hepworth and Ben Nicholson. No. 147, meanwhile, is the patriarch's domain, where Mr Green exhibits his stock of museum-quality old masters with a bias towards seventeenth-century Dutch and Flemish artists, such as Heem, Paulus Van Brussel and Pieter de Ring. Sales of earlier works by Pieter Bruegel the Elder and Younger, Corneille de Lyon and François Clouet keep Green in the international press.

147 New Bond Street W1
Tel. 020 7493 3939
33 New Bond Street W1
Tel. 020 7499 4738
Tube: Bond Street
www.richardgreen.com

For 19th- and 20th-century art

THE FINE ART SOCIETY
Established in 1876, the Fine Art Society is said to be the world's oldest art dealership. It was a pioneer of the solo show given to a living artist that the

society sponsored, and it funded Whistler's stay in Venice, from which came an exhibition, 'First Venice Etchings', in 1880. The society's choice of artist has proved sound, with living exhibitions in the late nineteenth and early twentieth century for Millais, Sargent, Sickert, Burne-Jones and Walter Crane. The works on display today are all far too pretty and the artists far too talented in painting, drawing and sculpture to have any credibility or relevance to the White Cube generation. But we happen to like Whistler's etchings and Tissot's rather gay late Victorian society folk. Artists currently for sale from the society's collection include Stanley Spencer, Graham Sutherland, Barbara Hepworth, Frank Auerbach and Henry Scott Tuke. There's also interest in important furniture from makers such as James Lamb, Liberty & Co. and Heal & Co. If your finances won't stretch to a tiny Tissot, the FAS regularly stages exhibitions that are open to the public, such as the triumphant bronzes in 'Frederic Leighton, Alfred Gilbert & the New Sculpture' (2015). In 2006 the FAS established a contemporary art department, which errs on the side of the exuberant and decorative rather than the scary factory-made conceptual school.

148 New Bond Street W1
Tel. 020 7629 5116
Tube: Bond Street
www.faslondon.com

MAAS GALLERY

Opened in 1960 by the self-confessed painfully shy, colour-blind and innumerate Jeremy Maas, this gallery almost single-handedly revived the market for Victorian paintings with its Pre-Raphaelite exhibition of 1961. At the time Victorian artists were hideously out of fashion, but Maas's exhibition of 126 drawings and 13 paintings made art collectors appreciate the work of Rossetti, Holman Hunt, Burne-Jones, Morris, Millais, Watts and Madox Brown. The National Portrait Gallery, Ashmolean Museum, Tate and Metropolitan Museum bought from Maas, as did the millionaire collector Paul Mellon and (later) Andrew Lloyd Webber. Maas bought perhaps the most popular Pre-Raphaelite painting of all, Lord Leighton's *Flaming June*, in 1963 for £1,000, and curated an exhibition of great Victorian paintings at the Royal Academy in 1977 to celebrate the Queen's Silver Jubilee.

Jeremy Maas's son Rupert has directed the gallery since his father's death in 1997. His knowledge is earned, not inherited, and Rupert has brought shoals of new clients to Clifford Street, not least for his witty asides as one of the experts on the BBC's *Antiques Roadshow*. Unlike the lion's share of Mayfair dealers in pre-twentieth-century art, the Maas Gallery does not sell only prohibitively expensive works that price most people out of the market. We've bought decent prints from Maas for the low hundreds, and particularly enjoyed the 'Small Oils' exhibition, featuring portraits by William Edward Frost, William Frederick Witherington and Allan Douglas Davidson, because – contrary to popular belief – not everyone who buys antique paintings lives in a house the size of

> *"Maas bought perhaps the most popular Pre-Raphaelite painting of all, Lord Leighton's Flaming June, in 1963 for £1,000 ..."*

Kenwood. Do watch out for the Maas Gallery's annual sale of nineteenth- and twentieth-century British pictures.

15A Clifford Street W1
Tel. 020 7734 2302
Tube: Bond Street
www.maasgallery.co.uk

For sculpture

SLADMORE GALLERY

The sculptor Nic Fiddian-Green's magnificent 30-foot bronze horse's head, currently on show at Marble Arch, is one of the most popular pieces of public sculpture to have been recently installed in London. The fourth plinth in Trafalgar Square would be a wonderful place to display it permanently. The Sladmore Gallery, a familiar presence on Jermyn Street since 1965, is a world authority on sculpture and represents the brightest and best of contemporary artists, including Fiddian-Green, Nick Bibby, Geoffrey Dashwood and Sophie Dickens. The imposing gallery on Jermyn Street, next to Wiltons, is where the work of the nineteenth- and twentieth-century sculptors is displayed. Here you will see Rodin thinkers, dainty Degas nudes, Bugatti lionesses and Antoine-Louis Barye wrestling wild beasts. Sladmore Contemporary

"... a world authority on sculpture and represents the brightest and best of contemporary artists ..."

(www.sladmorecontemporary.com) lives on the
incredibly smart if well-concealed Bruton Mews, and
the gallery also has a private sculpture garden next
to the British Museum in Bloomsbury, which can be
viewed by appointment. It is not coincidental that
the Duke of Bedford, who owns most of the property
in Bloomsbury, has installed various contemporary
sculptures from Sladmore at his family estate,
Woburn Abbey in Bedfordshire.

57 Jermyn Street SW1
Tel. 020 7629 1144
Tube: Green Park
www.sladmore.com

For photography

GETTY IMAGES GALLERY

The Getty Images Gallery is a world-class
photographic gallery led by the super-chic, coolly
efficient Louise Garczewska. The archive of negatives,
prints and transparencies (remember those?) is the
largest in the world, apparently exceeding 60 million,
with 1,500 individual collections, including the works
of Slim Aarons, Patrick Lichfield, Baron and Michael
Ochs. Getty's John Kobal Foundation Archive contains
arguably the greatest golden-age Hollywood portraits,
shot by Clarence Sinclair Bull, George Hurrell, Laszlo
Willinger and Ruth Harriet Louise, and moments in
world history are captured in the collections of *Picture
Post*, the *Daily Express* and the *Evening Standard*.

As one would expect, Getty Images has a slick
online operation, but the images displayed there

are merely the tip of the iceberg. The pleasure of commissioning art-quality prints from Getty is working with the team in the gallery, who will conduct a deeper search of the archive. Getty's darkrooms are among the best in Britain, and its staff know precisely how far they can push an archive image in scale.

The gallery keeps a rolling stock of Getty's 'greatest hits' on display in the office showrooms, such as glorious Aarons idylls of 1950s poolside high life and glamorous Hurrell studio portraits of Greta Garbo and Marlene Dietrich at their most fatale. In the main gallery space, exhibitions that change every three months or so zoom in on a newsworthy photographer, subject or theme.

46 Eastcastle Street W1
Tel. 020 7291 5380
Tube: Oxford Circus
www.gettyimagesgallery.com

HAMILTONS GALLERY

Hamiltons Gallery specializes in the works of the modern masters of twentieth- and twenty-first-century photography, such as Irving Penn, Richard Avedon, Helmut Newton and Robert Mapplethorpe. Tim Jefferies, director of the gallery since 1984, socialized with these giants of fashion photography, who now lead the market for photography as fine art. In his thirty or more years as a major international influence on collectors such as Elton John, Jefferies has seen photography increase in value and auction records exceed $6 million. The gallery is perfectly placed and proportioned to sell photographs of glamorous, sexually charged subjects such as Newton's glamazons, Albert Watson's dancers and Mapplethorpe's self-

portraits. Fashion is well represented, in particular
the works of Horst P. Horst, whom Jefferies has
championed for decades and whom the V&A
celebrated in a retrospective exhibition in 2014.

As a Mayfair art dealer, Jefferies is debonair
and handsome in the Central Casting style. To the
newspapers he is the Green Shield Stamp heir and
former escort of multiple supermodels. To the art
world he is a brave gallery director who doesn't merely
rely on 'greatest hits' twentieth-century masters
and will give more confrontational photographers
solo shows. Bettina Rheims's *Gender* portraits of
transsexuals aren't to everyone's taste, and some
might find Don McCullin's war photography hard to
live with, but Jefferies believes it is Hamiltons' role to
showcase the shock of the new by such artists as Guido
Mocafico, Tomio Seike and Erwin Olaf. We'd rather
a collection of Penn's 'Corner' portraits featuring
Duchamp, Dietrich, Capote and Gypsy Rose Lee …

13 Carlos Place W1
Tel. 020 7499 9493
Tube: Bond Street
www.hamiltonsgallery.com

Cecil Court

Exceptional Streets

Savile Row

Savile Row has been home to London's bespoke tailors since Henry Poole opened the first showroom door at Nos 36–39 in 1846. Poole's palatial shop was pulled down in 1960, as was the rest of the west side of the street. The Conduit Street end of Savile Row was demolished and rebuilt as a glass office block and art-gallery tower within the last decade. What is left? The magnificent mid-eighteenth-century **Gieves & Hawkes** town house **(No. 1)** stands square-jawed, facing Old Bond Street down Burlington Gardens. The listed building has had more changes of image than Lady Gaga in recent years, but appears to have settled under the creative direction of Jason Basmajian, who understands the naval and military history of the firm but can bring his ready-to-wear collections to a younger customer, for whom the traditions of Savile Row are a new proposition. The bespoke and military tailoring service at 1 Savile Row keeps the Chinese-owned firm credible.

A few doors down is **Kilgour (No. 5)**, once again under the creative direction of the modernist, minimalist Carlo Brandelli, who led the house in 2003, left in 2010 and returned in 2014. The space resembles a conceptual art gallery, the bespoke blocks floating on suspended mannequins its installations. Kilgour bespoke is for the man who doesn't want the attention or effort of a traditional Englishman's wardrobe. The soft, sculptural Kilgour coats are reminiscent of Prada in the mid-1990s and are a necessary key change on Savile Row.

The house of Hardy Amies, couturier to Her Majesty The Queen, is unrecognizable. Amies's town house atelier at No. 14 is now offices, and **Hardy Amies (No. 8)** is a Barber & Osgerby-designed concept store for contemporary menswear. **Alexander McQueen (No. 9)** quietly introduced a bespoke service in the basement, with its head tailor, Ritchie Charlton, developing a signature block incorporating the McQueen pagoda shoulder. The crossover between McQueen bespoke, Sarah Burton's collections and the couture work that the studio can access has the potential to revolutionize the Row.

Very few Savile Row tailors are still in the hands of the founding family, but **Dege & Skinner (No. 10)** is one of them. It has an impeccable record as a military tailor (including uniforms for princes William and Harry), and a dedication to the craft that means a minimum of sixty hours' work go into producing a three-piece suit. Dege is the only tailor on the Row to have a shirtmaker (head cutter, Mr Whittaker) working in the showroom.

Established in 1849, **Huntsman (No. 11)** is one of Savile Row's cornerstone bespoke firms. It developed a distinctive Huntsman cut that is strong of shoulder, shaped into the waist and suited to statuesque chaps like Tyrone Power and the precise, trim former head cutter Colin Hammick.

Chittleborough & Morgan (No. 12) are alumni of Tommy Nutter, who cut with a style and romance that are untroubled by the English gentleman cliché of Savile Row tailoring. **Richard Anderson (No. 13)** was head cutter at Huntsman before setting up under his own name with the charismatic salesman Brian Lishak, who has long passed his half-century on Savile Row and is still going strong. Anderson's memoir of his apprenticeship at Huntsman, *Bespoke: Savile Row Ripped & Smoothed* (2010), is one of the most amusing accounts of a notoriously tetchy trade. His cut is slim and elegant and his suits characterized by a bold choice of cloth.

At the time of writing, **Hardy Amies (No. 14)** still ran the bespoke service from a stateroom on the ground floor of this historic house, once occupied by the playwright Richard Brinsley Sheridan. The rest of the building – where once royal and aristocratic clients of Amies's haute couture sat on spindly gold chairs – now serves as offices. **Henry Poole & Co. (No. 15)** holds the world record for Royal Warrants, with over forty, some of them hanging in the showroom today. The first came from Emperor Napoleon III and the last from the Queen. Poole does not have a signature cut, but it has a roster of illustrious clients – recorded in ledgers dating back to 1845 – that will never be bettered. The first dinner jacket was cut for Poole's loyal royal the future King Edward VII in 1865. Other customers of fascination include Churchill, De Gaulle, Emperor Hirohito, William Randolph Hearst and William Frederick Cody (Buffalo Bill).

Patrick Grant, the owner of **Norton & Sons (No. 16)**, has had great success since buying the ailing bespoke house in 2005. With David Gandy, Grant has become the face of Savile Row and of London

Collections: Men, where his E. Tautz collection is presented biannually on the catwalk. From the beginning, Grant worked with such rising fashion stars as Giles Deacon and Henry Holland on tailored catwalk looks. Trading on his roots, Grant has made Norton & Sons the London home of Scottish tweeds, as well as producing more streamlined and modern but still correct City suits. Tautz now has its own flagship, on Duke Street in upper Mayfair.

Crossing Savile Row to the west side we find **Richard James (No. 29)**, a raised glass cube on a corner site with a face on Clifford Street. Richard James, which celebrated its twenty-first birthday in 2012, was the first tailor of the New Establishment school to open on the Row, and, instead of pursuing the traditional bespoke customer, James converted his peers who wore Westwood and Comme des Garçons to the magic of the handmade suit. In 2006 he opened a bespoke shop opposite 29 Savile Row on Clifford Street. It is the contemporary face of British bespoke.

With the closure of **Spencer Hart**, which now trades from an impressive showroom opposite Claridge's (22–24 Brook Street), the west side of Savile Row looks much diminished. The exception is **Davies & Son (No. 38)**. Founded in 1804, it was the only rival to Poole as a royal tailor, and listed Nelson, Robert Peel, King George V and the Duke of Windsor as customers. Davies is a small shop that contains huge talent. Like his father, its owner, Alan Bennett, has spent a life on the Row. Court tailoring for ambassadors remains a speciality.

Of course, other streets in Mayfair were colonized by tailors before Savile Row, so we recommend a stroll down Sackville Street, where **Meyer & Mortimer** (established in 1798) – the only surviving tailor to

George 'Beau' Brummell and the Prince Regent – resides. Do look up **Kathryn Sargent (6 Brook Street W1)**, who was the first female head cutter at Gieves & Hawkes and now has a delightful first-floor atelier just off Hanover Square. **Byrne & Burge (11 St George Street W1)** are a class-act husband and wife who trade above one of London's most charming tailoring shops, which contains **L. G. Wilkinson**, **A. J. Hewitt** and **Denman & Goddard**.

Lamb's Conduit Street

Lamb's Conduit Street was a shopping promenade as early as 1817, when you'd expect the Georgian terraced houses to have been private residences for lawyers practising in Gray's Inn or Lincoln's Inn. Today it is one of those four-leaf-clover streets that is almost entirely devoid of big brands. Starbucks, which muscled in in 2006, was soon seen off by locals who prefer a decent coffee from **The Espresso Room (31–35 Great Ormond Street)** or – better yet – a glass outside **Vats Wine Bar (No. 51)**. In addition to a bouquet of interior-design boutiques blooming up and down the street, Lamb's Conduit has become noted for independent men's fashion brands. Fortunately, the beards and brogues haven't been allowed to outnumber the eccentric Bloomsbury types, who still hold court in the cafés and restaurants en route to the **People's Supermarket (Nos 72–76)**, entirely staffed by volunteers.

The fashion brands face off against one another about halfway down Lamb's Conduit Street. **Folk**

(Nos 49 and 53) and **Oliver Spencer (Nos 58 and 62)** both have separate doors for menswear and womenswear. Spencer, who co-founded the fancy waistcoat and formal dress brand Favourbrook in the Piccadilly Arcade, is much more street in the style of his own label. Gently distressed military- and utility-themed lines are under-the-radar chic – London's answer to Brooklyn Heights luxurious workwear. Folk is what we would describe as grunge deluxe: ever-so-slightly dishevelled menswear for those who have grown up affecting not to care but now want a more expensive version of East End street style.

Grenson (No. 40) is a huge success story for its creative director, Tim Little, who turned the firm around in 2005 and took it over in 2010. Grenson (established in 1866) has to be the cult leather shoe brand for the beards and bikes, as the Doc Marten was for the skinheads of the 1970s. Grenson brogues are as robust and British as a bulldog. The Archie brogue, with wedge sole as thick as a slice of Warburton's bread, is the champion, although we think the Fred boot with triple sole, oversize punching and eyelets is the real bruiser.

The story behind **Private White VC (No. 55)** is a touching one. Private Jack White was awarded the Victoria Cross for service in the First World War. The Manchester factory in which he worked after being demobbed was saved in 2009 by his great-grandson James Eden (who had worked there as a teenager) and renamed in White's honour. The creative director of Private White is British fashion royalty: Nick 'son of Laura' Ashley. The brand takes clothing inspired by military tailoring and motorcycle racing as a starting point for an exclusively made-in-England collection. We were rather taken by the cotton three-piece working suit designed by Ashley in conjunction with Lord March for the Goodwood Revival.

Bloomsbury and Clerkenwell have no shortage of conceptual furniture shops with art-gallery aspirations selling a couple of twigs of Scandinavian design *c.* 1971 that our parents probably have in the loft. However, our taste is a little more catholic. The windows of **Darkroom (No. 52)**, which opened on the corner of Rugby Street in 2009, remind us of a canvas by Kandinsky: they are an explosion of graphic pattern-making, such as Eley Kishimoto's wallpaper designs, Christien Meindertsma's knitted pouffes, 'Off the Grid' plates designed by Darkroom, and vessels, mobiles, bags and vases that could pass for art installations if one didn't know better. Strong design and emerging talent are championed here.

Take a brief detour into Rugby Street to visit two of our favourite artistic independents. **Maggie Owen (13 Rugby Street)** began collecting important pieces of costume jewellery in 2003 when she fell in love with the extravagant, naturalistic work of Philippe Ferrandis, a protégé of Hubert de Givenchy no less. Owen is a discerning buyer and chooses statement pieces from the great costume jewellers that are reminiscent of the golden age of couture, when Verdura worked with Chanel and Dalí with Schiaparelli. A Ferrandis Mae necklace of rose quartz beads and amethysts is a fine example of Owen's impeccable taste. The pieces she stocks are set with the same artistry as high jewellery: just turn over one of Simon Harrison's glorious Claudette crystal necklaces to see what we mean.

Pentreath & Hall (17 Rugby Street), next door to Maggie Owen, is a delightful, diminutive interiors and gift shop belonging to the local architect and interior designer Ben Pentreath (see entry). Back on Lamb's Conduit Street, force yourself to walk past Vats for now, because once ensconced at the bar you will leave only under duress or anaesthetic. What we love about Lamb's Conduit Street is the mixture of the wildly fashionable and the incredibly useful, such as chemists, florists and even a Victorian funeral director, **France A. & Son (No. 45)**. **Dawson Flowers (No. 43)** is a lovely, unpretentious florist that sends a steady stream of hand-tied bouquets to the East and West Ends. It's much more Bloomsbury to pop in and order an armful of sunflowers or a few peonies than to buy anything too elaborate or Constance Spry.

On our last walk down Lamb's Conduit Street we were rather dismayed to see the shop of tailor **Connock & Lockie (No. 33)** empty. This jolly decent bespoke tailor was founded in 1902, and we'd always enjoyed walking past the shop and seeing the Japanese cutter Yusuke Nagashima sitting at his workbench handstitching. We found Connock & Lockie in temporary accommodation between the People's Supermarket and **Ciao Bella** (see entry), and we are assured that it will return to its original headquarters. Should you choose to end your promenade of Lamb's Conduit Street at Ciao, do stop on your way at **Persephone Books (No. 59)**, a welcoming independent bookshop that specializes in reprinting books by neglected female writers. One of its reprints, Winifred Watson's *Miss Pettigrew Lives For a Day* (1938), became a Hollywood film after being reissued. The success and kudos of Lamb's Conduit Street as a rich seam of independent menswear brands has attracted the big boys, such as **J Crew (No. 38)**; we sincerely hope success will not spoil it.

Redchurch Street

Every Londoner is familiar with the 'Peckham Rye
is the new Dalston' conversation, about cool creatives
turning the heat up in a previously rough area then
migrating when the rents rise. Although it was
stretching it a bit when the *Evening Standard* called
Redchurch Street the new Bond Street, there's no
denying that this humble, bleak East End backstreet
is the 'Alternative Miss World' of British fashion
compared to the mainstream, glossy brands of Bond
Street. If you struggle to find Redchurch Street,
orientate yourself with Shoreditch House (the East
End embassy of the private members' club Soho
House) then follow the shoals of fabulously dressed
secret shoppers from Calvin, Ralph, Prada et al.,
who spend their lives following swarms of Japanese
students cool-hunting in east London.

Les Trois Garçons, the stage name of creative
ménage-à-trois Hassan Abdullah, Michel Laserre and
Stefan Karlson, were the first to make this corner of
London a destination when they bought a Victorian
pub on the corner of Club Row and Redchurch Street
in 1996 and opened their celebrated restaurant in
2000. The food was pretty fancy, but it was the interior
– all stuffed tigers in tiaras, mad Murano chandeliers
and theatrical lighting – that made Les Trois Garçons
a scene. Their bar Loungelover was like a rookie
cocktail bar in the props department of Cinecittà
when Fellini was making movies. **Maison Trois
Garçons (No. 45)** is a corner site café-cum-interiors
shop stocked with gorgeous little things like teardrop
chandeliers, reupholstered French armchairs, simian

ceramic candle-holders and cushions embroidered with camp cats and canines in historic dress.

Labour and Wait (No. 85) is a good old-fashioned everyday hardware and homeware store, specializing in products made to last in traditional materials. Its name came from the American poet Longfellow's exhortation to 'learn to labour and to wait'. The original shop opened in Cheshire Street in 2000 and moved to Redchurch Street in 2010, in a green-tiled former Truman Brewery pub. If your heart beats that little bit faster on handling a robust aluminium housekeeper's bucket, a feather duster, a gorgeous red-leather tool roll or a reassuring enamel milk pan, then Labour and Wait is for you. In this ugly, aggressive world of technology, it is comforting to know that candles, lanterns, blankets and large spotted cotton handkerchiefs can still be found in this corner of east London.

A huge contributing factor to the cool of the streets off Shoreditch High Street is the collection of relatively untouched Victorian factories, pubs and workshops that suit the mood of honest, serious design sold on Redchurch Street. **Hostem (Nos 41–43)** – our third coveted corner site – has established itself as an authority on the austere, mysterious fashion designers popular in these parts, such as Yohji Yamamoto, Rick Owens, Simone Rocha, Dries Van Noten, Junya Watanabe and Casely-Hayford. The interiors are a perfect combination of Victorian workhouse austerity and clever design, such as the cluster of silk granny lampshades that form a Fagin's Den chandelier over the carved wooden cash register. The last time we visited Hostem, the cellar was inhabited by new East End bespoke tailoring from Casely-Hayford, shoemakers and jewellers. Bringing handcraft back to a street famed for cabinetmaking is a noble endeavour.

We should take a moment to appreciate Terence Conran's influence on fashionable London's restaurants, hotels and interior design. His Conran Shops have enjoyed a renaissance with Conran's son Jasper as creative director, and his **Boundary** hotel **(2–4 Boundary Street)**, which opened in 2008 on the corner of Redchurch Street, took the area to another level of influence beyond the young British fashion clique. Two years later, **Sunspel (No. 7)** demonstrated the 150-year-old heritage hero brand's unassailable instinct for retail that promises to be as astute as that of Margaret Howell. The makers of pioneering underwear of unprecedented luxury hired J. W. Anderson as creative director between 2011 and 2014, and he perfected small but perfectly formed collections of definitive white T-shirts made from 'Quality 82' fine-knit jersey cotton, fitted Aran fisherman's sweaters, grey cashmere hoodies and, of course, those boxer shorts that made fashion history when worn by Nick Kamen in the Levi's advertisement of 1985. Sunspel's polo shirts were worn by Daniel Craig as Bond, their underwear by the heir to the throne and those capsule collections by just about everyone with a membership to Shoreditch House.

Inevitably, Redchurch Street's frisson of street credibility and the promise of youth that seemingly every cool brand chases like a Labradoodle with a rubber ball have attracted the attention of more established brands. It was rumoured that Vivienne Westwood, Paul Smith and even Prada were scouting for locations. So far the guest brands with global reach have fitted in nicely: the Aussie skincare brand **Aesop (No. 44)**, with its minimalist apothecary-style shop, and **Aubin & Wills (Nos 64–66)**, whose 75,000-square-foot factory space with basement cinema couldn't be less high-street if it tried.

Burlington Arcade

The grand opening of Samuel Ware's Burlington Arcade, London's longest and loveliest covered shopping street, took place on 20 March 1819. The project was the grand plan of Lord and Lady George Cavendish, who lived in Burlington House and grew weary of hoi polloi hurling oyster shells over the courtyard wall as they passed down Piccadilly. The Burlington Arcade runs behind Bond Street from Burlington Gardens (the Savile Row side) to Piccadilly. After damage from fire and bombs, the Burlington Arcade has always been rebuilt in its original Regency style. It still has its Beadles to enforce order: in George Cavendish's day they were ex-servicemen of his regiment, the 10th Hussars; now they wear liveries tailored by Henry Poole & Co. and earpieces as they quietly ensure the rules of no bicycles, no whistling and no running are upheld.

The proportion of the shops lends itself to small but precious objects, hence the Arcade's reputation for fine antique jewellery, watches, fancy goods, perfume, and ladies' and gentlemen's accessories. The big brands have invaded, but one can't really complain if Chanel scents, Vilebrequin shorts and Ladurée macaroons court your company. With your back to the Burlington Gardens end of the Arcade, on your right is **Somlo Antiques (Nos 35–36)**, one of the world's authorities on collectible antique pocket watches and vintage wristwatches. Somlo has a remarkable collection of Omega watches, including a vintage chronograph pocket watch from 1906, an enamel dial chronograph from 1926 with eighteen-carat yellow-gold case, and a fabulous eighteen-carat yellow-gold Omega Constellation from 1952 with gold bracelet. Somlo also keeps watches by the great houses Breguet, Piaget, Rolex and Vacheron Constantin.

Across the floor is the luxury cashmere house **N. Peal (Nos 37–40)**, which has been in the Arcade since 1936. N. Peal's cashmere twinsets in a rainbow of colours from powdery pastels and monotones to jewel brights have attracted the attention of twentieth-century style icons Ava Gardner, Marilyn Monroe, Elizabeth Taylor, Grace Kelly and Diana, Princess of Wales. Cary Grant set a precedent for elegant, understated men shopping at N. Peal, and Daniel Craig wore an N. Peal navy V-neck in his third James Bond film, *Skyfall* (2012). The Duchess of Cambridge, a great supporter of the Burlington Arcade, is an N. Peal girl, as is Kate Moss.

The fourth-generation fine jeweller **Richard Ogden (Nos 28–29)** is directed by Robert Ogden, an authority on Victorian and Edwardian jewels and a trained designer and craftsman. The windows are ablaze with the sapphire jewels in which it specializes, as well as garland-style diamond tiaras, yellow-gold-and-amethyst mid-nineteenth-century combs, cameos, articulated ruby butterfly brooches and ropes of natural pearls. Ogden is famed for its Ring Room, in which engagement, wedding, civil-partnership and signet rings are designed and sold. The shop's ledgers record visits from Charlie Chaplin, Ingrid Bergman, Cary Grant and latterly Madonna.

You could put a sculptural yellow-gold piece of jewellery designed by **Wright & Teague (No. 27)** in the British Museum and it would be among friends, but W&T would be equally at home in the White Cube. There is a timeless quality to the work of husband-and-wife team Sheila Teague and Gary Wright because they bring together so many tribal, dynastic, organic and cultural influences. The work of the human hand is visible in pieces such as textured, misshapen eighteen-carat yellow-gold Waterbead bracelets, and W&T encourages secret engravings or messages concealed within the jewels. It is rather clever to offer each piece in sterling silver, eighteen-carat yellow gold, eighteen-carat rose gold and platinum, too, demonstrating the strength of the design. We're particularly partial to the thick, undulating yellow-gold Pacific ring, the yellow-gold Octet stacking rings (each set with a differently coloured gemstone) and the Isis rose-gold cufflinks, pavé set with white diamonds and influenced by a Romano-Egyptian form.

The jeweller **Hancocks (Nos 52–53)** dates from 1849, held Queen Victoria's Royal Warrant and has a reputation as a maker as well as a dealer. Window displays showcasing masterpieces by the great artist jewellers Boivin, Castellani, Flato, Giuliano, Grima, JAR, Cartier, Buccellati, Boucheron and Van Cleef & Arpels literally stop traffic in the Arcade as people point and stare in stupefied fashion. The emphasis on important signed jewellery sets Hancocks apart from the other antique jewellery shops. Be dazzled by a mystery-set sapphire-and-diamond VC&A ring from 1951, J. E. Caldwell's show-stopping diamond sautoir from 1920, a rare Lalique enamel-and-diamond butterfly brooch from 1895, and Sterle's audacious

blackamoor brooch in haematite, peridot, citrine
and diamond with plumed turban, dating from 1960.
Perfume is the perfect sell in the Burlington Arcade,
and although Chanel now has a foothold, we much
prefer **Penhaligon's (Nos 16–17)** terribly pretty
double-fronted shop and bespoke room upstairs.
Penhaligon's Blenheim Bouquet, formulated in
1902 for the dashing 9th Duke of Marlborough, is
still a best-seller.

Elizabeth Street

Built in the 1860s, Elizabeth Street was a shopping
promenade serving Thomas Cubitt's fashionable new
residential development Eaton Square (actually a
rectangle), built on the Grosvenor Estate and named
after the dukes of Westminster's country seat, Eaton
Hall in Cheshire. In the days before the London
property market started taking steroids, Eaton
Square was popular among such smart artistic types
as Robert Helpmann, Rex Harrison, Vivien Leigh
and Luise Rainer. Today the Eaton Square address is
a magnet for overseas wealth, and as a consequence
shutters remain closed for most of the year. Elizabeth
Street, however, is an oasis of village life in the
otherwise apparently deserted streets of Belgravia.
When the area's stucco mansions were built to rival
Mayfair, Benjamin Disraeli dismissed them as being
'as monotonous as Marylebone'. That's a bit harsh; the
shops that do well on Elizabeth Street suggest that
there is life behind the closed doors of Belgravia.

H. R. Stokes (No. 58) is the oldest shop in
Belgravia, London's most eminent stationer and

almost the same vintage as Elizabeth Street itself. It specializes in hand-engraved invitations, writing paper and calling cards that are still the common form of correspondence among the Belgravia set and the many embassies and ambassadors' residences in the area. Envelopes are still tissue-lined by hand, as they were in the 1890s when Lillie Langtry ordered her writing paper from H. R. Stokes. This is also Belgravia's preferred bookshop, stocking the best of the new titles (many of them penned by residents), and the sole UK stockist of Manhattan society stationer Crane & Co.

"Envelopes are still tissue-lined by hand, as they were in the 1890s when Lillie Langtry ordered her writing paper from H. R. Stokes."

The costume jeweller formerly known as Erickson Beamon rebranded in 2014 under the name of the wildly talented **Vicki Sarge (No. 38)**, who believed it was 'time for the solo album'. As her friend Hamish Bowles puts it, 'Vicki Sarge is a new age alchemist – a sorcerer who can take base metals, glass jewels and materials classical and innovative and spin them into dreams.' Sarge's inspiration comes from her misspent youth at Studio 54 and more than thirty years in the fashion industry, making couture showpieces for McQueen and Galliano. Clients as diverse as Michelle Obama, Madonna, Paloma Faith, Kate Moss and Beyoncé own her jewellery. Sarge is a magpie whose collections are Pop art in their collaging of inspirations, such as baroque Klimt, Pre-Raphaelite folk and African deco punk. Last time we popped in, Vicki showed off a wild collection of beads, pompoms, fringe and feather made for the Mario Testino Museum in Peru.

When the perfumer Jo Malone first came to London, she worked in a florist's shop on Elizabeth Street. In 2013 Malone chose to come full circle and open her new concept **Jo Loves (No. 42)**, having sold Jo Malone to Estée Lauder and quit as its creative director in 2006. Jo Loves is described as a 'fragrance brasserie' with scents and bath and body products served from a red glass bar in rather Roald Dahl fashion: shower gels in shot glasses and bath colognes from tagines. The fragrances – 'A Shot of Thai Lime over Mango', 'Pink Vetiver' and 'No. 42 The Flower Shop' – tell stories of Malone's life and are of intoxicating intensity. Belgravia's cellars are planned by **Jereboams (Nos 50–52)**, their humidors are filled with the finest Cuban cigars by **Tomtom Cigars & Coffee (No. 63)**, and **Oliveto (No. 49)** makes delicious gourmet pizzas when the locals can't be bothered to cook.

De Vroomen (No. 59) is the London flagship of the fine jeweller Leo de Vroomen, whose work in yellow gold, pearls, enamel and exceptional gemstones is absolutely unmistakable. The sensibility is baroque in so far as a design is imagined around fabulous stones such as mandarin garnets, aquamarines and cabochon amethysts the size of Edith Sitwell's rings. The gold work is absolutely sensational, as shown off in a beaten-gold necklace and a serpentine brooch of yellow gold flowing around two Tahitian pearls with diamond accents. We were most taken by the Bubbles ring, a cluster of yellow-gold baubles set with white diamonds in various shapes and sizes. De Vroomen also showcases contemporary silver design.

For friends with four paws, **Mungo & Maud (No. 79)** is to pets what Marie-Chantal on Walton Street is to children. We would be the first to agree that canines and cats are apt to give far more pleasure than children, and for a fraction of the cost, so pampering one's pooch with a sorbet cable-knit cashmere dog pullover (£135), an Amalfi dog lead in blush leather (£85) or a woven-leather dog bed (from £1,960) is entirely appropriate. There's an awful lot more available for dogs than cats, although we don't think Mungo & Maud have missed any tricks. There's a collection for new puppies as well as the more pedestrian requirements necessary for cleaning up after one's dog on the street. A small collection of Mungo & Maud products made for Mulberry appears to set a very dangerous precedent for designer dog clothing and accessories.

Philip Treacy (No. 69) is one of the most influential milliners in the history of the craft. There isn't a royal wedding or Royal Ascot that doesn't parade his polite work (he designed the feathered headdress worn by the Duchess of Cornwall for her wedding to Prince Charles), and those in the fashion and music industries adore his experiments in maximum millinery. So close was the muse–maestro relationship between the late fashion editor Isabella Blow and Treacy that their magnum opus was the subject of a Design Museum exhibition that toured the world. Treacy's black galleon hat rested on Blow's coffin at her funeral. Treacy has had many fashion moments since Blow adopted him: the birdcage cover of British *Vogue*, for which Linda Evangelista modelled the couture; Lady Gaga's lace geisha mask; Sarah Jessica Parker's gilded Mohican plume worn at the Met Ball; and Grace Jones's shocking-pink flying saucer. Treacy's first workshop was in the basement of Isabella and Detmar Blow's town house on Elizabeth Street, and he has remained loyal ever since.

Cecil Court

To echo Graham Greene, 'Thank God Cecil Court remains Cecil Court.' In the 1980s the West End still had time and space for curiosity shops specializing in such eclectibles as vintage film stills, vinyl records, coins, antique maps, theatre ephemera and postcards. The east side of Charing Cross Road was lined with second-hand bookshops, their stock spilling out on to the pavement from unruly trestle tables. We've watched many old favourites buckle under the weight of heavy rent rises, such as Monmouth Street's Centre Stage, a world authority on film and show soundtracks swept aside by iTunes and Amazon. We owe a debt of gratitude to the Marquess of Salisbury, who owns the land, for the preservation of Cecil Court – a pedestrianized conduit between St Martin's Lane and Charing Cross Road – and its eccentric, independent dealers.

Although we would agree that this terrace of nineteenth-century shopfronts is magic, we're afraid the shoals of tourists, told as part of their walking tour that Cecil Court was J. K. Rowling's model for Diagon Alley, are being duped. Cecil Court's claim to fame is much greater. Mozart lodged here when he first visited London as a child prodigy, and T. S. Eliot, Ellen Terry and John Gielgud lived in the apartments on the first floor. Authors and artists such as Charlie Chaplin,

T. E. Lawrence, Anton Dolin, Laurence Olivier, Judi Dench, Richard Harris and Kenneth Branagh all shopped here for first editions, photographs and theatrical gifts for co-stars. Cecil Court appears as a location in the Dirk Bogarde film *Victim* (1961), as is the Salisbury pub.

It was with great sadness that we saw Tracey Brett's **Notions Antiquaria (No. 24)** close its doors in late 2013. Tracey's father, Alan, opened Notions in 1977, since when its window displays festooned with *Vanity Fair* cartoons have been a welcome addition to Cecil Court. There wasn't a surface, shelf or wall in the tiny shop that wasn't groaning with stock amassed over two lifetimes. The joy of discovery was the great pleasure, as was Tracey herself.

Next door at **No. 22** is **Natalie Galustian Rare Books**. Galustian specializes in building catalogues of specialist books to sell to private collectors as fascinated as she is by poker, cocktails, pulp fiction, fashion monographs and male nudes. The parties in her basement gallery space – usually hosted by 69 Colebrooke Row (see entry) – are the rage in Cecil Court, and keep the spirit of sin and bohemian life alive. If coins, banknotes, cigarette cards and medals are of interest, do pop in to **Colin Narbeth & Son (No. 20)**. **Marchpane (No. 16)**, which specializes in illustrated children's books with a little sci-fi in the mix, is a fail-safe for christening presents, such as illustrated editions of Lewis Carroll's *Alice* books, a complete set of C. S. Lewis *Narnia* first editions or pretty prints of Winnie the Pooh, *The Tales of Beatrix Potter* and – if you must – *Harry Potter*. Like all Cecil Court dealers, Marchpane has a few surprises: we found a postcard signed by Charlie Chaplin and bought it for the Savoy collection.

The costume jeweller **Christopher St James (No. 12)** is a welcome newish facet to Cecil Court. His reproduction antique jewels have appeared in *Evita*, *Marie Antoinette*, *The Duchess*, *The Young Victoria*, *The Tudors* and *Moulin Rouge*. Mr St James has replicas of historic jewels, such as the infamous Marie Antoinette diamond necklace, Queen Alexandra's diamond kokoshnik tiara and the Cambridge emeralds. The jazzy shop shows off deco Bakelite, 1950s cocktail jewellery and Swarovski crystal by the yard. **Storey's Ltd (Nos 1 and 3)** is a lovely antique print and map gallery run by Tim Kingswood and occasionally favoured by his father, Ted. Storey's has a super stock of Gillray cartoons, London maps, *Vanity Fair* cartoons and a large selection of coloured prints from the *Illustrated London News*.

Mark Sullivan (No. 9) has what we would consider to be the most engaging shop window in London, filled with portrait miniatures, bronzes, ceramic figures and snuffboxes celebrating such historic figures as the Duke of Wellington, Napoleon, Churchill, Queen Victoria, Edward VII and Iron Chancellor Bismarck. Beyond the shop window are tall mahogany cabinets, tiers of shelves stacked to the ceiling and glass-topped counters filled with yet more curious decorative objects of historic provenance. The stock is quite overwhelming, and we defy you to walk over that threshold and come out empty-handed. **Travis & Emery (No. 17)** is an answered prayer for disciples of classical music. This deceptively small shop has an astonishingly comprehensive collection of antique sheet music for every conceivable instrument and composer of opera, ballet, symphonies and waltzes. It is the kind of shop that can in less than a minute lay hands on nineteenth-century sheet music for Donizetti's *Maria Stuarda*.

We can never pass the window of **Goldsboro Books (Nos 23–25)** without admiring the collection of signed first editions on display. For those who think of second-hand books as a dust trap and an irritant, look at Goldsboro's pristine first editions of Agatha Christie's complete works, with gleaming acetates protecting intact dust jackets like the old masters they undoubtedly are. Saving the best until last, we do urge you to make a pilgrimage to **Pleasures of Past Times (No. 11)**. This Aladdin's cave of theatrical books and memorabilia was opened in 1976 by the remarkable Mr David Drummond, who trod the boards as a clown but was known throughout theatreland for his encyclopaedic knowledge of the West End stage. He knew them all, my dear, and we have spent hours listening to his stories, which are much missed since his retirement in his early eighties. His sons now run the shop, and although it is less chaotic, David is much missed, as is the thrill of searching box upon box of sepia *cartes de visite* of obscure European or Russian royals for hours until you hit upon that rare portrait of the last tsar. We suspect it will be years before all David's hiding places for his treasures – a cape belonging to Ellen Terry or Ivor Novello's scrapbooks – are found.

Index

Acknowledgments

My gratitude and thanks go firstly to James B. Sherwood, who produced the original *Discriminating Guide to London*, allowed me to revive the title and encouraged the endeavour. This is my fourth book commissioned by Lucas Dietrich and published by Thames & Hudson. To misquote Rick Blaine, ours continues to be a beautiful friendship. This is my first T&H book almost exclusively written rather than illustrated, and I am hugely thankful for the talents of editor Rosanna Lewis for much fine-tuning. Claire Rollet's superb illustrations complement the text handsomely, and Kate Slotover's art direction is respectful of the original *Discriminating Guide* while reflecting the spirit of the writing. Simon Hesling, Susan Farmer, John Bowering, Scott Wimsett, Patricia Carruthers, Judith Watt and Katy Thomas (Mrs T) accompanied me on my adventures and offered wise advice on the manuscript. Having such amusing loved ones to share the city with makes me love London all the more.

www.james-sherwood.com